ABOUT THIS PUBLICATION

FOR SERVICE ASSISTANCE

Customer Service
1.980.299.5965

The records required by U.S. Code 2257(a) through (c) and the pertinent regulations 28 C.F.R. Cli. 1, Part 75 with respect to this publication and all materials associated with such records are maintained by The Multi-Media Group of Greater Charlotte, Publisher and available for review by Attorney General.

www.visionbooks.org

Copyright © 2015 by MMGGC
All rights reserved!

TID: 5061752
ISBN (10) digit: 1502915588
ISBN (13) digit: 978-1502915580

123-4-56789-01239-Paperback
123-4-56789-01239-Hardback

First Edition

090520140547

Printed in the United States of America

2015 EDITION

North Carolina Criminal Law

And Procedure-Pamphlet # 51

Printed In conjunction with the Administration of the Courts

North Carolina Criminal Law and Procedure
Pamphlet Reference Guide

11

12

13

§ 97-101.1. Commission may issue writs of habeas corpus.

The Industrial Commission may issue a writ of habeas corpus ad testificandum under Article 8 of Chapter 17 of the General Statutes although it is not a court of record. (1998-217, s. 31.1(a).)

Article 2.

Compensation Rating and Inspection Bureau.

§§ 97-102 through 97-104.6: Repealed by Session Laws 1977, c. 828, s. 8, as amended by Session Laws 1979, c. 824, s. 8.

Article 3.

Security Funds.

§§ 97-105 through 97-122: Repealed by Session Laws 1991 (Regular Session, 1992), c. 802, s. 12, as amended by Session Laws 1991 (Regular Session, 1992), c. 1030, s. 51.3.

§§ 97-123 through 97-129. Reserved for future codification purposes.

Article 4.

North Carolina Self-Insurance Security Association.

§ 97-130. Definitions.

As used in this Article:

(1)   "Association" means the North Carolina Self-Insurance Security Association established by G.S. 97-131.

15

(1a)   "Association Aggregate Security System" means the security system established by the Association under G.S. 97-133 whereby individual self-insurers collectively secure their aggregate self-insured workers' compensation liabilities through the North Carolina Self-Insurance Security Association.

(2)   "Board" means the Board of Directors of the Association established by G.S. 97-132.

(3)   "Commissioner" means the North Carolina Commissioner of Insurance.

(4)   "Covered claim" means an unpaid claim against an insolvent individual self-insurer or group self-insurer that relates to an injury that occurs while the individual self-insurer or group self-insurer is a member of the Association and that is compensable under this Chapter.

(5)   "Fund" means the North Carolina Self-Insurance Security Fund established by G.S. 97-133.

(5a)   "Group" or "Group self-insurer" means a group self-insurer licensed by the Commissioner under Part 1, Article 47 of Chapter 58 of the General Statutes.

(5b)   "Individual self-insurer" means an individual employer licensed by the Commissioner under Article 5 of this Chapter.

(6)   "Member self-insurer" or "member" means an individual self-insurer or group self-insurer that is required to be a member of the Association under this Article or Part 1, Article 47 of Chapter 58 of the General Statutes.

(7)   "Plan" means the Plan of Operation authorized by G.S. 97-134.

(8)   Repealed by Session Laws 2005-400, s. 1.2, effective January 1, 2006.

(9)   "Servicing facility" means those persons delegated by the Board to settle or compromise claims and to expend Fund assets to pay claims. (1985 (Reg. Sess., 1986), c. 1013, s. 1; 1987, c. 528, s. 1; 1997-362, s. 8; 2005-400, s. 1.2; 2011-196, s. 10.)

§ 97-131. Creation.

(a)   There is created a nonprofit unincorporated legal entity to be known as the North Carolina Self-Insurance Security Association. The Association is to provide mechanisms for the payment of covered claims against member self-insurers, to avoid excessive delay in payment of covered claims, to avoid financial loss to claimants because of the insolvency of a member self-insurer, to assist the Commissioner in the detection of self-insurer insolvencies, to fund the Association Aggregate Security System, and to capitalize the Fund to ensure the availability of financial resources to pay covered claims and to fund the activities of the Association.

(b)   All individual self-insurers and group self-insurers shall be and remain members of the Association as a condition of being licensed to self-insure in this State. The Association shall perform its functions under a Plan of Operation established or amended, or both, by the Board and shall exercise its powers through the Board.

(1)   An individual self-insurer or a group self-insurer shall be deemed to be a member of the Association for purposes of another member's insolvency, as defined in G.S. 97-135, when:

a.   The individual self-insurer or group self-insurer is a member of the Association when an insolvency occurs, or

b.   The individual self-insurer or group self-insurer has been a member of the Association at some point in time during the 12-month period immediately preceding the insolvency in question.

(2)   An individual self-insurer or a group self-insurer shall be deemed to be a member of the Association for purposes of its own insolvency if it is a member when the compensable injury occurs.

(3)   In determining the membership of the Association for the purposes of subdivisions (1) and (2) of this subsection for any date after the effective date of this Article, no individual self-insurer or group self-insurer may be deemed to be a member of the Association on any date after the effective date of this Article, unless that employer is on that date licensed as an individual self-insurer by the Commissioner under Article 5 of this Chapter or a group of employers is at that time licensed as a group self-insurer by the Commissioner under Article 47 of Chapter 58 of the General Statutes. (1985 (Reg. Sess., 1986), c. 1013, s. 1; 1987, c. 528, s. 2; 1997-362, s. 9; 2005-400, s. 2; 2011-196, s. 10.)

§ 97-132. Board of directors.

The Board shall consist of not less than nine directors serving terms as established in the Plan. The directors shall be selected by the members of the Association and shall serve for three-year terms and until a successor is elected and qualified. There is no limitation on the number of terms a director may serve. Directors may be reimbursed from the assets of the Association for expenses incurred by them as directors. (1985 (Reg. Sess., 1986), c. 1013, s. 1; 1987, c. 528, s. 3; 2005-400, s. 3; 2011-196, s. 10.)

§ 97-133. Powers and duties of the Association.

(a)   The Association shall:

(1)   Repealed by Session Laws 1999-219, s. 7.2, effective June 25, 1999.

(1a)   Administer a fund, to be known as the North Carolina Self-Insurance Security Fund, which shall receive the assets of the North Carolina Self-Insurance Guaranty Fund previously established under subdivision (2) of this subsection, the assessments required by subdivisions (2a) and (3a) of this subsection and any other sums received by the Association. The costs of administering the Association shall be borne by the Fund. The Association is authorized to secure insurance, primary excess insurance, reinsurance, bonds, other insurance, financial guarantees and related financial instruments to effectuate the purposes of the Association. The Board will invest the Fund assets pursuant to an investment policy adopted by the Board and reviewed and approved annually by the Department of the State Treasurer. The earnings from investment of Fund assets shall be placed in or credited to the Fund.

(2)   Repealed by Session Laws 2005-400, s. 4, effective January 1, 2006.

(2a)   Establish and operate the Association Aggregate Security System as defined in G.S. 97-130 and G.S. 97-165 as follows:

a.   The Association shall annually operate and provide an Association Aggregate Security System through a combination of cash on deposit in the Fund, securities, surety bonds, irrevocable letters of credit, insurance, reinsurance, or other financial instruments or guarantees owned or entered into by the Association. The Association shall assess the individual self-insurers that participate in the Association Aggregate Security System pursuant to subdivision (3a) of this subsection.

b.   through d. Repealed by Session Laws 2011-196, s. 10, effective July 1, 2011.

e.   If the Association determines it is not feasible or practical to operate the Association Aggregate Security System in any given year, it may terminate or suspend the Association Aggregate Security System and shall notify the Commissioner at least 90 days prior to the termination or suspension of the Association Aggregate Security System for that particular year. During any period that the Associate Aggregate Security System is terminated or suspended, every self-insurer shall deposit with the Commissioner, or continue to deposit, the amount required by G.S. 97-185(b3) in the manner prescribed by G.S. 97-185(c).

f.   Group self-insurers shall not participate in the Association Aggregate Security System.

(3)   Repealed by Session Laws 2005-400, s. 4, effective January 1, 2006.

(3a)   Assess members of the Association as follows:

a.   Association Aggregate Security System assessments. - The Association shall assess each individual self-insurer participating in the Association Aggregate Security System a security system assessment. The amount of the security system assessment charged to each individual self-insurer participating in the Association Aggregate Security System shall be based on the Association's reasonable consideration of all of the following factors:

1.   The total amount of assessments necessary to provide aggregate security for all participating individual self-insurers.

2.   The individual self-insurer's total workers' compensation liabilities under the Act.

3.   The financial strength and creditworthiness of the participating individual self-insurer.

4.   Any other relevant factors.

b.   Special assessment. - In the event that there are covered claims against an insolvent member or members and the assets of the Fund are not sufficient to pay the obligations of the Association, then the Association may collect a special assessment from the members in an amount sufficient to pay the aggregate value of such covered claims. Each member's special assessment shall be determined by the Board and shall be based on the proportion of the member's total obligations under the Act to the aggregate total of all members' obligations under the Act.

c.   Initial assessments. - An individual self-insurer that becomes a member and does not initially participate in the Association Aggregate Security System shall pay an initial assessment to the Association in an amount determined by the Board. A group self-insurer, upon receiving its initial license from the Commissioner, shall pay an initial assessment to the Association in an amount determined by the Board.

d.   Each member shall be notified of assessments no later than 30 days before the assessment is due.

e.   Delinquent assessments, except as otherwise provided, shall bear interest at a rate to be established by the Board.

f.   Group assessments. - The Association may annually assess each member group self-insurer in an amount not to exceed two percent (2%) of the group self-insurer's annual gross premiums for the preceding calendar year, as determined under G.S. 105-228.5(b), (b1), and (c).

(4)   Be obligated to pay covered claims.

(5)   After paying any covered claim, be subrogated to the rights of the injured employee and dependents and be entitled to enforce liability against the self-insurer or any third party by any appropriate action brought in its own name or in the name of the injured employee and dependents.

(6)   Expend Fund assets in amounts necessary to pay all of the following:

a.   The obligations of the Association under this Article subsequent to an insolvency.

b.   The expenses of handling covered claims subsequent to an insolvency.

c.   The cost of examinations under G.S. 97-137.

d.   The costs of implementing and operating the Association Aggregate Security System.

e.   All other expenses authorized by this Article.

(7)   Investigate claims brought against the Association and adjust, compromise, settle, and pay covered claims to the extent of the Association's obligation; and deny all other claims. The Association may review settlements to which the insolvent member was a party to determine the extent to which such settlements may be properly contested.

(8)   Notify such persons as the Commissioner directs under G.S. 97-136.

(9)   Handle claims through its directors, its employees, or through one or more members or other persons designated as servicing facilities. Designation of a member as a servicing facility may be declined by such member.

(10)   Reimburse each servicing facility for obligations of the Association paid by the facility and for expenses incurred by the facility while handling claims on behalf of the Association.

(11)   Pay any other expenses of the Association authorized by this section.

(12)   Repealed by Session Laws 2005-400, s. 4, effective January 1, 2006.

(13)   Require each member to annually determine its total undiscounted workers' compensation claims liability and require each member to notify the Association of this determination.

(b)   The Association may:

(1)   Employ or retain such persons, including, but not limited to, adjustors, brokers, accountants, attorneys, financial advisors, investment bankers, placement agents, and consultants, as the Board may determine are necessary to handle claims, perform other duties of, provide services to, and consult with the Association.

(2)   Borrow funds necessary to effect the purposes of this Article in accord with the Plan, including entering into standby lines of credit.

21

(3)   Sue or be sued.

(4)   Negotiate and become a party to such contracts as are necessary to carry out the purpose of this section.

(5)   Perform such other acts as are necessary or proper to effectuate the purpose of this section.

(6)   Repealed by Session Laws 2011-196, s. 10, effective July 1, 2011.

(c)   Repealed by Session Laws 2005-400, s. 4, effective January 1, 2006.

(c1)   The Association shall provide in its Plan that the functions of administration and adjusting claims shall not be performed by the same entity that provides legal representation to the Association for claims.

(d)   Repealed by Session Laws 2005-400, s. 4, effective January 1, 2006. (1985 (Reg. Sess., 1986), c. 928, s. 1(a); 1985 (Reg. Sess., 1986), c. 1013, s. 1; 1987, c. 528, ss. 4-10; 1989, c. 485, s. 27; 1995, c. 533, s. 1; 1997-475, ss. 2.3, 2.4; 1999-219, s. 7.2; 2003-115, ss. 1, 2; 2005-400, s. 4; 2009-242, s. 1; 2011-196, s. 10.)

§ 97-134. Plan of Operation.

The Plan is as follows:

(1)   The Board shall adopt a Plan of Operation and any amendments necessary or suitable to assure the fair, reasonable, and equitable administration of the Association.

(2)   All member self-insurers shall comply with the Plan.

(3)   The Plan shall:

a.   Establish the procedures whereby all the powers and duties of the Association under G.S. 97-133 will be performed.

b.   Establish procedures for investing and managing Fund assets.

c. Adopt a reasonable mechanism and procedure to achieve equity in assessing members under G.S. 97-133.

d. Establish the amount and method of reimbursing members of the Board under G.S. 97-132.

e. Establish procedures by which claims may be filed with the Association and establish acceptable forms of proof of covered claims.

f. Establish regular places and times for meetings of the Board.

g. Establish procedures for records to be kept of all financial transactions of the Association, its agents, and the Board.

h. Provide that any member self-insurer aggrieved by any final action or decision of the Association may appeal to the Commissioner within 30 days after the action or decision.

i. Repealed by Session Laws 2011-196, s. 10, effective July 1, 2011.

j. Contain additional provisions necessary or proper for the execution of the powers and duties of the Association. (1985 (Reg. Sess., 1986), c. 1013, s. 1; 1987, c. 528, s. 11; 2005-400, s. 5; 2011-196, s. 10.)

§ 97-135. Insolvency.

A member self-insurer shall be insolvent for the purposes of this Article under any of the following circumstances:

(1) Determination of insolvency by a court of competent jurisdiction.

(2) Institution of bankruptcy proceedings by or regarding the member self-insurer.

(3) The Board determines that the member self-insurer's total liabilities exceed its total assets or the member self-insurer is unable or ceases to pay its debts as they fall due or in the ordinary course of business.

(4)　　A member self-insurer is deemed to be insolvent, bankrupt, or in default as defined by the terms of any security instrument created pursuant to the Association Aggregate Security System. (1985 (Reg. Sess., 1986), c. 1013, s. 1; 1987, c. 528, s. 12; 2005-400, s. 6.1.)

§ 97-136. Powers and duties of the Commissioner.

(a)　　The Commissioner shall:

(1)　　Notify the Association of the existence of an insolvent member self-insurer not later than 30 days after he receives notice of an insolvency pursuant to the standards set forth in G.S. 97-135.

(2)　　Repealed by Session Laws 2011-196, s. 10, effective July 1, 2011.

(b)　　The Commissioner may:

(1)　　Require that the Association notify the insureds of the insolvent member self-insurer and any other interested parties of the insolvency and of their rights under this Article. The notifications shall be by mail at their last known addresses, where available; but if required information for notification is not available, notice by publication in a newspaper of general circulation in this State shall be sufficient; and

(2)　　Revoke the designation of any servicing facility if the Commissioner finds claims are being handled unsatisfactorily. (1985 (Reg. Sess., 1986), c. 1013, s. 1; 2005-400, s. 6.2; 2011-196, s. 10.)

§ 97-137. Examination of the Association.

The Association shall be subject to examination and regulation by the Commissioner. The Board shall submit, not later than June 1 of each year, a financial report for the preceding calendar year in a form approved by the Commissioner. (1985 (Reg. Sess., 1986), c. 1013, s. 1; 2011-196, s. 10.)

§ 97-138. Tax exemption.

The Association shall be exempt from payment of all fees and all taxes levied by this State or any of its political subdivisions, except taxes levied on real or personal property. (1985 (Reg. Sess., 1986), c. 928, s. 1(b).)

§ 97-139. Immunity.

There shall be no liability on the part of and no cause of action of any nature may arise against any member self-insurer, the Association, or its agents or employees, the Board or its individual members, or the Commissioner or his representatives for any acts or omissions taken by them in the performance of their powers and duties under this Article. The immunity established by this section shall not extend to willful neglect or malfeasance that would otherwise be actionable. (1985 (Reg. Sess., 1986), c. 1013, s. 1.)

§ 97-140. Nonduplication of recovery.

Any person having a covered claim that may be recovered under more than one insurance or self-insurance guaranty or security association or its equivalent shall seek recovery first from the association of the place or residence of the claimant. Any recovery under this Article shall be reduced by the amount of recovery from any other insurance guaranty or security association or its equivalent. (1985 (Reg. Sess., 1986), c. 1013, s. 1; 2005-400, s. 7.)

§ 97-141. Stay of proceedings.

All claims or proceedings under this Chapter to which the insolvent member self-insurer is a party either before the Industrial Commission or a court in this State and the running of all time periods against either the insolvent member self-insurer or the Association under this Chapter shall be stayed for 60 days from the later of the date of notice to the Association of the insolvency or the date the Association is notified of a claim or proceeding under this Chapter in order to permit the Association to investigate, prosecute, or defend properly any petition, claim, or appeal under this Chapter, provided that the payment of weekly compensation for incapacity is made whenever time periods or proceedings affecting the payment of weekly compensation are stayed. (1985 (Reg. Sess., 1986), c. 1013, s. 1; 2003-115, s. 6.)

§ 97-142. Disposition of assets upon dissolution.

In the event of dissolution of the Association, all assets remaining after provision for satisfaction of all outstanding claims shall be distributed to the State Treasurer for establishment of a reserve to satisfy potential claims against the Association and, all such claims being satisfied, for inclusion in the general fund of the State. (1985 (Reg. Sess., 1986), c. 1013, s. 1.)

§ 97-143. Use of deposits made by insolvent member self-insurers.

After the Commissioner has notified the Association, under G.S. 97-136(a), that a member is insolvent, the Commissioner shall assign and deliver to the Association, and the Association is authorized to expend any deposit made by the insolvent member under G.S. 58-47-90 or G.S. 97-185, to the extent the deposit is needed by the Association to pay covered claims against the insolvent member as required by this Article, and to the extent the deposit is needed to pay expenses of the Association relating to covered claims against the insolvent member. For insolvent individual member self-insurers that participate in the Association Aggregate Security System, the Association is authorized to pursue recovery under every instrument, contract, and form of security comprising the composite security. The Association shall account to the Commissioner and the insolvent member or its successor for all deposits received from the Commissioner under this section. (1991, c. 644, s. 25; 1997-362, s. 6; 2005-400, s. 8.)

§§ 97-144 through 97-164. Reserved for future codification purposes.

Article 5.

Individual Employers.

§ 97-165. Definitions.

As used in this Article:

(1)   "Act" means the Workers' Compensation Act established in Article 1 of this Chapter.

(1a)   "Affiliate of" or "person affiliated with" a specific person means a person that indirectly through one or more intermediaries or directly controls, is controlled by, or is under common control with the person specified.

(1b)   "Association Aggregate Security System" means the security system established pursuant to G.S. 97-133 whereby individual self-insurers collectively secure their aggregate self-insured workers' compensation liabilities under the Act through the North Carolina Self-Insurance Security Association.

(2)   "Certified audit" means an audit on which a certified public accountant or a foreign registered public accounting firm expresses his or her professional opinion that the accompanying statements fairly present the financial position of the self-insurer or the guarantor, in conformity with accounting principles generally accepted in the United States or prepared in accordance with International Financial Reporting Standards.

(3)   "Certified public accountant" or "CPA" means a CPA who is in good standing with the American Institute of Certified Public Accountants and in all states in which the CPA is licensed to practice. A CPA shall be recognized as independent as long as the CPA conforms to the standards of the profession, as contained in the Code of Professional Ethics of the American Institute of Certified Public Accountants and Rules and Regulations and Code of Ethics and Rules of Professional Conduct of the North Carolina State Board of Certified Public Accountant Examiners, or similar code. The Commissioner may hold a hearing to determine whether a CPA is independent and, considering the evidence presented, may rule that the CPA is not independent for purposes of expressing an opinion on financial statements prepared in accordance with United States Generally Accepted Accounting Principles or International Financial Reporting Standards. The Commission may require the self-insurer or the guarantor to replace the CPA with another whose relationship with the self-insurer or the guarantor is independent within the meaning of this definition.

(4)   "Commissioner" means the Commissioner of Insurance.

(4a)   "Control", "controlling", "controlled by", and "under common control with" mean the direct or indirect possession of the power to direct or cause the direction of the management and policies of a person through ownership of or through proxies for voting of greater than fifty percent (50%) of the voting securities, or in the case of a not-for-profit entity, the power to direct or cause the direction of the management and policies of the entity.

(5)   "Corporate surety" means an insurance company authorized by the Commissioner to write surety business in this State.

(5a)   "Financial statement" means a financial statement as defined by accounting principles generally accepted in the United States or a financial statement prepared in accordance with International Financial Reporting Standards.

(6)   "Foreign registered public accounting firm" means a public accounting firm that is organized and operates under the laws of a non-United States jurisdiction, government, or political subdivision and is registered and in good standing with the Public Company Accounting Oversight Board and authorized by the Board to prepare or issue any audit report with respect to any issuer.

(6a)   "Guarantor" means a person within the same holding company system who controls the applicant, whose financial statement is used by the applicant to become a self-insurer under the Act, and who has guaranteed the payment of the self-insurer's liability under the Act.

(7)   "Hazardous financial condition" means that, based on its present or reasonably anticipated financial condition, a self-insurer or guarantor is insolvent or, although not yet financially impaired or insolvent, is unlikely to be able to meet its obligations with respect to known claims and reasonably anticipated claims or to pay other obligations in the normal course of business.

(7a)   "Holding company system" means an entity comprising two or more affiliated persons.

(8)   "Management" means those persons who are authorized to direct or control the operations of a self-insurer.

(8a)   "Person" means an individual, corporation, partnership, limited liability company, association, joint stock company, trust, unincorporated organization, or any similar entity or any combination of the foregoing acting in concert.

(9)   "Qualified actuary" means a member in good standing of the Casualty Actuarial Society or a member in good standing of the American Academy of Actuaries, who has been approved as qualified for signing casualty loss reserve opinions by the Casualty Practice Council of the American Academy of Actuaries, and is in compliance with G.S. 58-2-171.

(10)   "Self-insurer" means an individual self-insurer as defined by G.S. 97-130(5b).

(11)   "Subsidiary of" a specific person means an affiliate controlled by such person indirectly through one or more intermediaries or an affiliate directly controlled by such person. (1997-362, s. 4; 1999-132, s. 13.5; 2004-199, s. 20(h); 2005-400, s. 9; 2009-172, s. 5.)

§ 97-170. License applications; required information.

(a)   No employer shall self-insure its workers' compensation liabilities under the Act unless it is licensed by the Commissioner under this Article. This subsection does not apply to an employer authorized to self-insure its workers' compensation liabilities under the Act prior to December 1, 1997, whose authority to self-insure its workers' compensation liabilities under the Act has not terminated after that date.

(b)   An applicant for a license as a self-insurer shall file with the Commissioner the information required by subsection (d) of this section on a form prescribed by the Commissioner at least 90 days before the proposed licensing date. No application is complete until the Commissioner has received all required information. A copy of the application must also be filed with the North Carolina Self-Insurance Security Association at least 90 days before the proposed licensing date.

(c)   Only an applicant whose total fixed assets amount to five hundred thousand dollars ($500,000) or more may apply for a license. In judging the applicant's financial strength and liquidity relative to its ability to comply with the Act, the Commissioner shall consider all of the following relative to the applicant:

(1)   Organizational structure and management.

(2)   Financial strength.

(3)   Source and reliability of financial information.

(4)   Risks to be retained.

(5)   Workers' compensation loss history.

(6)   Number of employees.

(7)   Claims administration.

(8)   Excess insurance.

(9)   Access to excess insurance.

(d)   The license application shall be comprised of the following information:

(1)   Applicant name; organizational structure of the applicant, including any controlling entity, subsidiaries, or affiliates; location of principal office; contact person; organization date; type of operations within this State; management background; and addresses of all plants or offices in this State.

(2)   Certified audited financial statements prepared by a CPA or submitted by a foreign registered public accounting firm for the two most recent years. The financial statement presentation shall facilitate application of ratio and trend analysis.

(3)   Evidence of the insurance required by G.S. 97-190.

(4)   Repealed by Session Laws 1999-132, s. 13.7, effective June 4, 1999.

(5)   For applicants with 20 or more full-time employees, a certificate or other evidence of safety inspection, satisfactory to the Commissioner, that certifies that all safety requirements of the Department of Labor have been met.

(6)   Summary of workers' compensation benefits paid for the last three calendar years and the total liability for all open claims within 30 days or some

other period acceptable to the Commissioner not to exceed 90 days, before the filing of the application.

(7)   Summary, by risk classification, of annual payroll and number of employees within the State.

(8)   Repealed by Session Laws 2005-400, s. 10, effective January 1, 2006.

(9)   Proof of compliance with the claims administration provisions of Article 47 of Chapter 58 of the General Statutes.

(10)   A letter of approval for membership by the North Carolina Self-Insurance Security Association.

(e)   Every applicant shall execute and file with the Commissioner an agreement, as part of the application, in which the applicant agrees to participate in the Association Aggregate Security System, or if excluded from the Association Aggregate Security System, to deposit with the Commissioner pursuant to G.S. 97-185 cash, acceptable securities, an irrevocable letter of credit in a form acceptable to the Commissioner issued by a bank acceptable to the Commissioner, or a surety bond issued by a corporate surety, or a combination thereof, that will guarantee the applicant's compliance with this Article and the Act. (1997-362, s. 4; 1999-132, ss. 13.6, 13.7; 2003-212, s. 25; 2005-400, s. 10; 2009-172, s. 6.)

§ 97-175. License.

(a)   After the review of the application and all supporting materials, the Commissioner shall either grant or deny a license. If a license is denied, the Commissioner shall notify the applicant of the denial and inform the applicant of the deficiencies that constitute the basis for denial.

(b)   If the deficiencies are resolved within 60 days after the Commissioner's notice of denial, the applicant shall be granted a license. The applicant may be granted additional time to remedy the deficiencies in its application. A request for an extension of time shall be made in writing by the applicant within 30 days after notice of denial by the Commissioner. If the requirements of this Article have not been met, the application shall be withdrawn or denied. (1997-362, s. 4.)

§ 97-177. License covering applicant and any subsidiary or applicant relying on a guarantor; procedure; requirements.

(a)   The Commissioner may, in the Commissioner's discretion, upon request by an applicant, issue a license to an applicant or to an applicant and one or more of its subsidiaries if all of the following requirements are satisfied:

(1)   The applicant or a guarantor of the applicant executes a guaranty agreement, in a form prescribed by the Commissioner, for the payment of all workers' compensation liabilities covered under the Act. For any applicant or guarantor that is a corporation, there shall be submitted, along with the guaranty agreement, a board of directors' resolution from the respective corporation authorizing the guaranty of the liabilities of the subsidiary company or companies and granting signature authority to each person or officer executing the agreement.

(2)   The applicant or guarantor files a statement with the Commissioner that lists the percentage of ownership of voting securities or proxies representing voting securities owned or held by the applicant or guarantor for each subsidiary, or in the case of a not-for-profit entity, documentation acceptable to the Commissioner evidencing control.

(3)   The applicant and its guarantor or the applicant and its subsidiaries, whichever applies, satisfy the requirements of G.S. 97-170(c).

(4)   All other applicable requirements for licensure under the Act are satisfied.

(b)   A license issued by the Commissioner pursuant to this section shall include the name of the applicant, the name of each licensed subsidiary, and the date of issuance for each licensed subsidiary.

(c)   If a self-insurer requests to add a subsidiary to its license, the Commissioner shall review the request in accordance with this section. Upon approval, the Commissioner shall issue to the self-insurer a new license that includes the newly licensed subsidiary and the date of license issuance for the newly licensed subsidiary, and the self-insurer shall return the original license to the Commissioner.

(d)   A self-insurer shall neither include nor delete a subsidiary from its license without the Commissioner's prior written approval.

(e)   If a controlling relationship or guaranty agreement terminates, the self-insurer shall retain all liabilities under the Act that were incurred by the self-insurer during the period of self-insurance and shall account for all such liabilities until discharged, as evidenced by reports filed with the Commissioner. Termination of a guaranty agreement does not affect the guarantor's liability for payment of liabilities arising prior to termination of the agreement. (2005-400, s. 11.)

§ 97-180. Reporting and records.

(a)   Every self-insurer shall submit, within 120 days after the end of its fiscal year, a certified audited financial statement, prepared by a CPA or submitted by a foreign registered public accounting firm, for that fiscal year. The financial statement presentation shall facilitate the application of ratio and trend analysis. If the self-insurer was issued a license pursuant to G.S. 97-177, the financial statement required under this subsection shall be that of the guarantor.

(b)   Every self-insurer shall submit within 120 days after the end of its fiscal year a report from a qualified actuary setting forth an opinion certifying the loss and loss adjustment expense reserves for workers' compensation obligations in North Carolina. The report shall show liabilities, excess insurance carrier and other qualifying credits, if any, and net retained workers' compensation liabilities.

(c)   Every self-insurer shall submit within 120 days after the end of its fiscal year a report in the form of a sworn statement prescribed by the Commissioner, setting forth the total workers' compensation benefits paid in the previous fiscal year, and the total outstanding workers' compensation liabilities for each loss year, recorded at the close of its fiscal year for the net retained liability.

(d)   Upon the request of the Commissioner, every self-insurer shall submit a report of its annual payroll information. The report shall summarize payroll, by annual amount paid, and the number of employees, by classification, using the rules, classifications, and rates in the most recently approved Workers' Compensation and Employers' Liability Insurance Manual governing the audits of payrolls and the adjustments of premiums. Every self-insurer shall maintain true and accurate payroll records. These payroll records shall be maintained to allow for verification of the completeness and accuracy of the annual payroll report.

33

(e)   Every self-insurer shall report promptly to the Commissioner changes in the name or address of the self-insurer or guarantor; significant changes in the financial condition of the self-insurer, guarantor, or any affiliate, including bankruptcy filings; and changes in its organizational structure, including its subsidiaries and affiliates. Any change shall be reported in writing to the Commissioner within 10 days after the effective date of the change. Upon request by the Commissioner, a self-insurer shall provide the Commissioner copies of documents or information deemed necessary to determine whether any change has affected the privilege of the employer to self-insure. (1997-362, s. 4; 1999-132, ss. 13.8, 13.9; 2005-400, s. 12; 2009-172, s. 7.)

§ 97-185. Deposits; surety bonds; letters of credit.

(a)   Repealed by Session Laws 2005-400, s. 13, effective January 1, 2006.

(a1)   All individual self-insurers as defined in G.S. 97-130(5b) shall participate in the Association Aggregate Security System established under G.S. 97-131 unless excluded by the Board of Directors of the North Carolina Self-Insurance Security Association. The Board of Directors of the North Carolina Self-Insurance Security Association shall exclude all of the following from the Association Aggregate Security System:

(1)   Individual self-insurers whose licenses have previously been revoked by the Commissioner.

(2)   Individual self-insurers with a debt rating as established by Standard & Poor's Rating Service or by Moody's Investor Service, below the minimum Standard & Poor's or Moody's ratings if a minimum debt rating has been established by the Board of Directors of the North Carolina Self-Insurance Security Association for the Association Aggregate Security System.

(3)   Individual self-insurers that have defaulted on the payment of their self-insured workers' compensation liabilities.

(4)   Individual self-insurers that fail to submit sufficient financial information to enable the Association to determine their total outstanding workers' compensation liabilities, or their creditworthiness, or both.

The Board of Directors of the North Carolina Self-Insurance Security Association shall notify the Commissioner of the individual self-insurers that are excluded from participating in the Association Aggregate Security System.

(b) Repealed by Session Laws 2003-115, s. 3, effective January 1, 2004.

(b1) Repealed by Session Laws 2005-400, s. 13, effective January 1, 2006.

(b2) An individual self-insurer that is excluded from participation in the Association Aggregate Security System, including individual self-insurers that are granted a license to self-insure after the North Carolina Self-Insurance Security Association annually implements the Association Aggregate Security System, shall deposit with the Commissioner an amount not less than one hundred percent (100%) of the individual self-insurer's total undiscounted outstanding claims liability per the most recent report from a qualified actuary as required by G.S. 97-180(b), but not less than five hundred thousand dollars ($500,000), or such greater amount as the Commissioner prescribes based on, but not limited to, the financial condition of the individual self-insurer and the risk retained by the individual self-insurer.

(b3) During any period of time that no Association Aggregate Security System is in effect, individual self-insurers with a debt rating of BBB or better from Standard & Poor's Rating Service, a division of McGraw Hill, Inc., or an equivalent rating from another national rating agency shall deposit with the Commissioner an amount not less than fifty percent (50%) of the individual self-insurer's total undiscounted outstanding claims liability per the most recent report from a qualified actuary as required by G.S. 97-180(b), but not less than five hundred thousand dollars ($500,000). An individual self-insurer licensed pursuant to G.S. 97-177 may utilize the debt rating of its guarantor for the purpose of establishing the application of this subsection. The Commissioner shall consider and may, in the Commissioner's discretion, increase or reduce the deposit to a greater or lesser percentage of the individual self-insurer's claims liability based on the financial strength of the individual self-insurer and other financial information submitted by the individual self-insurer. All other individual self-insurers shall deposit with the Commissioner an amount not less than one hundred percent (100%) of the individual self-insurer's total undiscounted outstanding claims liability per the most recent report from a qualified actuary as required by G.S. 97-180(b), but not less than five hundred thousand dollars ($500,000), or such greater amount as the Commissioner prescribes based on, but not limited to, the financial condition of the individual self-insurer and the risk retained by the individual self-insurer.

35

(c)   Deposits received, changes to existing deposits, or deposits exchanged after the effective date of this section, shall be comprised of one or more of the following:

(1)   Interest-bearing bonds of the United States of America.

(2)   Interest-bearing bonds of the State of North Carolina, or of its cities or counties.

(3)   Certificates of deposit issued by any solvent bank domesticated in the State of North Carolina that have a maturity of one year or greater.

(4)   Surety bonds in a form acceptable to the Commissioner and issued by a corporate surety. A surety bond deposited pursuant to this subsection shall require that the surety reimburse the Commissioner, or his successors, assigns, or transferees, for any costs incurred in the collection of the proceeds of the surety bond, including reasonable attorneys' fees, and any costs incurred in administering the insolvent self-insurer's workers' compensation claims.

(4a)   Irrevocable letters of credit in a form acceptable to the Commissioner issued by a bank acceptable to the Commissioner. An irrevocable letter of credit deposited pursuant to this subsection shall require that the bank reimburse the Commissioner, or his successors, assigns, or transferees for any costs incurred in the collection of the proceeds of the letter of credit, including reasonable attorneys' fees.

(4b)   The reimbursement of attorneys' fees and collections cost provided for in subdivisions (4) and (4a) of this subsection shall be no greater than fifteen percent (15%) of the penal amount of the bond and shall not come from the proceeds of the bond or the letter of credit but shall be in addition to the proceeds of the bond or the letter of credit.

(5)   Any other investments that are approved by the Commissioner.

(d)   All bonds or securities that are posted as a security deposit shall be valued annually at market value. If the market value is less than the face value, the Commissioner may require the self-insurer to post additional securities. In making this determination, the Commissioner shall consider the self-insurer's or guarantor's financial condition, the amount by which market value is less than face value, and the likelihood that the securities will be needed to provide benefits.

(e)   Securities deposited under this section shall be assigned to the Commissioner, the Commissioner's successors, assigns, or trustees, on a form prescribed by the Commissioner in a manner that renders the securities negotiable by the Commissioner. If a self-insurer or guarantor is deemed by the Commissioner to be in a hazardous financial condition, the Commissioner may sell or collect, or both, such amounts that will yield sufficient funds to meet the self-insurer's obligations under the Act. In the case of a letter of credit, the Commissioner may draw the full amount of a letter of credit if the letter of credit is not renewed within 90 days prior to its expiration or at any time that the bank issuing the letter of credit is no longer acceptable to the Commissioner. Interest accruing on any negotiable security deposited under this Article shall be collected and transmitted to the self-insurer if the self-insurer or guarantor is not in a hazardous financial condition.

(f)   No judgment creditor, other than a claimant entitled to benefits under the Act, may levy upon any deposits made under this section.

(g)   Pursuant to the provisions of this section and with the approval of the Commissioner, deposits held by the Commissioner may be replaced with other acceptable forms of deposit in amount determined by the Commissioner. Any deposit to be replaced with another form of deposit shall not be released until the approved replacement deposit is received by the Commissioner.

(h)   Any self-insurer that ceases to self-insure, whether by voluntary termination or by revocation of license, shall continue to secure and be liable for its obligations under the Act and shall continue to report to the Commissioner pursuant to G.S. 97-180. Upon the request of the Commissioner, a self-insurer that ceases to self-insure shall submit filings, as prescribed in G.S. 97-180, to determine whether the deposit is sufficient to satisfy those workers' compensation obligations incurred during the period that the self-insurer was licensed as a self-insurer. The Commissioner may require an increase in the deposit amount or may grant a reduction in the deposit amount to ensure that the deposit is sufficient to cover all existing and future obligations incurred by the self-insurer while subject to the provisions of the Act.

(i)   An endorsement to a surety bond shall be filed with the Commissioner within 90 days after the effective date of the endorsement. (1997-362, s. 4; 2003-115, ss. 3, 4, 5; 2005-400, s. 13; 2009-242, ss. 2, 3, 4; 2011-196, s. 11.)

§ 97-190. Excess insurance.

(a)   Every self-insurer, as a prerequisite for licensure under this Article, shall maintain specific and aggregate excess loss coverage through an insurance policy. A self-insurer shall maintain limits and retentions commensurate with its risk. A self-insurer's retention shall be the lowest retention suitable for the self-insurer's exposures and level of annual premium. The Commissioner may require different levels, or waive the requirement, of specific and aggregate excess loss coverage consistent with the market availability of excess loss coverage, the self-insurer's claims experience, and the self-insurer's or guarantor's financial condition.

(b)   An excess insurance policy required by this section shall be issued by either an insurance company licensed in this State, a captive insurance company licensed in this State, or an eligible surplus lines insurer as defined in G.S. 58-21-10 and shall:

(1)   Provide for at least 30 days' written notice of cancellation by registered or certified mail, return receipt requested, to the self-insurer and to the Commissioner.

(2)   Be renewable automatically at its expiration, except upon 30 days' written notice of nonrenewal by certified mail, return receipt requested, to the self-insurer and to the Commissioner.

(c)   Every self-insurer shall provide to the Commissioner evidence of coverage and any amendments within 30 days after their effective dates. Every self-insurer shall, at the request of the Commissioner, furnish copies of its excess insurance policies and amendments. (1997-362, s. 4; 2005-400, s. 14; 2013-116, s. 5.)

§ 97-195. Revocation, suspension or restriction of license.

(a)   Repealed by Session Laws 2005-400, s. 15, effective January 1, 2006.

(a1)   The Commissioner may, upon at least 45 days notice and opportunity for a hearing, revoke, suspend, or restrict the license of a self-insurer if any of the following apply:

(1)   The self-insurer fails or refuses to comply with any law, order, or rule applicable to the self-insurer.

(2)   There is a determination of insolvency by a court of competent jurisdiction.

(3)   The self-insurer is in a hazardous financial condition.

(4)   The self-insurer has experienced a material loss or deteriorating operating trends, or has reported a deficit financial position.

(5)   Any affiliate or subsidiary is insolvent, threatened with insolvency, or delinquent in payment of its monetary or any other obligation.

(6)   The self-insurer has failed to pay premium taxes pursuant to Article 8B of Chapter 105 of the General Statutes.

(7)   Contingent liabilities, pledges, or guaranties that either individually or collectively involve a total amount that in the Commissioner's opinion may affect a self-insurer's solvency.

(8)   The management of a self-insurer has failed to respond to the Commissioner's inquiries about the condition of the self-insurer or has furnished false and misleading information in response to an inquiry by the Commissioner.

(9)   The management of a self-insurer has filed any false or misleading sworn financial statement, has released a false or misleading financial statement to a lending institution or to the general public, or has made a false or misleading entry or omitted an entry of material amount in the filed financial information.

(10)   The self-insurer has experienced, or will experience in the foreseeable future, cash flow or liquidity problems.

(11)   The self-insurer has failed to make proper and timely payment of claims, as required by this Article.

(12)   Failure to pay any North Carolina Self-Insurance Security Association assessments made pursuant to G.S. 97-133.

(13)   Failure to participate in the Association Aggregate Security System or, if excluded from participation in the Association Aggregate Security System, failure to provide and maintain the deposit required by G.S. 97-185.

(b)   Repealed by Session Laws 2005-400, s. 15, effective January 1, 2006.

(c)   Any self-insurer subject to license revocation, suspension, or restriction under subsection (a1) of this section may request an administrative hearing before the Commissioner to review that order. If a hearing is requested, a notice of hearing shall be served, and the notice shall state the time and place of hearing and the conduct, condition, or ground on which the Commissioner based the order. Unless mutually agreed upon between the Commissioner and the self-insurer, the hearing shall occur not less than 10 days nor more than 30 days after notice is served and shall be either in Wake County or in some other place designated by the Commissioner. The Commissioner shall hold all hearings under this section privately unless the self-insurer requests a public hearing, in which case the hearing shall be public. The request for a hearing shall not stay the effect of the order. (1997-362, s. 4; 2003-221, s. 15; 2005-400, s. 15.)

§ 97-196. Civil penalties or restitution for violations; administrative procedure.

(a)   Whenever the Commissioner has reason to believe that a self-insurer has violated any of the provisions of this Article, and the violation subjects the license of the self-insurer to suspension or revocation, the Commissioner may, after notice and opportunity for a hearing, proceed under the appropriate subsections of this section.

(b)   If the Commissioner finds a violation of this Article, the Commissioner may, in addition to or instead of suspending or revoking the license, order the payment or a monetary penalty as provided in subsection (c) of this section or petition the Superior Court of Wake County for an order directing payment of restitution as provided in subsection (d) of this section, or both. Each day during which a violation occurs constitutes a separate violation.

(c)   If the Commissioner orders the payment of a monetary penalty pursuant to subsection (b) of this section, the penalty shall not be less than one hundred dollars ($100.00) nor more than one thousand dollars ($1,000). In determining the amount of the penalty, the Commissioner shall consider the degree and extent of harm caused by the violation, the amount of money that inured to the benefit of the violator as a result of the violation, whether the violation was committed willfully, and the prior record of the violator in complying or failing to comply with laws, rules, or orders applicable to the violator. The clear proceeds of the penalty shall be remitted to the Civil Penalty and Forfeiture Fund in accordance with G.S. 115C-457.2. Payment of the civil penalty under this section shall be in addition to payment of any other penalty for a violation of the criminal laws of this State.

(d)   Upon petition of the Commissioner, the court may order the self-insurer who committed a violation specified in subsection (b) of this section to make restitution in an amount that would make whole any person harmed by the violation. The petition may be made at any time, and the petition may be made in any appeal of the Commissioner's order.

(e)   Restitution to any State agency for extraordinary administrative expenses incurred in the investigation and hearing of the violation may also be ordered by the court in such amount that would reimburse the agency for the expenses.

(f)   Nothing in this section prevents the Commissioner from negotiating a mutually acceptable agreement with any self-insurer as to the status of the self-insurer's license or as to any civil penalty or restitution.

(g)   Unless otherwise specifically provided for, all administrative proceedings under this Article are governed by Chapter 150B of the General Statutes. Appeals of the Commissioner's orders under this section shall be governed by G.S. 58-2-75. (2005-400, s. 16.)

§ 97-200. Claims administration.

(a)   A self-insurer shall not utilize any claims adjuster unless the adjuster is licensed under G.S. 58-33-25.

(b)   Every self-insurer shall comply with the provisions of Article 47 of Chapter 58 of the General Statutes that are related to claims administration. (1997-362, s. 4.)

41

Chapter 98.

Burnt and Lost Records.

§ 98-1. Copy of destroyed record as evidence; may be recorded.

When the office of any registry is destroyed by fire or other accident, and the records and other papers thereof are burnt or destroyed, the copies of all such proceedings, instruments and papers as are of record or registry, certified by the proper officer, though without the seal of office, shall be received in evidence whenever the original or duly certified exemplifications would be. Such copies, when the court is satisfied of their genuineness, may be ordered to be recorded or registered. (1865-6, c. 41, ss. 1, 2; Code, s. 55; Rev., s. 327; C.S., s. 365.)

§ 98-2. Originals may be again recorded.

All original papers, once admitted to record or registry, whereof the record or registry is destroyed, may, on motion, be again recorded or registered, on such proof as the court shall require. (1865-6, c. 41, s. 3; Code, s. 56; Rev., s. 328; C.S., s. 366.)

§ 98-3. Establishing boundaries and interest, where conveyance and copy lost.

When any conveyance of real estate, or of any right or interest therein, is lost, the registry thereof being also destroyed, any person claiming under the same may cause the boundaries thereof to be established in the manner provided in the Chapter entitled Boundaries, or he may proceed in the following manner to establish both the boundaries and the nature of his estate:

He shall file his petition before the clerk of the superior court, setting forth the whole substance of the conveyance as truly and specifically as he can, the location and boundaries of his land, whose land it adjoins, the estate claimed therein, and a prayer to have his own boundaries established and the nature of his estate declared.

All persons claiming any estate in the premises, and those whose lands adjoin, shall be notified of the proceedings. Unless they or some of them, by answer on oath, deny the truth of all or some of the matters alleged, the clerk shall order a surveyor to run and designate the boundaries of the petitioner's land, and return his survey, with a plot thereof, to the court. This, when confirmed, shall, with the declaration of the court as to the nature of the estate of the petitioner, be registered and have, as to the persons notified, the effect of a deed for the same, executed by the person possessed of the same next before the petitioner. But in all cases, however, wherein the process of surveying is disputed, and the surveyor is forbidden to proceed by any person interested, the same proceedings shall be had as under the Chapter entitled Boundaries.

If any of the persons notified deny by answer the truth of the conveyance, the clerk shall transfer the issues of fact to the superior court, to be tried as other issues of fact are required by law to be tried; and on the verdict and the pleadings the judge shall adjudge the rights of the parties, and declare the contents of the deed, if any deed is found by the jury, and allow the registration of such judgment and declaration, which shall have the force and effect of a deed. (1865-6, c. 41, s. 3; Code, s. 56; Rev., s. 328; C.S., s. 367; 1973, c. 108, s. 44.)

§ 98-4. Copy of lost will may be probated.

In counties where the original wills on file in the office of the clerk of superior court, and will books containing copies, are lost or destroyed, if the executor or any other person has preserved a copy of a will (the original being so lost or destroyed) with a certificate appended, signed by a clerk of the court in whose office the will was, or is required to be filed, stating that said copy is a correct one, this copy may be admitted to probate, under the same rules and in the same manner as now prescribed by law for proving wills. The proceedings in such cases shall be the same as though such copy was the original offered for the first time for probate, except that the clerk who signed such certificate shall, on oath, acknowledge his signature, or in case it appears that he has died or left the State, then his signature shall be proved by a competent witness; and the witness or witnesses to the original, who may be examined, shall be required to swear that he or they signed in the presence of the testator and by his direction a paper-writing purporting to be his last will and testament. (1868-69, c. 160, s. 1; Code, s. 57; Rev., s. 329; C.S., s. 368.)

§ 98-5. Copy of lost will as evidence; letters to issue.

In any action or proceeding at law, where it becomes necessary to introduce such will to establish title, or for any other purpose, a copy of the will and of the record of the probate, with a certificate signed by the clerk of the superior court for the county where the will may be recorded, stating that said record and copy are full and correct, shall be admitted as competent evidence; and when a copy of a will is admitted to probate, the clerk shall thereupon issue letters testamentary. (1868-69, c. 160, s. 2; Code, s. 58; Rev., s. 330; C.S., s. 369.)

§ 98-6. Establishing contents of will, where original and copy destroyed.

Any person desirous of establishing the contents of a will destroyed as aforesaid, there being no copy thereof, may file a petition in the office of the clerk of the superior court, setting forth the entire contents thereof, according to the best of the person's knowledge, information and belief. All persons having an interest under the same shall be made parties, and if the truth of such petition is denied, the issues of fact shall be transferred to the superior court for trial by a jury, whether the will was recorded, and if so recorded, the contents thereof, and the declarations of the judge shall be recorded as the will of the testator. Any devisee is a competent witness as to the contents of every part of said will, except such as may concern his own interest in the same. (1865-6, c. 41, s. 4; Code, s. 59; Rev., s. 331; C.S., s. 370; 1973, c. 108, s. 45; 2011-284, s. 68.)

§ 98-7. Perpetuating destroyed judgments and proceedings.

Every person desirous of perpetuating the contents of destroyed judgments, orders or proceedings of court, or any paper admitted to record or registration, or directed to be filed for safekeeping, other than wills or conveyances of real estate, or some right or interest therein, or any deed or other instrument of writing, required to be recorded or registered, but not having been recorded or registered, it being competent to register or record said deed or other instrument at the time of its loss or destruction, may file his petition in the court having jurisdiction of like matters with the original proceeding, setting forth the substance of the whole record, deed, proceeding, or paper, which he desires to perpetuate. If, on the hearing, the court shall declare the existence of such record, deed, or proceeding, or paper at the time of the burning of the office wherein the same was lodged or kept, or other destruction thereof, and that the same was there destroyed, and shall declare the contents thereof, such declaration shall be recorded or registered, or filed, according to the nature of the paper destroyed. (1865-6, c. 41, s. 5; Code, s. 60; Rev., s. 332; C.S., s. 371.)

§ 98-8. Color of title under destroyed instrument.

Every person who has been in the continual, peaceable and quiet possession of land, tenements, or hereditaments, situated in the county, claiming, using and occupying them as his own, for the space of seven years, under known boundaries, the title thereto being out of the State, is deemed to have been lawfully possessed, under color of title, of such estate therein as has been claimed by him during his possession, although he may exhibit no conveyance therefor: Provided, that such possession commenced before the destruction of the registry office, or other destruction as aforesaid, and also that any such person, or any person claiming by, through or under him, makes affidavit and produces such proof as is satisfactory to the court that the possession was rightfully taken; and if taken under a written conveyance, that the registry thereof was destroyed by fire or other means, or was destroyed before registry as aforesaid, and that neither the original nor any copy thereof is in existence: Provided further, that such presumption shall not arise against infants, persons of nonsane memory, and persons residing out of the State, who were such at the time of possession taken, and were not therefore barred, nor were so barred at the time of the burning of the office or other destruction. (1865-6, c. 41, s. 6; Code, s. 61; Rev., s. 333; C.S., s. 372.)

§ 98-9. Action on destroyed bond.

Actions on official or other bonds lodged in any office which are destroyed with the registry thereof may be prosecuted by petition against the principal and sureties thereto, and the proceedings shall be as in the former courts of equity. (1865-6, c. 41, s. 7; Code, s. 62; Rev., s. 334; C.S., s. 373.)

§ 98-10. Destroyed witness tickets; duplicates may be filed.

The court having jurisdiction of the action may allow other witness tickets to be filed in place of such as may be destroyed, upon the oath of the witness or other satisfactory proof. (1865-6, c. 41, s. 8; Code, s. 63; Rev., s. 335; C.S., s. 374.)

§ 98-11. Replacing lost official conveyances.

Where any conveyance executed by any person, sheriff, clerk and master, or commissioner of court has been lost, and registry thereof destroyed as aforesaid, and there is no copy thereof, such persons, whether in or out of office, may execute another of like tenor and date, reciting therein that the same is a duplicate, and such deed shall be evidence of the facts therein recited, in all cases wherein the parties thereto are dead, or are incompetent witnesses to prove the same, to the extent as if it was the original conveyance. (1865-6, c. 41, s. 9; Code, s. 64; Rev., s. 336; C.S., s. 375.)

§ 98-12. Court records as proof of destroyed instruments set out therein.

The records of any court in or out of the State, and all transcripts of such records, and the exhibits filed therewith in any case, are admissible to prove the existence and contents of all deeds, wills, conveyances, depositions and other papers, copies whereof are therein set forth or exhibited, in all cases where the records and registry of such as were or ought to have been recorded and registered, or the originals of such as were not proper to be recorded or registered, have been destroyed as aforesaid, although such transcripts or exhibits have been informally certified; and when offered in evidence have the like effect as though the transcript or record was the record of the court whose records are destroyed, and the deeds, wills and conveyances, depositions and other papers therein copied or therewith exhibited were original. (1865-6, c. 41, s. 10; Code, s. 65; Rev., s. 337; C.S., s. 376.)

§ 98-13. Copies contained in court records may be recorded.

The copies aforesaid of all such deeds, wills, conveyances and other instruments proper to be recorded or registered, as are mentioned in G.S. 98-12, may be recorded or registered on application to the clerk of the superior court and due proof that the original thereof was genuine. (1865-6, c. 41, s. 11; Code, s. 66; Rev., s. 338; C.S., s. 377.)

§ 98-14. Rules for petitions and motions.

The following rules shall be observed in petitions and motions under this Chapter:

(1)   The facts stated in every petition or motion shall be verified by affidavit of the petitioner that they are true according to the best of his knowledge, information, and belief.

(2)   The instrument or paper sought to be established by any petition shall be fully set forth in its substance, and its precise language shall be stated when the same is remembered.

(3)   All persons interested in the prayers of the petition or decree shall be made parties.

(4)   Petitions to establish a record of any court shall be filed in the superior court of the county where the record is sought to be established. Other petitions may be filed in the office of the clerk.

(5)   The costs shall be paid as the court may decree.

(6)   Appeals shall be allowed as in all other cases, and where the error alleged shall be a finding by the superior court of a matter of fact, the same may be removed on appeal to the appellate division, and the proper judgments directed to be entered below.

(7)   It shall be presumed that any order or record of the court of pleas and quarter sessions, which was made and has been lost or destroyed, was made by a legally constituted court, and the requisite number of justices, without naming said justices. (1865-6, c. 41, s. 12; 1874-5, c. 51; c. 254, s. 3; Code, s. 67; 1893, c. 295; Rev., s. 339; C.S., s. 378; 1969, c. 44, s. 64; 1973, c. 108, s. 46.)

§ 98-15. Records allowed under this Chapter to have effect of original records.

The records and registries allowed by the court in pursuance of this Chapter shall have the same force and effect as original records and registries. (1865-6, c. 41, s. 14; Code, s. 68; Rev., s. 340; C.S., s. 379.)

§ 98-16. Destroyed court records proved prima facie by recitals in conveyances executed before their destruction.

The recitals, reference to, or mention of any decree, order, judgment or other record of any court of record of any county in which the courthouse, or records of said courts, or both, have been destroyed by fire or otherwise, contained, recited or set forth in any deed of conveyance, paper-writing, or other bona fide written evidence of title, executed prior to the destruction of the courthouse and records of said county, by any executor or administrator with a will annexed, or by any clerk and master, superior court clerk, clerk of the court of pleas and quarter sessions, sheriff, or other officer, or commissioners appointed by either of said courts, and authorized by law to execute said deed or other paper-writing, are deemed, taken and recognized as true in fact, and are prima facie evidence of the existence, validity and binding force of said decree, order, judgment or other record so referred to or recited in said deed or paper-writing, and are to all intents and purposes binding and valid against all persons mentioned or described in said instrument of writing, deed, etc., as purporting to be parties thereto, and against all persons who were parties to said decree, judgment, order or other record so referred to or recited, and against all persons claiming by, through or under them or either of them. (1870-1, c. 86, s. 1; 1871-2, c. 64, s. 1; Code, s. 69; Rev., s. 341; C.S., s. 380.)

§ 98-17. Conveyances reciting court records prima facie evidence thereof.

Such deed of conveyance, or other paper-writing, executed as aforesaid, and registered according to law, may be read in any suit now pending or which may hereafter be instituted in any court of this State, as prima facie evidence of the existence and validity of the decree, judgment, order, or other record upon which the same purports to be founded, without any other or further restoration or reinstatement of said decree, order, judgment, or record than is contained in this Chapter. (1870-1, c. 86, s. 2; Code, s. 70; Rev., s. 342; C.S., s. 381.)

§ 98-18. Court records and conveyances to which Chapter extends.

This Chapter shall extend to records of any court which have been or may be destroyed by fire or otherwise, and to any deed of conveyance, paper-writing, or other bona fide evidence of title executed before the destruction of said records. (1871-2, c. 64, s. 2; 1874-5, c. 254, s. 2; Code, s. 71; Rev., s. 343; C.S., s. 382.)

§§ 98-19 through 98-20. Repealed by Session Laws 1971, c. 780, s. 37.

Chapter 99.

Libel and Slander.

§ 99-1. Libel against newspaper; defamation by or through radio or television station; notice before action.

(a)   Before any action, either civil or criminal, is brought for the publication, in a newspaper or periodical, of a libel, the plaintiff or prosecutor shall at least five days before instituting such action serve notice in writing on the defendant, specifying the article and the statements therein which he alleges to be false and defamatory.

(b)   Before any action, either civil or criminal, is brought for the publishing, speaking, uttering, or conveying by words, acts or in any other manner of a libel or slander by or through any radio or television station, the plaintiff or prosecutor shall at least five days before instituting such action serve notice in writing on the defendant, specifying the time of and the words or acts which he or they allege to be false and defamatory. (1901, c. 557; Rev., s. 2012; C.S., s. 2429; 1943, c. 238, s. 1.)

§ 99-2. Effect of publication or broadcast in good faith and retraction.

(a)   If it appears upon the trial that said article was published in good faith, that its falsity was due to an honest mistake of the facts, and that there were reasonable grounds for believing that the statements in said article were true, and that within 10 days after the service of said notice a full and fair correction, apology and retraction was published in the same editions or corresponding issues of the newspaper or periodical in which said article appeared, and in as conspicuous place and type as was said original article, then the plaintiff in such case, if a civil action, shall recover only actual damages, and if, in a criminal proceeding, a verdict of "guilty" is rendered on such a state of facts, the defendant shall be fined a penny and the costs, and no more.

(b)   If it appears upon the trial that such words or acts were conveyed and broadcast in good faith, that their falsity was due to an honest mistake of the facts, or without prior knowledge or approval of such station, and if with prior knowledge or approval that there were reasonable grounds for believing that the words or acts were true, and that within 10 days after the service of said notice a full and fair correction, apology and retraction was conveyed or broadcast by or over such radio or television station at approximately the same time of day and by the same sending power so as to be as visible and audible as the original acts or words complained of, then the plaintiff in such case, if a civil action, shall recover only actual damages, and if, in a criminal proceeding, a verdict of "guilty" is rendered on such state of facts, the defendant shall be fined a penny and costs, and no more. (1901, c. 557; Rev., s. 2013; C.S., s. 2430; 1943, c. 238, s. 2.)

§ 99-3. Anonymous communications.

The two preceding sections [G.S. 99-1 and 99-2] shall not apply to anonymous communications and publications. (1901, c. 557, s. 3; Rev., s. 2014; C.S., s. 2431.)

§ 99-4. Repealed by Session Laws 1975, c. 402.

§ 99-5. Negligence in permitting defamatory statements by others essential to liability of operator, etc., of broadcasting station.

The owner, licensee or operator of a visual or sound radio broadcasting station or network of stations, and the agents or employees of any such owner, licensee or operator, shall not be liable for any damage for any defamatory statement published or uttered in or as a part of a visual or sound radio broadcast, by one other than such owner, licensee or operator, or agent or employee thereof, unless such owner, licensee or operator shall be guilty of negligence in permitting any such defamatory statement. (1949, c. 262.)

Chapter 99A.

Civil Remedies for Criminal Actions.

§ 99A-1. Recovery of damages for interference with property rights.

Notwithstanding any other provisions of the General Statutes of North Carolina, when personal property is wrongfully taken and carried away from the owner or person in lawful possession of such property without his consent and with the intent to permanently deprive him of the use, possession and enjoyment of said property, a right of action arises for recovery of actual and punitive damages from any person who has or has had, possession of said property knowing the property to be stolen.

An agent having possession, actual or constructive, of property lawfully owned by his principal, shall have a right of action in behalf of his principal for any unlawful interference with that possession by a third person.

In cases of bailments where the possession is in the bailee, a trespass committed during the existence of the bailment shall give a right of action to the bailee for the interference with his special property and a concurrent right of action to the bailor for the interference with his general property.

Any abuse of, or damage done to, the personal property of another or one who is in possession thereof, unlawfully, is a trespass for which damages may be recovered. (1973, c. 809.)

Chapter 99B.

Products Liability.

§ 99B-1. Definitions.

When used in this Chapter, unless the context otherwise requires:

(1)   "Claimant" means a person or other entity asserting a claim and, if said claim is asserted on behalf of an estate, an incompetent or a minor, "claimant" includes plaintiff's decedent, guardian, or guardian ad litem.

(2)   "Manufacturer" means a person or entity who designs, assembles, fabricates, produces, constructs or otherwise prepares a product or component part of a product prior to its sale to a user or consumer, including a seller owned in whole or significant part by the manufacturer or a seller owning the manufacturer in whole or significant part.

(3)   "Product liability action" includes any action brought for or on account of personal injury, death or property damage caused by or resulting from the manufacture, construction, design, formulation, development of standards, preparation, processing, assembly, testing, listing, certifying, warning, instructing, marketing, selling, advertising, packaging, or labeling of any product.

(4)   "Seller" includes a retailer, wholesaler, or distributor, and means any individual or entity engaged in the business of selling a product, whether such sale is for resale or for use or consumption. "Seller" also includes a lessor or bailor engaged in the business of leasing or bailment of a product. (1979, c. 654, s. 1; 1995, c. 522, s. 1.)

§ 99B-1.1. Strict liability.

There shall be no strict liability in tort in product liability actions. (1995, c. 522, s. 1.)

§ 99B-1.2. Breach of warranty.

Nothing in this act shall preclude a product liability action that otherwise exists against a manufacturer or seller for breach of warranty. The defenses provided for in this Chapter shall apply to claims for breach of warranty unless expressly excluded under this Chapter. (1995, c. 522, s. 1.)

§ 99B-2. Seller's opportunity to inspect; privity requirements for warranty claims.

(a)   No product liability action, except an action for breach of express warranty, shall be commenced or maintained against any seller when the product was acquired and sold by the seller in a sealed container or when the product was acquired and sold by the seller under circumstances in which the seller was afforded no reasonable opportunity to inspect the product in such a manner that would have or should have, in the exercise of reasonable care, revealed the existence of the condition complained of, unless the seller damaged or mishandled the product while in his possession; provided, that the provisions of this section shall not apply if the manufacturer of the product is not subject to the jurisdiction of the courts of this State or if such manufacturer has been judicially declared insolvent.

(b)   A claimant who is a buyer, as defined in the Uniform Commercial Code, of the product involved, or who is a member or a guest of a member of the family of the buyer, a guest of the buyer, or an employee of the buyer may bring a product liability action directly against the manufacturer of the product involved for breach of implied warranty; and the lack of privity of contract shall not be grounds for the dismissal of such action. (1979, c. 654, s. 1; 1989, c. 420; 1995, c. 522, s. 1.)

§ 99B-3. Alteration or modification of product.

(a)   No manufacturer or seller of a product shall be held liable in any product liability action where a proximate cause of the personal injury, death, or damage to property was either an alteration or modification of the product by a party other than the manufacturer or seller, which alteration or modification occurred after the product left the control of such manufacturer or such seller unless:

(1)   The alteration or modification was in accordance with the instructions or specifications of such manufacturer or such seller; or

(2)   The alteration or modification was made with the express consent of such manufacturer or such seller.

(b)   For the purposes of this section, alteration or modification includes changes in the design, formula, function, or use of the product from that originally designed, tested, or intended by the manufacturer. It includes failure to observe routine care and maintenance, but does not include ordinary wear and tear. (1979, c. 654, s. 1; 1995, c. 522, s. 1.)

§ 99B-4. Knowledge or reasonable care.

No manufacturer or seller shall be held liable in any product liability action if:

(1)   The use of the product giving rise to the product liability action was contrary to any express and adequate instructions or warnings delivered with, appearing on, or attached to the product or on its original container or wrapping, if the user knew or with the exercise of reasonable and diligent care should have known of such instructions or warnings; or

(2)   The user knew of or discovered a defect or dangerous condition of the product that was inconsistent with the safe use of the product, and then unreasonably and voluntarily exposed himself or herself to the danger, and was injured by or caused injury with that product; or

(3)   The claimant failed to exercise reasonable care under the circumstances in the use of the product, and such failure was a proximate cause of the occurrence that caused the injury or damage complained of. (1979, c. 654, s. 1; 1995, c. 522, s. 1.)

§ 99B-5. Claims based on inadequate warning or instruction.

(a)   No manufacturer or seller of a product shall be held liable in any product liability action for a claim based upon inadequate warning or instruction unless the claimant proves that the manufacturer or seller acted unreasonably in failing to provide such warning or instruction, that the failure to provide adequate warning or instruction was a proximate cause of the harm for which damages are sought, and also proves one of the following:

(1)   At the time the product left the control of the manufacturer or seller, the product, without an adequate warning or instruction, created an unreasonably dangerous condition that the manufacturer or seller knew, or in the exercise of

ordinary care should have known, posed a substantial risk of harm to a reasonably foreseeable claimant.

(2)   After the product left the control of the manufacturer or seller, the manufacturer or seller became aware of or in the exercise of ordinary care should have known that the product posed a substantial risk of harm to a reasonably foreseeable user or consumer and failed to take reasonable steps to give adequate warning or instruction or to take other reasonable action under the circumstances.

(b)   Notwithstanding subsection (a) of this section, no manufacturer or seller of a product shall be held liable in any product liability action for failing to warn about an open and obvious risk or a risk that is a matter of common knowledge.

(c)   Notwithstanding subsection (a) of this section, no manufacturer or seller of a prescription drug shall be liable in a products liability action for failing to provide a warning or instruction directly to a consumer if an adequate warning or instruction has been provided to the physician or other legally authorized person who prescribes or dispenses that prescription drug for the claimant unless the United States Food and Drug Administration requires such direct consumer warning or instruction to accompany the product. (1995, c. 522, s. 1.)

§ 99B-6. Claims based on inadequate design or formulation.

(a)   No manufacturer of a product shall be held liable in any product liability action for the inadequate design or formulation of the product unless the claimant proves that at the time of its manufacture the manufacturer acted unreasonably in designing or formulating the product, that this conduct was a proximate cause of the harm for which damages are sought, and also proves one of the following:

(1)   At the time the product left the control of the manufacturer, the manufacturer unreasonably failed to adopt a safer, practical, feasible, and otherwise reasonable alternative design or formulation that could then have been reasonably adopted and that would have prevented or substantially reduced the risk of harm without substantially impairing the usefulness, practicality, or desirability of the product.

(2)   At the time the product left the control of the manufacturer, the design or formulation of the product was so unreasonable that a reasonable person, aware of the relevant facts, would not use or consume a product of this design.

(b)   In determining whether the manufacturer acted unreasonably under subsection (a) of this section, the factors to be considered shall include, but are not limited to, the following:

(1)   The nature and magnitude of the risks of harm associated with the design or formulation in light of the intended and reasonably foreseeable uses, modifications, or alterations of the product.

(2)   The likely awareness of product users, whether based on warnings, general knowledge, or otherwise, of those risks of harm.

(3)   The extent to which the design or formulation conformed to any applicable government standard that was in effect when the product left the control of its manufacturer.

(4)   The extent to which the labeling for a prescription or nonprescription drug approved by the United States Food and Drug Administration conformed to any applicable government or private standard that was in effect when the product left the control of its manufacturer.

(5)   The utility of the product, including the performance, safety, and other advantages associated with that design or formulation.

(6)   The technical, economic, and practical feasibility of using an alternative design or formulation at the time of manufacture.

(7)   The nature and magnitude of any foreseeable risks associated with the alternative design or formulation.

(c)   No manufacturer of a product shall be held liable in any product liability action for a claim under this section to the extent that it is based upon an inherent characteristic of the product that cannot be eliminated without substantially compromising the product's usefulness or desirability and that is recognized by the ordinary person with the ordinary knowledge common to the community.

(d)   No manufacturer of a prescription drug shall be liable in a product liability action on account of some aspect of the prescription drug that is unavoidably unsafe, if an adequate warning and instruction has been provided pursuant to G.S. 99B-5(c). As used in this subsection, "unavoidably unsafe" means that, in the state of technical, scientific, and medical knowledge generally prevailing at the time the product left the control of its manufacturer, an aspect of that product that caused the claimant's harm was not reasonably capable of being made safe.

(e)   Nothing in this section precludes an action against a manufacturer in accordance with the provisions of G.S. 99B-5. (1995, c. 522, s. 1.)

§§ 99B-7 through 99B-9. Reserved for future codification purposes.

§ 99B-10. Immunity for donated food.

(a)   Notwithstanding the provisions of Article 12 of Chapter 106 of the General Statutes, or any other provision of law, any person, including but not limited to a seller, farmer, processor, distributor, wholesaler, or retailer of food, who donates an item of food for use or distribution by a nonprofit organization or nonprofit corporation shall not be liable for civil damages or criminal penalties resulting from the nature, age, condition, or packaging of the donated food, unless an injury is caused by the gross negligence, recklessness, or intentional misconduct of the donor.

(b)   Notwithstanding any other provision of law, any nonprofit organization or nonprofit corporation that uses or distributes food that has been donated to it for such use or distribution shall not be liable for civil damages or criminal penalties resulting from the nature, age, condition, or packaging of the donated food, unless an injury is caused by the gross negligence, recklessness, or intentional misconduct of the organization or corporation. (1979, 2nd Sess., c. 1188, s. 1; 1989, c. 365; 1991 (Reg. Sess., 1992), c. 935, s. 2; 1995, c. 522, s. 1.)

§ 99B-11. Claims based on defective design of firearms.

(a)   In a products liability action involving firearms or ammunition, whether a firearm or ammunition shell is defective in design shall not be based on a

57

comparison or weighing of the benefits of the product against the risk of injury, damage, or death posed by its potential to cause that injury, damage, or death when discharged.

(b)   In a products liability action brought against a firearm or ammunition manufacturer, importer, distributor, or retailer that alleges a design defect, the burden is on the plaintiff to prove, in addition to any other elements required to be proved:

(1)   That the actual design of the firearm or ammunition was defective, causing it not to function in a manner reasonably expected by an ordinary consumer of firearms or ammunition; and

(2)   That any defective design was the proximate cause of the injury, damage, or death. (1987 (Reg. Sess., 1988), c. 1059, s. 1; 1995, c. 522, s. 1.)

§ 99B-12. Burden of proof in certain cases.

(a)   A commodity producer shall be entitled to a rebuttable presumption that the commodity producer was not negligent when death or injury is proximately caused by the consumption of the producer's raw agricultural commodity if the producer (i) is certified by the United States Department of Agriculture Agricultural Marketing Service Good Agricultural Practices and Good Handling Practices Audit Verification Program or other third-party certification program designated by the Commissioner for purposes of this section; (ii) has a written food safety policy that complies with the certification program's standard and can provide evidence that the producer trains employees on the policy on an annual basis; (iii) has had no formal administrative findings or sanctions or legal judgments entered against the producer during the previous three years based on a claim that the commodity producer's negligence was the proximate cause of a plaintiff's death or injury; and (iv) has had no settlement agreements concluding litigation where the settlement exceeded twenty-five thousand dollars ($25,000), or in which the producer admitted liability, during the previous three years based on a claim that the commodity producer's negligence was the proximate cause of a plaintiff's death or injury. This presumption may be overcome only by clear and convincing evidence that the commodity producer's negligence was the proximate cause of the death or injury.

(b)   As used in this section:

(1)   Commodity producer means a producer of raw agricultural commodities.

(2)   Raw agricultural commodity means any food in its raw or natural state, including all fruits that are washed, colored, or otherwise treated in their unpeeled natural form prior to marketing, and which is covered by the United States Department of Agriculture Agricultural Marketing Service Good Agricultural Practices and Good Handling Practices Audit Verification Program. (2013-265, s. 2.)

Chapter 99C.

Actions Relating to Winter Sports Safety and Accidents.

§ 99C-1. Definitions.

When used in this Chapter, unless the context otherwise requires:

(1)   Competitor. - A skier actually engaged in competition or in practice therefor with the permission of the ski area operator on any slope or trail or portion thereof designated by the ski area operator for the purpose of competition.

(1a)   Freestyle terrain. - Constructed and natural features in ski areas intended for winter sports including, but not limited to, terrain parks and terrain park features such as jumps, rails, fun boxes, half-pipes, quarter-pipes, and freestyle-bump terrain.

(2)   Passenger. - Any person who is being transported or is awaiting transportation, or being conveyed on a passenger tramway or is moving from the disembarkation point of a passenger tramway or is in the act of embarking upon or disembarking from a passenger tramway.

(3)   Passenger tramway. - Any device used to transport passengers uphill on skis or other winter sports devices, or in cars on tracks, or suspended in the air, by the use of steel cables, chains, belts or ropes. Such definition shall include such devices as a chair lift, J Bar, or platter pull, rope tow, and wire tow.

(4)   Ski area. - All winter sports slopes, alpine and Nordic ski trails, freestyle terrain and passenger tramways, that are administered or operated as a ski area enterprise within this State.

(5)   Ski area operator. - A person, corporation, or organization that is responsible for the safe operation and maintenance of the ski area.

(6)   Skier. - Any person who is wearing skis or other winter sports devices or any person who for the purpose of skiing or other winter sports is on a designated and clearly marked winter sports slope, alpine or Nordic ski trail or freestyle terrain that is located at a ski area, or any person who is a passenger or spectator at a ski area.

(7)   Winter sports. - Any use of skis, snowboards, snowshoes, or any other device for skiing, sliding, jumping, or traveling on snow or ice. (1981, c. 939, s. 1; 2009-353, s. 1.)

§ 99C-2. Duties of ski area operators and skiers.

(a)   A ski area operator shall be responsible for the maintenance and safe operation of any passenger tramway in his ski area and insure that such is in conformity with the rules and regulations prescribed and adopted by the North Carolina Department of Labor pursuant to G.S. 95-120(1) as such appear in the North Carolina Administrative Procedures Act. The North Carolina Department of Labor shall conduct certifications and inspections of passenger tramways.

A ski area operator's responsibility regarding passenger tramways shall include, but is not limited to, insuring operating personnel are adequately trained and are adequate in number; meeting all standards set forth for terminals, stations, line structures, and line equipment; meeting all rules and regulations regarding the safe operation and maintenance of all passenger lifts and tramways, including all necessary inspections and record keeping.

(b)   A skier shall have the following responsibilities:

(1)   To know the range of the skier's abilities to negotiate any ski slope or trail and to ski within the limits of such ability;

(2)   To maintain control of the skier's speed and course at all times when skiing and to maintain a proper lookout so as to be able to avoid other skiers and obvious hazards and inherent risks, including variations in terrain, snow, or

ice conditions, bare spots and rocks, trees and other forms of forest growth or forest debris;

(3)   To stay clear of snow grooming equipment, all vehicles, pole lines, lift towers, signs, snowmaking equipment, and any other equipment on the ski slopes and trails;

(4)   To heed all posted information and other warnings and to refrain from acting in a manner which may cause or contribute to the injury of the skier or others;

(5)   To wear retention straps, ski brakes, or other devices to prevent runaway skis or snowboards;

(6)   Before beginning to ski from a stationary position or before entering a ski slope or trail from the side, to avoid moving skiers already on the ski slope or trail;

(7)   To not move uphill on any passenger tramway or use any ski slope or trail while such person's ability to do so is impaired by the consumption of alcohol or by the use of any narcotic or other drug or while such person is under the influence of alcohol or any narcotic or any drug;

(8)   If involved in a collision with another skier or person, to not leave the vicinity of the collision before giving his name and current address to an employee of the ski area operator, a member of the ski patrol, or the other skier or person with whom the skier collided, except in those cases when medical treatment is required; in which case, said information shall be provided as soon as practical after the medical treatment has been obtained. If the other person involved in the collision is unknown, the skier shall leave the personal identification required by this subsection with the ski area operator;

(9)   Not to embark upon or disembark from a passenger tramway except at an area that is designated for such purpose;

(10)   Not to throw or expel any object from a passenger tramway;

(11)   Not to perform any action that interferes with the operation or running of a passenger tramway;

(12)   Not to use such tramway unless the skier has the ability to use it with reasonable safety;

(13)   Not to engage willfully or negligently in any type conduct that contributes to or causes injury to another person or his properties;

(14)   Not to embark upon a passenger tramway without the authority of the ski area operator;

(15)   If using freestyle terrain, to know the range of the skier's abilities to negotiate the terrain and to avoid conditions and obstacles beyond the limits of such ability that a visible inspection should have revealed.

(c)   A ski area operator shall have the following responsibilities:

(1)   To mark all trails and maintenance vehicles and to furnish such vehicles with flashing or rotating lights that shall be in operation whenever the vehicles are working or moving in the ski area;

(2)   To mark with a visible sign or other warning implement the location of any hydrant or similar equipment that is used in snowmaking operations and located anywhere in the ski area;

(3)   To indicate the relative degree of difficulty of a slope or trail by appropriate signs. Such signs are to be prominently displayed at the base of a slope where skiers embark on a passenger tramway serving the slope or trail, or at the top of a slope or trail. The signs must be of the type that have been approved by the National Ski Areas Association and are in current use by the industry;

(4)   To post at or near the top of or entrance to, any designated slope or trail, signs giving reasonable notice of unusual conditions on the slope or trail;

(5)   To provide adequate ski patrols;

(6)   To mark clearly any hidden rock, hidden stump, or any other hidden hazard known by the ski area operator to exist;

(6a)   To inspect the winter sports slopes, alpine and Nordic ski trails, and freestyle terrains that are open to the public at least twice daily and maintain a log recording: (i) the time of the inspection and the name of the inspector(s); and

(ii) the general surface conditions, based on industry standards, for the entire ski area at the time of the inspections;

(6b)   To post, in a conspicuous manner, the general surface conditions for the entire ski area twice daily; and

(7)   Not to engage willfully or negligently in any type conduct that contributes to or causes injury to another person or his properties. (1981, c. 939, s. 1; 2009-353, s. 1.)

§ 99C-3. Violation constitutes negligence.

A violation of any responsibility placed on the skier, passenger or ski area operator as set forth in G.S. 99C-2, to the extent such violation proximately causes injury to any person or damage to any property, shall constitute negligence on the part of the person violating the provisions of that section. (1981, c. 939, s. 1.)

§ 99C-4. Competition.

The ski area operator shall, prior to the beginning of a competition, allow each competitor a reasonable visual inspection of the course or area where the competition is to be held. The competitor shall be held to assume risk of all course conditions including, but not limited to, weather and snow conditions, course construction or layout, and obstacles which a visual inspection should have revealed. No liability shall attach to a ski area operator for injury or death of any competitor proximately caused by such assumed risk. (1981, c. 939, s. 1.)

§ 99C-5. Operation of passenger tramway.

The operation of a passenger tramway shall not constitute the operation of a common carrier. (1981, c. 939, s. 1.)

Chapter 99D.

Civil Rights.

§ 99D-1. Interference with Civil Rights.

(a)   It is a violation of this Chapter if:

(1)   Two or more persons, motivated by race, religion, ethnicity, or gender, but whether or not acting under color of law, conspire to interfere with the exercise or enjoyment by any other person or persons of a right secured by the Constitutions of the United States or North Carolina, or of a right secured by a law of the United States or North Carolina that enforces, interprets, or impacts on a constitutional right; and

(2)   One or more persons engaged in such a conspiracy use force, repeated harassment, violence, physical harm to persons or property, or direct or indirect threats of physical harm to persons or property to commit an act in furtherance of the object of the conspiracy; and

(3)   The commission of an act described in subdivision (2) interferes, or is an attempt to interfere, with the exercise or enjoyment of a right, described in subdivision (1), of another person.

(b)   Any person whose exercise or enjoyment of a right described in subdivision (a)(1) has been interfered with, or against whom an attempt has been made to interfere with the exercise or enjoyment of such a right, by a violation of this Chapter may bring a civil action. The court may restrain and enjoin such future acts, and may award compensatory and punitive damages to the plaintiff. The court may award court costs and attorneys' fees to the prevailing party. However, a prevailing defendant may be awarded reasonable attorneys' fees only upon a showing that the case is frivolous, unreasonable, or without foundation.

(b1)   The North Carolina Human Relations Commission may bring a civil action on behalf, and with the consent, of any person subjected to a violation of this Chapter. In any such action, the court may restrain and enjoin such future acts, and may award compensatory damages and punitive damages to the person on whose behalf the action was brought. Court costs may be awarded to the Commission or the defendant, whichever prevails. Notwithstanding the provisions of G.S. 114-2, the Commission shall be represented by the Commission's staff attorney.

(c)   No civil action may be brought or maintained, and no liability may be imposed, under this Chapter against a governmental unit, a government official with respect to actions taken within the scope of his official governmental duties, or an employer or his agent with respect to actions taken concerning his employees within the scope of the employment relationship. (1987, c. 718; 1991, c. 433, ss. 1, 2.)

Chapter 99E.

Special Liability Provisions.

Article 1.

Equine and Farm Animal Activity Liability.

Part 1. Equine Activity Liability.

§ 99E-1. Definitions.

As used in this Part, the term:

(1)   "Engage in an equine activity" means participate in an equine activity, assist a participant in an equine activity, or assist an equine activity sponsor or equine professional. The term "engage in an equine activity" does not include being a spectator at an equine activity, except in cases in which the spectator places himself in an unauthorized area and in immediate proximity to the equine activity.

(2)   "Equine" means a horse, pony, mule, donkey, or hinny.

(3)   "Equine activity" means any activity involving an equine. Actions to preserve, maintain, or regulate the use of land for equestrian recreation shall not be considered an equine activity.

(4)   "Equine activity sponsor" means an individual, group, club, partnership, or corporation, whether the sponsor is operating for profit or nonprofit, which sponsors, organizes, or provides the facilities for an equine activity. The term includes operators and promoters of equine facilities. A landowner who allows

equine recreation on the landowner's property shall not be considered an equine activity sponsor.

(5)   "Equine professional" means a person engaged for compensation in any one or more of the following:

a.   Instructing a participant.

b.   Renting an equine to a participant for the purpose of riding, driving, or being a passenger upon the equine.

c.   Renting equipment or tack to a participant.

d.   Examining or administering medical treatment to an equine.

e.   Hooftrimming or placing or replacing horseshoes on an equine.

(5a)   "Equine recreation" means use of a landowner's property for an equine activity (i) where the landowner is neither the equine activity sponsor nor the equine professional and (ii) when the landowner permits use of the property without charge. For purposes of this subdivision, "charge" has the meaning set forth in G.S. 38A-2 and G.S. 38A-3.

(6)   "Inherent risks of equine activities" means those dangers or conditions that are an integral part of engaging in an equine activity, including any of the following:

a.   The possibility of an equine behaving in ways that may result in injury, harm, or death to persons on or around them.

b.   The unpredictability of an equine's reaction to such things as sounds, sudden movement, unfamiliar objects, persons, or other animals.

Inherent risks of equine activities does not include a collision or accident involving a motor vehicle.

(7)   "Participant" means any person, whether amateur or professional, who engages in an equine activity, whether or not a fee is paid to participate in the equine activity. (1997-376, s. 1; 2013-265, s. 3.2.)

§ 99E-2. Liability.

(a)   Except as provided in subsection (b) of this section, an equine activity sponsor, an equine professional, or any other person engaged in an equine activity, including a corporation or partnership, shall not be liable for an injury to or the death of a participant resulting from the inherent risks of equine activities and, except as provided in subsection (b) of this section, no participant or participant's representative shall maintain an action against or recover from an equine activity sponsor, an equine professional, or any other person engaged in an equine activity for injury, loss, damage, or death of the participant resulting exclusively from any of the inherent risks of equine activities. In any action for damages against an equine activity sponsor or an equine professional for an equine activity, the equine activity sponsor or equine professional must plead the affirmative defense of assumption of the risk of the equine activity by the participant.

(b)   Nothing in subsection (a) of this section shall prevent or limit the liability of an equine activity sponsor, an equine professional, or any other person engaged in an equine activity if the equine activity sponsor, equine professional, or person engaged in an equine activity does any one or more of the following:

(1)   Provides the equipment or tack, and knew or should have known that the equipment or tack was faulty, and such faulty equipment or tack proximately caused the injury, damage, or death.

(2)   Provides the equine and failed to make reasonable and prudent efforts to determine the ability of the participant to engage safely in the equine activity or to safely manage the particular equine.

(3)   Commits an act or omission that constitutes willful or wanton disregard for the safety of the participant, and that act or omission proximately caused the injury, damage, or death.

(4)   Repealed by Session Laws 2013-265, s. 3.2, effective August 1, 2013, and applicable to claims arising on or after that date.

(c)   Nothing in subsection (a) of this section shall prevent or limit the liability of an equine activity sponsor, an equine professional, or any other person engaged in an equine activity under liability provisions as set forth in the products liability laws.

(d)   Nothing in this section shall be construed to conflict with or render ineffectual a liability release, indemnification, assumption, or acknowledgment of risk agreement between a participant and an equine activity sponsor or an equine professional. (1997-376, s. 1; 2013-265, s. 3.2.)

§ 99E-3. Warning required.

(a)   Every equine professional and every equine activity sponsor shall post and maintain signs which contain the warning notice specified in subsection (b) of this section. The signs required by this section shall be placed in a clearly visible location on or near stables, corrals, or arenas where the equine professional or the equine activity sponsor conducts equine activities. The warning notice specified in subsection (b) of this section shall be designed by the Department of Agriculture and Consumer Services and shall consist of a sign in black letters, with each letter to be a minimum of one inch in height. Every written contract entered into by an equine professional or by an equine activity sponsor for the providing of professional services, instruction, or the rental of equipment or tack or an equine to a participant, whether or not the contract involves equine activities on or off the location or site of the equine professional's or the equine activity sponsor's business, shall contain in clearly readable print the warning notice specified in subsection (b) of this section.

(b)   The signs and contracts described in subsection (a) of this section shall contain the following warning notice:

"WARNING

Under North Carolina law, an equine activity sponsor or equine professional is not liable for an injury to or the death of a participant in equine activities resulting exclusively from the inherent risks of equine activities. Chapter 99E of the North Carolina General Statutes."

(c)   Failure to comply with the requirements concerning warning signs and notices provided in this Part shall prevent an equine activity sponsor or equine professional from invoking the privileges of immunity provided by this Part. (1997-376, s. 1; 2013-265, s. 3.2.)

§ 99E-4. Exception.

The liability of a landowner for injury or death associated with participation in equine recreation shall be subject to the limitation set forth in G.S. 38A-4 and shall not be subject to this Part. (2013-265, s. 3.3.)

§ 99E-5. Reserved for future codification purposes.

Part 2. Farm Animal Activity Liability.

§ 99E-6. Definitions.

As used in this Part, the term:

(1)   "Engage in a farm animal activity" means participate in a farm animal activity, assist a participant in a farm animal activity, or assist a farm animal activity sponsor or farm animal activity professional. The term "engage in a farm animal activity" does not include being a spectator at a farm animal activity, except in cases in which the spectator voluntarily places himself or herself in an unauthorized area and in immediate proximity to the farm animal activity.

(2)   "Equine" means a horse, pony, mule, donkey, or hinny.

(3)   "Equine activity" means a farm animal activity involving only equines.

(4)   "Farm animal" means one or more of the following domesticated animals: cattle, oxen, bison, sheep, swine, goats, horses, ponies, mules, donkeys, hinnies, llamas, alpacas, lagomorphs, ratites, and poultry.

(5)   "Farm animal activity" means an activity in which participants engage with one or more farm animals, including, but not limited to, all of the following:

a.   Shows, fairs, exhibits, competitions, performances, or parades that involve farm animals.

b.   Training or teaching activities, or both, involving farm animals.

c. Boarding farm animals, including normal daily care.

d. Rides, trips, shows, clinics, hunts, parades, games, exhibitions, or other activities of any kind that are sponsored by a farm animal activity sponsor.

e. Testing, riding, inspecting, or evaluating a farm animal belonging to another, whether or not the owner has received some monetary consideration or other thing of value for the use of the farm animal or is permitting a prospective purchaser of the farm animal to ride, inspect, or evaluate the farm animal.

f. Placing or repairing horseshoes, trimming the hooves on a farm animal, or otherwise providing farrier services.

g. Examining or administering medical treatment to a farm animal by a veterinarian.

(6) "Farm animal activity sponsor" means an individual, group, club, partnership, corporation, educational organization, or other legally constituted entity, whether the sponsor is operating for profit or nonprofit, which sponsors, organizes, allows, or provides the facilities for a farm animal activity, including, but not limited to, pony clubs; 4-H clubs; Future Farmers of America organizations; hunt clubs; riding clubs; polo clubs; school-and college-sponsored classes, programs, and activities; therapeutic riding programs; and operators, instructors, and promoters of farm animal facilities, including, but not limited to, stables, clubhouses, ponyride strings, fairs, exhibitions, and arenas at which the activity is held.

(7) "Farm animal facility" means any area used for any farm animal activity, including, but not limited to, farms, ranches, riding arenas, training stables or barns, pastures, riding trails, show rings, polo fields, petting zoos, and other areas or facilities used or provided by farm animal activity sponsors or where participants engage in farm animal activities.

(8) "Farm animal professional" means a person engaged for compensation in any of the following:

a. Instructing a participant.

b. Renting a farm animal to a participant for the purpose of riding, driving, or being a passenger upon the farm animal.

c.   Providing daily care of farm animals boarded at a farm animal facility.

d.   Renting equipment or tack to a participant.

e.   Training a farm animal.

f.   Examining or administering medical treatment to a farm animal.

g.   Providing farrier services to a farm animal.

h.   Hooftrimming or placing or replacing horseshoes on a farm animal.

(9)   "Inherent risks of farm animal activities" means those dangers or conditions that are an integral part of engaging in a farm animal activity, including any of the following:

a.   The possibility of a farm animal behaving in ways that may result in injury, harm, or death to persons on or around them.

b.   The unpredictability of a farm animal's reaction to such things as sounds, sudden movement, unfamiliar objects, persons, or other animals.

c.   The risk of contracting an illness due to coming into physical contact with animals, animal feed, animal waste, or surfaces that have been in contact with animal waste.

Inherent risks of farm animal activities does not include a collision or accident involving a motor vehicle.

(10)   "Participant" means any person, whether amateur or professional, who engages in a farm animal activity, whether or not a fee is paid to participate in the farm animal activity. (2013-265, s. 3.3.)

§ 99E-7. Liability.

(a)   Except as provided in subsection (b) of this section, a farm animal activity sponsor, a farm animal professional, or any other person engaged in a farm animal activity, including a corporation or partnership, shall not be liable for an injury to or the death of a participant resulting from the inherent risks of farm

71

animal activities, and, except as provided in subsection (b) of this section, no participant or participant's representative shall maintain an action against or recover from a farm animal sponsor, a farm animal professional, or any other person engaged in a farm animal activity for injury, loss, damage, or death of the participant resulting exclusively from any of the inherent risks of farm animal activities. In any action for damages against a farm animal activity sponsor or a farm animal professional for a farm animal activity, the farm animal activity sponsor or farm animal professional must plead the affirmative defense of assumption of the risk of the farm animal activity by the participant.

(b) Nothing in subsection (a) of this section shall prevent or limit the liability of a farm animal activity sponsor, a farm animal professional, or any other person engaged in a farm animal activity if the farm animal activity sponsor, professional, or person engaged in a farm animal activity does any one or more of the following:

(1) Provides the equipment or tack and knew or should have known that the equipment or tack was faulty, and such faulty equipment or tack proximately caused the injury, damage, or death.

(2) Provides the farm animal and failed to make reasonable and prudent efforts to determine the ability of the participant to engage safely in the farm animal activity or to safely manage the particular farm animal.

(3) Commits an act or omission that constitutes willful or wanton disregard for the safety of the participant, and that act or omission proximately caused the injury, damage, or death.

(c) Nothing in subsection (a) of this section shall prevent or limit the liability of a farm animal activity sponsor, a farm animal professional, or any other person engaged in a farm animal activity under liability provisions as set forth in the products liability laws. (2013-265, s. 3.3.)

§ 99E-8. Warning required.

(a) Every farm animal activity sponsor and every farm animal professional shall post and maintain signs which contain the warning notices specified in subsection (b) or (c) of this section. The signs required by this section shall be placed in a clearly visible location on or near stables, corrals, arenas, or other farm animal facilities where the farm animal professional or the farm animal activity sponsor conducts animal activities. The warning notices specified in subsections (b) and (c) of this section shall be designed by the Department of Agriculture and Consumer Services and shall consist of a sign in black letters, with each letter to be a minimum of one inch in height. Every written contract entered into by a farm animal professional or by a farm animal activity sponsor for the providing of professional services, instruction, or the rental of equipment or tack or a farm animal to a participant, whether or not the contract involves farm animal activities on or off the location or site of the farm animal professional's or farm animal activity sponsor's business, shall contain in clearly readable print the warning notice specified in subsection (b) or (c) of this section.

(b)   The signs and contracts described in subsection (a) of this section shall contain the following warning notice:

"WARNING

Under North Carolina law, a farm animal activity sponsor or farm animal professional is not liable for an injury to or the death of a participant in farm animal activities resulting exclusively from the inherent risks of farm animal activities. Chapter 99E of the North Carolina General Statutes."

(c)   If a farm animal activity sponsor or farm animal professional sponsors or engages in farm animal activities only involving equines, the signs and contracts described in subsection (a) of this section may contain the following warning notice:

"WARNING

Under North Carolina law, an equine activity sponsor or equine professional is not liable for an injury to or the death of a participant in equine activities resulting exclusively from the inherent risks of equine activities. Chapter 99E of the North Carolina General Statutes."

(d)   Failure to comply with the requirements concerning warning signs and notices provided in this Part shall prevent a farm animal activity sponsor or farm animal professional from invoking the privileges of immunity provided by this Part. (2013-265, s. 3.3.)

§ 99E-9. Reserved for future codification purposes.

Article 2.

Roller Skating Rink Safety and Liability.

§ 99E-10. Definitions.

As used in this Article:

(1)   "Operator" means a person or entity who owns, manages, controls, or directs, or who has operational responsibility for a roller skating rink.

(2)   "Roller skater" means an individual wearing roller skates while in a roller skating rink for the purpose of recreational or competitive roller skating. "Roller skater" includes any individual in the roller skating rink who is an invitee, whether or not this individual pays consideration.

(3)   "Roller skating rink" means a building, facility, or premises that provide an area specifically designed to be used by the public for recreational or competitive roller skating.

(4)   "Spectator" means an individual who is present in a roller skating rink only for the purpose of observing recreational or competitive roller skating. (1997-376, s. 2.)

§ 99E-11. Duties of an operator.

The operator, to the extent practicable, shall:

(1)   Post the duties of roller skaters and spectators and the duties, obligations, and liabilities of the operator as prescribed in this Article in conspicuous places in at least three locations in the roller skating rink.

(2)   Maintain the stability and legibility of all signs, symbols, and posted notices required under subdivision (1) of this section.

(3)   Comply with all roller skating rink safety standards published by the Roller Skating Rink Operators Association, including, but not limited to, the proper maintenance of roller skating equipment and roller skating surfaces.

(4)   When the rink is open for sessions, have at least one floor guard on duty for approximately every 200 skaters.

(5)   Maintain the skating surface in reasonably safe condition and clean and inspect the skating surface before each session.

(6)   Maintain in good condition the railings, kickboards, and walls surrounding the skating surface.

(7)   In rinks with step-up or step-down skating surfaces, ensure that the covering on the riser is securely fastened.

(8)   Install fire extinguishers and inspect fire extinguishers at recommended intervals.

(9)   Provide reasonable security in parking areas during operational hours.

(10)   Inspect emergency lighting units periodically to ensure the lights are in proper order.

(11)   Keep exit lights and lights in service areas on when skating surface lights are turned off during special numbers.

(12)   Check rental skates on a regular basis to ensure the skates are in good mechanical condition.

(13)   Prohibit the sale or use of alcoholic beverages on the premises.

(14)   Comply with all applicable State and local safety codes.

(15)   Not engage willfully or negligently in any conduct that may proximately cause injury, damage, or death to a roller skater or spectator. (1997-376, s. 2.)

§ 99E-12. Duties of a roller skater.

Each roller skater shall, to the extent commensurate with the person's age:

(1)   Maintain reasonable control of his or her speed and course at all times.

(2)   Heed all posted signs and warnings.

(3)   Maintain a proper lookout to avoid other roller skaters and objects.

(4)   Accept the responsibility for knowing the range of his or her ability to negotiate the intended direction of travel while on roller skates and to skate within the limits of that ability.

(5)   Refrain from acting in a manner that may cause or contribute to the injury of himself, herself, or any other person. (1997-376, s. 2.)

§ 99E-13. Assumption of risk.

Roller skaters and spectators are deemed to have knowledge of and to assume the inherent risks of roller skating, insofar as those risks are obvious and necessary. The obvious and necessary inherent risks include, but are not limited to, injury, damage, or death that:

(1)   Results from incidental contact with other roller skaters or spectators,

(2)   Results from falls caused by loss of balance, or

(3)   Involves objects or artificial structures properly within the intended path of travel of the roller skater,

and that is not otherwise attributable to a rink operator's breach of the operator's duties as set forth in G.S. 99E-11. (1997-376, s. 2.)

§ 99E-14. Defense to suit.

Assumption of risk pursuant to G.S. 99E-13 is a complete defense to a suit against an operator by a roller skater or a spectator for injuries resulting from any obvious and necessary inherent risks, unless the operator has violated the operator's duties under G.S. 99E-11. (1997-376, s. 2.)

§§ 99E-15 through 99E-20. Reserved for future codification purposes.

Article 3.

Hazardous Recreation Parks Safety and Liability.

§ 99E-21. Purpose.

The purpose of this Article is to encourage governmental owners or lessees of property to make land available to a governmental entity for skateboarding, inline skating, or freestyle bicycling. It is recognized that governmental owners or lessees of property have failed to make property available for such activities because of the exposure to liability from lawsuits and the prohibitive cost of insurance, if insurance can be obtained for such activities. It is also recognized that risks and dangers are inherent in these activities, which risks and dangers should be assumed by those participating in the activities. (2003-334, s. 1.)

§ 99E-22. Definitions.

The following definitions apply in this Article:

(1)   Governmental entity. -

a.   The State, any county or municipality, or any department, agency, or other instrumentality thereof.

b.   Any school board, special district, authority, or other entity exercising governmental authority.

77

(2)   Hazardous recreational activity. - Skateboarding, inline skating, or freestyle bicycling.

(3)   Inherent risk. - Those dangers or conditions that are characteristic of, intrinsic to, or an integral part of skateboarding, inline skating, and freestyle bicycling. (2003-334, s. 1.)

§ 99E-23. Duties of operators of skateboard parks.

(a)   No operator of a skateboard park shall permit any person to ride a skateboard therein, unless that person is wearing a helmet, elbow pads, and kneepads.

(b)   For any facility owned or operated by a governmental entity that is designed and maintained for the purpose of recreational skateboard use, and that is not supervised on a regular basis, the requirements under subsection (a) of this section are satisfied when all of the following occur:

(1)   The governmental entity adopted an ordinance requiring any person riding a skateboard at the facility to wear a helmet, elbow pads, and kneepads.

(2)   Signs are posted at the facility affording reasonable notice that any person riding a skateboard in the facility must wear a helmet, elbow pads, and kneepads and that any person failing to do so will be subject to citation under the ordinance under subdivision (1) of this subsection. (2003-334, s. 1.)

§ 99E-24. Duties of persons engaged in hazardous recreational activities.

(a)   Any person who participates in or assists in hazardous recreational activities assumes the known and unknown inherent risks in these activities, irrespective of age, and is legally responsible for all damages, injury, or death to himself or herself or other persons or property that result from these activities. Any person who observes hazardous recreational activities assumes the known and unknown inherent risks in these activities, irrespective of age, and is legally responsible for all damages, injury, or death to himself or herself that result from these activities. No public entity that sponsors, allows, or permits skateboarding, inline skating, or freestyle bicycling on its property is required to eliminate, alter, or control the inherent risks in these activities.

(b)   While engaged in hazardous recreational activities, irrespective of where such activities occur, a participant is responsible for doing all of the following:

(1)   Acting within the limits of his or her ability and the purpose and design of the equipment used.

(2)   Maintaining control of his or her person and the equipment used.

(3)   Refraining from acting in any manner that may cause or contribute to death or injury of himself or herself or other persons.

(c)   Failure to comply with the requirement of subsection (b) of this section constitutes negligence. (2003-334, s. 1.)

§ 99E-25. Liability of governmental entities.

(a)   This section does not grant authority or permission for a person to engage in hazardous recreational activities on property owned or controlled by a governmental entity unless such governmental entity has specifically designated such area for these activities.

(b)   No governmental entity or public employee who has complied with G.S. 99E-23 shall be liable to any person who voluntarily participates in hazardous recreation activities for any damage or injury to property or persons that arises out of a person's participation in the activity and that takes place in an area designated for the activity.

(c)   This section does not limit liability that would otherwise exist for any of the following:

(1)   The failure of the governmental entity or public employee to guard against or warn of a dangerous condition of which a participant does not have and cannot reasonably be expected to have had notice.

(2)   An act of gross negligence by the governmental entity or public employee that is the proximate cause of the injury.

(d)   Nothing in this section creates a duty of care or basis of liability for death, personal injury, or damage to personal property. Nothing in this section shall be deemed to be a waiver of sovereign immunity under any circumstances.

(e)   Nothing in this section limits the liability of an independent concessionaire or any person or organization other than a governmental entity or public employee, whether or not the person or organization has a contractual relationship with a governmental entity to use the public property, for injuries or damages suffered in any case as a result of the operation of equipment for hazardous recreational activities on public property by the concessionaire, person, or organization.

(f)   The fact that a governmental entity carries insurance that covers any activity subject to this Article does not constitute a waiver of the liability limits under this section, regardless of the existence or limits of the coverage. (2003-334, s. 1.)

§ 99E-26. Reserved for future codification purposes.

§ 99E-27. Reserved for future codification purposes.

§ 99E-28. Reserved for future codification purposes.

§ 99E-29. Reserved for future codification purposes.

Article 4.

Agritourism Activity Liability.

§ 99E-30. Definitions.

As used in this Article, the following terms mean:

(1)   Agritourism activity. - Any activity carried out on a farm or ranch that allows members of the general public, for recreational, entertainment, or educational purposes, to view or enjoy rural activities, including farming, ranching, historic, cultural, harvest-your-own activities, or natural activities and

attractions. An activity is an agritourism activity whether or not the participant paid to participate in the activity. "Agritourism activity" includes an activity involving any animal exhibition at an agricultural fair licensed by the Commissioner of Agriculture pursuant to G.S. 106-520.3.

(2)   Agritourism professional. - Any person who is engaged in the business of providing one or more agritourism activities, whether or not for compensation.

(3)   Inherent risks of agritourism activity. - Those dangers or conditions that are an integral part of an agritourism activity including certain hazards, including surface and subsurface conditions, natural conditions of land, vegetation, and waters, the behavior of wild or domestic animals, and ordinary dangers of structures or equipment ordinarily used in farming and ranching operations. Inherent risks of agritourism activity also include the potential of a participant to act in a negligent manner that may contribute to injury to the participant or others, including failing to follow instructions given by the agritourism professional or failing to exercise reasonable caution while engaging in the agritourism activity.

(4)   Participant. - Any person, other than the agritourism professional, who engages in an agritourism activity.

(5)   Person. - An individual, fiduciary, firm, association, partnership, limited liability company, corporation, unit of government, or any other group acting as a unit. (2005-236, s. 1; 2007-171, s. 1.)

§ 99E-31. Liability.

(a)   Except as provided in subsection (b) of this section, an agritourism professional is not liable for injury to or death of a participant resulting from the inherent risks of agritourism activities, so long as the warning contained in G.S. 99E-32 is posted as required and, except as provided in subsection (b) of this section, no participant or participant's representative can maintain an action against or recover from an agritourism professional for injury, loss, damage, or death of the participant resulting exclusively from any of the inherent risks of agritourism activities. In any action for damages against an agritourism professional for agritourism activity, the agritourism professional must plead the affirmative defense of assumption of the risk of agritourism activity by the participant.

(b)   Nothing in subsection (a) of this section prevents or limits the liability of an agritourism professional if the agritourism professional does any one or more of the following:

(1)   Commits an act or omission that constitutes willful or wanton disregard for the safety of the participant, and that act or omission proximately causes injury, damage, or death to the participant.

(2)   Has actual knowledge or reasonably should have known of an existing dangerous condition on the land, facilities, or equipment used in the activity or the dangerous propensity of a particular animal used in such activity and does not make the danger known to the participant, and the danger proximately causes injury, damage, or death to the participant.

(c)   Nothing in subsection (a) of this section prevents or limits the liability of an agritourism professional under liability provisions as set forth in Chapter 99B of the General Statutes.

(d)   Any limitation on legal liability afforded by this section to an agritourism professional is in addition to any other limitations of legal liability otherwise provided by law. (2005-236, s. 1; 2013-265, s. 4.)

§ 99E-32. Warning required.

(a)   Every agritourism professional must post and maintain signs that contain the warning notice specified in subsection (b) of this section. The sign must be placed in a clearly visible location at the entrance to the agritourism location and at the site of the agritourism activity. The warning notice must consist of a sign in black letters, with each letter to be a minimum of one inch in height. Every written contract entered into by an agritourism professional for the providing of professional services, instruction, or the rental of equipment to a participant, whether or not the contract involves agritourism activities on or off the location or at the site of the agritourism activity, must contain in clearly readable print the warning notice specified in subsection (b) of this section.

(b)   The signs and contracts described in subsection (a) of this section must contain the following notice of warning:

"WARNING

Under North Carolina law, there is no liability for an injury to or death of a participant in an agritourism activity conducted at this agritourism location if such injury or death results from the inherent risks of the agritourism activity. Inherent risks of agritourism activities include, among others, risks of injury inherent to land, equipment, and animals, as well as the potential for you to act in a negligent manner that may contribute to your injury or death. You are assuming the risk of participating in this agritourism activity."

(c)   Failure to comply with the requirements concerning warning signs and notices provided in this subsection will prevent an agritourism professional from invoking the privileges of immunity provided by this Article. (2005-236, s. 1.)

§ 99E-33: Reserved for future codification purposes.

§ 99E-34: Reserved for future codification purposes.

§ 99E-35: Reserved for future codification purposes.

§ 99E-36: Reserved for future codification purposes.

§ 99E-37: Reserved for future codification purposes.

§ 99E-38: Reserved for future codification purposes.

§ 99E-39: Reserved for future codification purposes.

Article 5.

Commonsense Consumption Act.

§ 99E-40. Title.

This act shall be known and may be cited as the "Commonsense Consumption Act." (2013-309, s. 1.)

§ 99E-41. Definitions.

The following definitions apply in this Article:

(1)   Claim. - Any claim by or on behalf of a natural person, as well as any derivative or other claim arising from a common set of facts or circumstances and asserted by or on behalf of any other person.

(2)   Knowing and willful conduct. - Conduct which meets all of the following criteria:

a.   The conduct was committed with any of the following:

1.   The intent to deceive or injure consumers.

2.   Actual knowledge that such conduct was injurious to consumers.

3.   Reason to know there is a reasonable probability of injury to consumers.

b.   The conduct constituting the violation was not required by regulations, orders, rules, or other pronouncement of, or any statute administered by, a federal, State, or local government agency.

(3)   Other person. - Any individual, corporation, company, association, firm, partnership, society, joint-stock company, or any other entity, including any governmental entity or private attorney general. (2013-309, s. 1.)

§ 99E-42. Claims arising from weight gain, obesity, associated health conditions, or long-term consumption of food - Limitation on liability.

Except as set forth in G.S. 99E-43, a packer, distributor, manufacturer, carrier, holder, seller, marketer, or advertiser of a food, as defined in section 201(f) of the federal Food, Drug, and Cosmetic Act, 21 U.S.C. § 321(f), or an association of one or more such entities, shall not be liable in any civil action for any claim arising out of weight gain, obesity, a health condition associated with weight gain or obesity, or other generally known condition allegedly caused by or allegedly likely to result from long-term consumption of food. For purposes of this section, a health condition arising from a single instance of consumption

84

shall not be considered to result from long-term consumption of food. (2013-309, s. 1.)

§ 99E-43. Claims arising from weight gain, obesity, associated health conditions, or long-term consumption of food - Exceptions to limit on liability.

G.S. 99E-42 shall not preclude liability in a civil action in which the claim of weight gain, obesity, health condition associated with weight gain or obesity, or other generally known condition allegedly caused by or allegedly likely to result from long-term consumption of food meets either of the following:

(1)   The claim includes as an element of the cause of action a material violation of an adulteration or misbranding requirement prescribed by statute or rule of this State or the United States of America and the claimed injury was proximately caused by such violation.

(2)   The claim is based on knowing and willful conduct applicable to the manufacturing, marketing, distribution, advertising, labeling, or sale of food, in violation of any other State or federal law and the claimed injury was proximately caused by such violation. (2013-309, s. 1.)

§ 99E-44. Construction of Article.

(a)   Nothing in this Article shall be construed to create any new claim, right of action, or civil liability not previously existing under State law.

(b)   Nothing in this Article shall be construed to interfere with any agency's exclusive or primary jurisdiction to find or declare violations of a food adulteration or misbranding statute or rule. (2013-309, s. 1.)

Chapter 100.

Monuments, Memorials and Parks.

Article 1.

Approval of Memorials, Works of Art, etc.

§ 100-1. Repealed by Session Laws 1973, c. 476, s. 48.

§ 100-2. Approval of memorials before acceptance by State; regulation of existing memorials, etc.; "work of art" defined; highway markers.

No memorial or work of art shall hereafter become the property of the State by purchase, gift or otherwise, unless such memorial or work of art or a design of the same, together with the proposed location of the same, shall first have been submitted to and approved by the North Carolina Historical Commission; nor shall any memorial or work of art, until so submitted and approved, be contracted for, placed in or upon or allowed to extend over any property belonging to the State. No existing memorial or work of art owned by the State shall be removed, relocated, or altered in any way without approval of the North Carolina Historical Commission. The term "work of art" as used in this section shall include any painting, portrait, mural decoration, stained glass, statue, bas-relief, sculpture, monument, tablet, fountain, or other article or structure of a permanent character intended for decoration or commemoration. This section, however, shall not apply to markers set up by the Board of Transportation in cooperation with the Department of Environment and Natural Resources and the Department of Cultural Resources as provided by Chapter 197 of the Public Laws of 1935. (1941, c. 341, s. 2; 1957, c. 65, s. 11; 1973, c. 476, s. 48; c. 507, s. 5; c. 1262, s. 86; 1977, c. 771, s. 4; 1979, 2nd Sess., c. 1306, ss. 3, 4; 1989, c. 727, s. 218(27); 1997-443, s. 11A.119(a).)

§ 100-3. Approval of design, etc., of certain bridges and other structures.

No bridge, arch, gate, fence or other structure intended primarily for ornamental or memorial purposes and which is paid for either wholly or in part by appropriation from the State treasury, or which is to be placed on or allowed to extend over any property belonging to the State, shall be begun unless the design and proposed location thereof shall have been submitted to the North Carolina Historical Commission and approved by it. Furthermore, no existing structures of the kind named and described in the preceding part of this section owned by the State, shall be removed or remodeled without submission of the plans therefor to the North Carolina Historical Commission and approval of said plans by the North Carolina Historical Commission. This section shall not be construed as amending or repealing Chapter 197 of the Public Laws of 1935. (1941, c. 341, s. 3; 1973, c. 476, s. 48; 1979, 2nd Sess., c. 1306, s. 3.)

§ 100-4. Governor to accept works of art approved by North Carolina Historical Commission.

The Governor of North Carolina is hereby authorized to accept, in the name of the State of North Carolina, gifts to the State of works of art as defined in G.S. 100-2. But no work of art shall be so accepted unless and until the same shall have been first submitted to the North Carolina Historical Commission and by it judged worthy of acceptance. (1941, c. 341, s. 4; 1973, c. 476, s. 48; 1979, 2nd Sess., c. 1306, s. 3.)

§ 100-5. Duties as to buildings erected or remodeled by State.

Upon request of the Governor and the Board of Public Buildings and Grounds, the North Carolina Historical Commission shall act in an advisory capacity relative to the artistic character of any building constructed, erected, or remodeled by the State. The term "building" as used in this section shall include structures intended for human occupation, and also bridges, arches, gates, walls, or other permanent structures of any character not intended primarily for purposes of decoration or commemoration. (1941, c. 341, s. 5; 1973, c. 476, s. 48; 1979, 2nd Sess., c. 1306, s. 3.)

§ 100-6. Disqualification to vote on work of art, etc.; vacancy.

Any member of the North Carolina Historical Commission who shall be employed by the State to execute a work of art or structure of any kind requiring submission to the North Carolina Historical Commission, or who shall take part in a competition for such work of art or structure, shall be disqualified from voting thereon, and the temporary vacancy thereby created may be filled by appointment by the Governor. (1941, c. 341, s. 6; 1973, c. 476, s. 48; 1979, 2nd Sess., c. 1306, s. 3.)

§ 100-7. Construction.

The provisions of this Article shall not be construed to include exhibits of an educational nature arranged by museums or art galleries administered by the State or any of its agencies or institutions, or to prevent the placing of portraits of officials, officers, or employees of the State in the offices or buildings of the departments, agencies, or institutions with which such officials, officers, or employees are or have been connected. But upon request of such museums or agencies, the North Carolina Historical Commission shall act in an advisory capacity as to the artistic qualities and appropriations of memorial exhibits or works of art submitted to it. (1941, c. 341, s. 7; 1973, c. 476, s. 48; 1979, 2nd Sess., c. 1306, s. 3.)

§ 100-8. Memorials to persons within 25 years of death; acceptance of commemorative funds for useful work.

No monument, statue, tablet, painting, or other article or structure of a permanent nature intended primarily to commemorate any person or persons shall be purchased from State funds or shall be placed in or upon or allowed to extend over State property within 25 years after the death of the person or persons so commemorated: Provided, nevertheless, that nothing in this Article shall be interpreted as prohibiting the acceptance of funds by State agencies or institutions from individuals or societies who wish to commemorate some person or persons by providing funds for educational, health, charitable, or other useful work. The agency or institution to which such funds are offered for memorial enterprises shall exercise its discretion as to the acceptance and expenditure of such funds. Nothing in this Article shall be interpreted as prohibiting the erection on the lands of the Cliffs of the Neuse State Park an appropriate tablet or plaque honoring the life and memory of the late Lionel Weil of Wayne County. Nothing in this Article shall be interpreted as prohibiting the erection on the lands of the Morrow Mountain State Park an appropriate tablet or plaque honoring the life and memory of the late James McKnight Morrow of Stanly County. Nothing in this Article shall be interpreted as prohibiting the erection on the lands of the Cliffs of the Neuse State Park an appropriate tablet or plaque, of such size and containing such language, as may be agreed upon by the donors and Director of State Parks, honoring the Whitfield heirs for their contributions to the establishment of the said park. (1941, c. 341, s. 8; 1957, c. 181; 1961, c. 976; 1963, c. 1128; 1979, 2nd Sess., c. 1306, s. 4.)

Chapter 101.

Names of Persons.

§ 101-1. Legislature may regulate change by general but not private law.

The General Assembly shall not have power to pass any private law to alter the name of any person, but shall have power to pass general laws regulating the same. (Const., Art. II, s. 11; Rev., s. 2146; C.S., s. 2970.)

§ 101-2. Procedure for changing name; petition; notice.

(a)   A person who wishes, for good cause shown, to change his or her name must file an application before the clerk of the superior court of the county in which the person lives, after giving 10 days' notice of the application by publication at the courthouse door.

(b)   The publication in subsection (a) of this section is not required if the applicant:

(1)   Is a participant in the address confidentiality program under Chapter 15C of the General Statutes; or

(2)   Provides evidence that the applicant is a victim of domestic violence, sexual offense, or stalking. This evidence may include any of the following:

a.   Law enforcement, court, or other federal or state agency records or files.

b.   Documentation from a program receiving funds from the Domestic Violence Center Fund, if the applicant is alleged to be a victim of domestic violence.

(c)   The application and the court's entire record of the proceedings relating to the applicant's name change is not a matter of public record where the applicant has complied with subsection (b)(1) or (b)(2) of this section. Records qualifying under this subsection shall be maintained separately from other records, shall be withheld from public inspection, and may be examined only by order of the court or with the written consent of the applicant.

(d)   An application to change the name of a minor child may be filed by the child's parent or parents, guardian appointed under Article 6 of Chapter 35A of the General Statutes, or guardian ad litem appointed under Rule 17 of the Rules of Civil Procedure, and this application may be joined in the application for a change of name filed by the parent or parents. A change of parentage or the addition of information relating to parentage on the birth certificate of any person is governed by G.S. 130A-118. An application to change the name of a minor child may not be filed without the consent of both parents if both parents are living, unless one of the following applies:

(1)   A minor who has reached the age of 16 may file an application to change his or her name with the consent of the parent who has custody of the minor and has supported the minor, without the necessity of obtaining the consent of the other parent, when the clerk of court is satisfied that the other parent has abandoned the minor.

(2)   A parent may file an application on behalf of the minor without the consent of the other parent if the other parent has abandoned the minor child.

(3)   A parent may file an application on behalf of the minor without the consent of the other parent if the other parent has been convicted of any of the following offenses against the minor or a sibling of the minor:

a.   Felonious or misdemeanor child abuse.

b.   Taking indecent liberties with a minor in violation of G.S. 14-202.1.

c.   Rape or any other sex offense in violation of Article 7A of Chapter 14 of the General Statutes.

d.   Incest in violation of G.S. 14-178.

e.   Assault, communicating a threat, or any other crime of violence.

For purposes of subdivisions (1) and (2) of this subsection, abandonment may be shown by filing a copy of an order of a court of competent jurisdiction adjudicating that parent's abandonment of the minor. If a court of competent jurisdiction has not declared the minor to be an abandoned child, the clerk, on 10 days' written notice by registered or certified mail, directed to the last known address of the parent alleged to have abandoned the child, may determine whether the parent has abandoned the child. If the parent denies that the parent abandoned the child, this issue of fact shall be transferred and determined as provided in G.S. 1-301.2. If abandonment is determined, the consent of the parent is not required. Upon final determination of this issue of fact the proceeding shall be transferred back to the special proceedings docket for further action by the clerk. A parent who files an application on behalf of a minor pursuant to subdivision (3) of this subsection shall submit proof of the other parent's conviction to the clerk at the time of filing. (1891, c. 145; Rev., s. 2147; C.S., s. 2971; 1947, c. 115; 1953, c. 678; 1955, c. 951, s. 3; 1957, c. 1442; 1959, c. 1161, s. 7; 1971, c. 444, s. 1; 1995, c. 509, s. 135.2(f); 1999-216, s. 13; 2007-116, s. 1; 2013-42, s. 1.)

§ 101-3. Contents of petition.

The applicant shall state in the application his true name, county of birth, date of birth, the full name of parents as shown on birth certificate, the name he desires to adopt, his reasons for desiring such change, and whether his name has ever before been changed by law, and, if so, the facts with respect thereto. (1891, c. 145; Rev., s. 2147; C.S., s. 2972; 1945, c. 37, s. 1; 1957, c. 1233, s. 1.)

§ 101-4. Proof of good character to accompany petition.

The applicant shall also file with said petition proof of his good character, which proof must be made by at least two citizens of the county who know his standing: Provided, however, proof of good character shall not be required when the application is for the change of name of a child under 16 years of age. (1891, c. 145; Rev., s. 2148; C.S., s. 2973; 1963, c. 206.)

§ 101-5. Name change application requirements; grounds for clerk to order or deny name change; certificate and record.

(a)   A person who desires to change his or her true name may apply to the clerk of superior court of the county where the person resides and must submit all of the following information to the clerk in support of the application for a name change:

(1)   The applicant's true name, county of birth, date of birth, the full name of parents as shown on birth certificate, and the name sought to be adopted.

(2)   The results of a state and national criminal history record check conducted within 90 days of the date of application by the State Bureau of Investigation, the Federal Bureau of Investigation, or a Channeler approved by the Federal Bureau of Investigation. The requirements of this subdivision shall not apply to an application to change the name of a minor less than 16 years of age.

(3)   A sworn statement as to the following:

a.   That the applicant is a bona fide resident of, and domiciled in, the county where the change of name is sought.

b.   Whether or not the applicant has outstanding tax or child support obligations.

(b)   The clerk shall instruct the applicant on the process for having fingerprints taken and submitted for the criminal history record check, including providing information on law enforcement agencies or acceptable service providers. The clerk may require the applicant to provide any other information that the clerk determines is reasonably necessary for the fair and complete review of the name change application.

(c)   The clerk shall review all the information contained in the application and otherwise available to the clerk to determine whether there is good and sufficient reason to grant or to deny the name change.

(d)   Except as prohibited by G.S. 101-6(c), if the clerk finds that good and sufficient reasons exist for the change of name, and the applicant has met the requirements of subsection (a) of this section, it is the clerk's duty to issue an order changing the name of the applicant from that person's true name to the name sought to be adopted. The order shall contain all of the following:

(1)   The true name, the county of birth, the date of birth, the full name of parents as shown on birth certificate, and the name sought to be adopted.

(2)   The clerk's summary of the information reviewed in connection with the application.

The clerk shall issue to the applicant a certificate under the clerk's hand and seal of office, stating the change made in the applicant's name, and shall also record the application and order on the docket of special proceedings in his court.

(e)   The clerk shall forward the order granting the name change to:

(1)   The State Registrar of Vital Statistics on a form provided by the Registrar. If the applicant was born in North Carolina, the State Registrar shall note the change of name of the individual or individuals specified in the order on the birth certificate of that individual or those individuals and shall notify the register of deeds in the county of birth. If the applicant was born in another state of the United States, the State Registrar shall forward the notice of change of name to the registration office of the state of birth. If the name change is not a matter of public record pursuant to G.S. 101-2(c), the clerk shall notify the State Registrar; however, the State Registrar shall not notify the register of deeds in the applicant's county of birth or the registration office of the state of birth.

(2)   The Division of Criminal Information at the State Bureau of Investigation, which shall update its records to show the name change.

(f)   If the clerk finds that good and sufficient reasons exist to deny the applicant's request for a name change, it is the clerk's duty not to issue an order changing the name of the applicant from that person's true name to the name sought to be adopted. The order denying the name change shall state the reasons for the denial. If the applicant desires to appeal the clerk's decision, the applicant must petition the resident superior court judge within 30 days of the date of the order denying the name change to request a reconsideration of the application. The reconsideration decision of the resident superior court judge is final and not subject to appeal. An unsuccessful applicant on reconsideration is subject to a waiting period of 12 months from the date of the adverse decision of the resident superior court judge before the applicant may submit another name change application. A successful applicant on reconsideration shall be granted the name change by the clerk in like manner as prescribed by subsection (d) of this section.

(g)   Upon information obtained by the clerk of fraud or material misrepresentation in the application for a name change, the clerk on his or her own motion may set aside the order granting the name change after notice to the applicant and opportunity to be heard. If the clerk sets aside the name change order, the clerk shall notify the State Registrar of Vital Statistics and the

Division of Criminal Information. (1891, c. 145; Rev., ss. 2149, 2150; C.S., s. 2974; 1955, c. 951, s. 4; 1957, c. 1233, s. 2; 1971, c. 444, s. 2; 2011-61, s. 8; 2011-303, s. 1; 2012-194, s. 19; 2013-42, s. 2.)

§ 101-6. Effect of change; only one change, except as provided.

(a)   When the order is made and the applicant's name changed, he is entitled to all the privileges and protection under his new name as he would have been under the old name. No person shall be allowed to change his name under this Chapter but once, except that he shall be permitted to resume his former name upon compliance with the requirements and procedure set forth in this Chapter for change of name, and except as provided in subsection (b) of this section.

(b)   For good cause shown, and upon compliance with the requirements and procedure set forth in this Chapter for change of name, the name of a minor child may be changed not more than two times under this Chapter.

(c)   A sex offender who is registered in accordance with Article 27A of Chapter 14 of the General Statutes is prohibited from obtaining a change of name under this Chapter. (1891, c. 145; Rev., ss. 2147, 2149; C.S., s. 2975; 1945, c. 37, s. 2; 1991, c. 333, s. 1; 2008-218, s. 9.)

§ 101-7. Recording name change.

When the name of any individual, corporation, partnership, or association has been changed in a manner provided by law, any attorney licensed to practice law in this State may file an affidavit with the clerk of superior court stating facts concerning the change of name. The clerk shall cause the affidavit to be filed and indexed among the records of his office, pursuant to G.S. 7A-180(3) and G.S. 7A-343(3). The clerk shall also forward a copy of the affidavit under the seal of his office to the clerk of superior court of any other county named in the affidavit where it shall also be filed and indexed in accordance with this section. Affidavits filed and indexed under this section are for informational purposes only and neither the affidavit nor the manner of its filing and indexing shall in any manner affect the rights or liabilities of any person. (1971, c. 592, s. 1.)

§ 101-8. Resumption of name by widow or widower.

A person at any time after the person is widowed may, upon application to the clerk of court of the county in which the person resides setting forth the person's intention to do so, resume the use of her maiden name or the name of a prior deceased husband or of a previously divorced husband in the case of a widow, or his premarriage surname in the case of a widower. The application shall set forth the full name of the last spouse of the applicant, shall include a copy of the spouse's death certificate, and shall be signed by the applicant in the applicant's full name. The clerks of court of the several counties of this State shall record and index such applications in the manner required by the Administrative Office of the Courts. (1979, c. 768; 1981, c. 564, s. 2; 1993 (Reg. Sess., 1994), c. 565, s. 2.)

Chapter 102.

Official Survey Base.

§ 102-1. Name and description.

The official survey base for the State of North Carolina shall be a system of plane coordinates to be known as the "North Carolina Coordinate System," said system being defined as a Lambert conformal projection of Clarke's spheroid of 1866, having a central meridian of 79°-00' west from Greenwich and standard parallels of latitude of 34°-20' and 36°-10' north of the equator, along which parallels the scale shall be exact. All coordinates of the system are expressed in feet, the x coordinate being measured easterly along the grid and the y coordinate being measured northerly along the grid. The origin of the coordinates is hereby established on the meridian 79°-00' west from Greenwich at the intersection of the parallels 33°-45' north latitude, such origin being given the coordinates x=2,000,000 feet, y=0 feet. The precise position of said system shall be as marked on the ground by triangulation or traverse stations or monuments established in conformity with the standards adopted by the United States Coast and Geodetic Survey for first-and second-order work, whose geodetic positions have been rigidly on the North American datum of 1927, and whose plane coordinates have been computed on the system defined. (1939, c. 163, s. 1.)

§ 102-1.1. Name and description in relation to 1983 North American Datum.

From and after the date and time the North Carolina Geodetic Survey Section in the Division of Emergency Management of the Department of Public Safety receives from the National Geodetic Survey, official notice of a complete, published definition of the North American Datum of 1983 including the State plane coordinate constants applicable to North Carolina, the official survey base for North Carolina shall be a system of plane coordinates to be known as the "North Carolina Coordinate System of 1983," said system being defined as a Lambert conformal projection of the "Geodetic Reference System (GRS 80 Ellipsoid)" having a central meridian of 79° - 00' west from Greenwich and standard parallels of latitude of 34° - 20' and 36° - 10' north of the equator, along which parallels the scale shall be exact. All coordinates of the system are expressed in metres, the x coordinate being measured easterly along the grid and the y coordinate being measured northerly along the grid. The U.S. Survey Foot, 1 meter = 39.37 inches or 3.2808333333 feet, shall be used as a conversion factor. The origin of the coordinates is hereby established on the meridian 79° - 00' west from Greenwich at the intersection of the parallels 33° - 45' north latitude, such origin being given the coordinates x = 609,601.22 metres, y = 0 metres. The precise position of said system shall be as marked on the ground by triangulation or traverse stations or monuments established in conformity with the standards adopted by the National Geodetic Survey for first- and second-order work, whose geodetic positions have been rigidly adjusted on the North American Datum of 1983, and whose plane coordinates have been computed on the system defined. Whenever plane coordinates are used in the description or identification of surface area or location within this State, the coordinates shall be identified as "NAD 83", indicating North American Datum of 1983, or as "NAD 27", indicating North American Datum of 1927. (1979, c. 4; 1987, c. 148; 1989, c. 727, s. 218(33); 1997-443, s. 11A.119(a); 2005-386, s. 1.2; 2012-142, s. 12.4(b).)

§ 102-2. Physical control.

Any triangulation or traverse station or monument established as described in G.S. 102-1 may be used in establishing a connection between any survey and the above-mentioned system of rectangular coordinates. (1939, c. 163, s. 2.)

§ 102-3. Use of name.

The use of the term "North Carolina Coordinate System" on any map, report, or survey, or other document, shall be limited to coordinates based on the North Carolina Coordinate System as defined in this Chapter. (1939, c. 163, s. 3.)

§ 102-4. Damaging, defacing, or destroying monuments.

If any person shall willfully damage, deface, destroy, or otherwise injure a station, monument or permanent mark of the North Carolina Coordinate System, or shall oppose any obstacles to the proper, reasonable, and legal use of any such station or monument, such person shall be guilty of a Class 1 misdemeanor. (1939, c. 163, s. 4; 1993, c. 539, s. 683; 1994, Ex. Sess., c. 24, s. 14(c).)

§ 102-5. Repealed by Session Laws 1963, c. 783.

§ 102-6. Legality of use in descriptions.

For the purpose of describing the location of any survey station or land boundary corner in the State of North Carolina, it shall be considered a complete, legal, and satisfactory description to define the location of such point or points by means of coordinates of the North Carolina Coordinate System as described herein. (1963, c. 163, s. 6; c. 783.)

§ 102-7. Use not compulsory.

Nothing contained in this Chapter shall be interpreted as requiring any purchaser or mortgagee to rely wholly on a description based upon the North Carolina Coordinate System. (1939, c. 163, s. 7.)

§ 102-8. Administrative agency.

The administrative agency of the North Carolina Coordinate System shall be the Department of Public Safety through its appropriate division hereinafter called the "agency." (1939, c. 163, s. 8; 1973, c. 1262, s. 86; 1977, c. 771, s. 4; 1989, c. 727, s. 218(34); 1997-443, s. 11A.119(a); 2012-142, s. 12.4(c).)

§ 102-9. Duties and powers of the agency.

It shall be the duty of the agency to make or cause to be made from time to time such surveys and computations as are necessary to further or complete the North Carolina Coordinate System. The agency shall endeavor to carry to completion as soon as practicable the field monumentation and office computations of the coordinate system. For the purpose of this work the agency shall have the power to accept grants for the specific purpose of carrying on the work; to coordinate, organize, and direct any federal or other assistance which may be offered to further the work; to cooperate with any individual, firm, company, public or private agency, State or federal agencies, in the prosecution of the work; to enter into contracts or cooperative agreements with other state or federal agencies in promoting the work of the coordinating system. The agency shall further have the power to adopt necessary rules, regulations, and specifications relating to the establishment and use of the coordinate system as defined in this Chapter, consistent with the standards and practice of the United States Coast and Geodetic Survey. (1939, c. 163, s. 9; 1997-443, s. 11A.119(a).)

§ 102-10. Prior work.

The system of stations, monuments, traverses, computations, and other work which has been done or is under way in North Carolina by the so-called North Carolina Geodetic Survey, under the supervision of the United States Coast and Geodetic Survey, is, where consistent with the provisions of this Chapter, hereby made a part of the North Carolina Coordinate System. The surveys, notes, computations, monuments, stations, and all other work relating to the coordinate system, which has been done by said North Carolina Geodetic Survey, under the supervision of and in cooperation with the United States Coast and Geodetic Survey and federal relief agencies, hereby are placed under the direction of, and shall become the property of, the administrative agency. All persons or agencies having in their possession any surveys, notes, computations, or other data pertaining to the aforementioned coordinate system, shall turn over to the Department of Public Safety such data upon request. (1939, c. 163, s. 10; 1959, c. 1315, s. 1; 1973, c. 1262, s. 86; 1977, c. 771, s. 4; 1989, c. 727, s. 218(35); 1997-443, s. 11A.119(a); 2012-142, s. 12.4(d).)

§ 102-11. Vertical control.

Whereas the foregoing provisions of this Chapter heretofore are related to horizontal control only, the administrative agency may adopt standards for vertical control or levying surveys consistent with those recommended by and used by the United States Coast and Geodetic Survey, and make or cause to be made such surveys as are necessary to complete the vertical control of North Carolina, in accordance with the provisions for horizontal control surveys as defined in this Chapter. (1939, c. 163, s. 11.)

§ 102-12. Control system map.

The agency shall prepare for publication and cause to be published a map or maps setting forth the location of monuments for both horizontal and vertical control, together with such other pertinent data as the agency may direct for implementation of the North Carolina Coordinate System. The agency shall furnish such map or maps to any person or may make such charge as will defray the expense of printing and distribution. It shall be the responsibility of the agency to maintain this map, make revisions as often as necessary to provide up-to-date information and furnish up-to-date copies to the register of deeds of each county in the State. (1959, c. 1315, s. 2; 2012-142, s. 12.4(e).)

§ 102-13. Repealed by Session Laws 1975, c. 183, s. 1.

§ 102-14. Repealed by Session Laws 1973, c. 1262, s. 86.

§ 102-15. Improvement of land records.

There is hereby established a statewide program for improvement of county land records to be administered by the Secretary of State (hereafter called the Secretary). First emphasis shall be given to the completion of countywide base maps. Counties with a base map system prepared to acceptable standards will be encouraged to undertake subsequent logical improvements in their respective land records systems. Work undertaken by any county under this program will be eligible for financial assistance out of funds appropriated for this purpose to the Department of the Secretary of State. The amount allotted to each project is to be determined by the Secretary, but in no case shall such allotments exceed one dollar for every dollar of local tax funds expended on the project by the county. Federal or other State funds available to the project will not be eligible as matching money under the State program. (1977, c. 1099, s. 1; 1985, c. 479, s. 165(b); 1989, c. 727, s. 218(36); 1989 (Reg. Sess., 1990), c. 1004, s. 19(b); 1997-443, s. 11A.119(a); 1999-119, s. 1.)

§ 102-16. Board of county commissioners to apply for assistance.

The board of county commissioners of each county may apply to the Secretary, upon forms provided by him and in accordance with directives and requirements outlined in G.S. 102-17, for assistance in completing one or more projects. Such project or projects shall constitute one or more phases of a plan for the improvement of the county's land records. The work to be undertaken shall be described in relation to the county's revaluation schedule, and it shall be shown to be a part of a larger undertaking for achieving ultimate long-term improvements in the land records maintained by the county register of deeds, the county tax supervisor, or other county office. (1977, c. 1099, s. 1.)

§ 102-17. County projects eligible for assistance.

All projects funded under this assistance program shall be described as conforming to one or more of the project outlines defined herein. All projects shall achieve a substantial measure of conformity with the objectives set forth in these project outlines such that a greater degree of statewide standardization of land records will result. The Secretary shall prepare and make available to all counties administrative regulations designed to assist the counties in preparing project plans and applications for assistance, and to assure compliance with the objectives and other requirements of G.S. 102-15, 102-16, and this section.

County projects shall be eligible for assistance subject to availability of funds, compliance with administrative regulations, and conformity with one or more of the project outlines as follows:

(1)   Base Maps. - Preparation of accurate planimetric or orthophoto maps with countywide coverage at one or more scale ratios suitable as a base for the development and maintenance of current cadastral maps. These maps shall have additional information included where appropriate to increase their utility for other purposes. The formulation of technical standards and detailed specifications and the coordination of all such mapping projects with other State mapping programs shall be the responsibility of the Department of the Secretary of State. Insofar as possible mapping projects funded under this assistance program shall utilize existing photography, geodetic control surveys, and previously mapped information, and be coordinated or combined with adjacent or related mapping projects to achieve the best efficiency and economy consistent with the maintenance of high quality map production.

(2)   Cadastral Maps. - Preparation of accurate maps of all property boundaries together with other supporting information and based on up-to-date planimetric or orthophoto maps conforming to the specifications for base maps outlined in subdivision (1) of this section. The formulation of specifications and standards for these cadastral maps shall be the responsibility of the Department of the Secretary of State. These specifications and standards shall be designed to conform to the best acceptable practice for county land records in North Carolina. The cadastral maps shall be scheduled as nearly as possible to be completed and made available for the next revaluation cycle to be undertaken by each county and the maps shall include references to subdivision plat numbers, property codes, and other related information considered useful to the appraisal process or to the public generally.

(3)   Standardized Parcel Identifiers. - Adoption of a system of parcel identifiers which will serve to provide unique identification of each parcel of land, a permanent historical record of change and the chain of title, and any necessary cross-reference to other preexisting parcel identifiers. The proposed system of parcel identifiers shall conform to such minimum specifications and standards as may be promulgated by the Secretary for the purpose of achieving consistency and compatibility among all counties throughout the State. Said minimum specifications and standards for parcel identifier systems shall be adopted and administered by the Secretary only after consultation with the recommendation from an advisory committee on land records with a

101

membership representative of professional organizations concerned with public land records and map making.

(4)   Automated Processing of Land Parcel Records. - Preparation and implementation of a system of automated record keeping and processing which will expedite the maintenance of accurate up-to-date files, improve the appraisal process, and facilitate analytical operations needed to respond to requirements for current information. Technical standards and minimum specifications shall be the joint responsibility of the Department of the Secretary of State, the Department of Revenue, and the Department of Cultural Resources. (1977, c. 771, s. 4; c. 1099, s. 1; 1985, c. 479, s. 165(c); 1989, c. 727, s. 218(37); 1997-443, s. 11A.119(a); 1999-119, s. 2.)

Chapter 103.

Sundays, Holidays and Special Days.

§ 103-1. Repealed by Session Laws 1951, c. 73.

§ 103-2. Hunting on Sunday.

If any person shall, except in defense of his own property, hunt on Sunday, having with him a shotgun, rifle, or pistol, he shall be guilty of a Class 3 misdemeanor. Provided, that the provisions hereof shall not be applicable to military reservations, the jurisdiction of which is exclusively in the federal government, or to field trials authorized by the Wildlife Resources Commission. Wildlife protectors are granted authority to enforce the provisions of this section. (1868-9, c. 18, ss. 1, 2; Code, s. 3783; Rev., s. 3842; C.S., s. 3956; 1945, c. 1047; 1967, c. 1003; 1979, c. 830, s. 13; 1989, c. 642, s. 3; 1993, c. 539, s. 684; 1994, Ex. Sess., c. 24, s. 14(c).)

§ 103-3. Execution of process on Sunday.

It shall be lawful for any sheriff or other lawful officer to execute any summons, capias, or other process on Sunday. (1957, c. 1052; 1973, c. 108, s. 47.)

§ 103-4. Dates of public holidays.

(a)   The following are declared to be legal public holidays:

(1)   New Year's Day, January 1.

(1a)   Martin Luther King, Jr.'s, Birthday, the third Monday in January.

(2)   Robert E. Lee's Birthday, January 19.

(3)   Washington's Birthday, the third Monday in February.

(3a)   Greek Independence Day, March 25.

(4)   Anniversary of signing of Halifax Resolves, April 12.

(5)   Confederate Memorial Day, May 10.

(6)   Anniversary of Mecklenburg Declaration of Independence, May 20.

(7)   Memorial Day, the last Monday in May.

(8)   Good Friday.

(9)   Independence Day, July 4.

(10)   Labor Day, the first Monday in September.

(11)   Columbus Day, the second Monday in October.

(11a)   Yom Kippur.

(12)   Veterans Day, November 11.

(13)   Tuesday after the first Monday in November in years in which a general election is to be held.

(14)   Thanksgiving Day, the fourth Thursday in November.

(15)   Christmas Day, December 25.

(b)   Whenever any public holiday shall fall upon Sunday, the Monday following shall be a public holiday. (1881, c. 294; Code, s. 3784; 1891, c. 58; 1899, c. 410; 1901, c. 25; Rev., s. 2838; 1907, c. 996; 1909, c. 888; 1919, c. 287; C.S., s. 2959; 1935, c. 212; 1959, c. 1011; 1969, c. 521; 1973, c. 53; 1979, c. 84; 1981, c. 135; 1983, c. 1; 1987, c. 25, s. 1, c. 851, ss. 1, 2, c. 853, s. 2.)

§ 103-5. Acts to be done on Sunday or holidays.

(a)   Except as otherwise provided by law, when the day or the last day for doing any act required or permitted by law to be performed in a public office or courthouse falls on a Saturday, Sunday, or legal holiday when the public office or courthouse is closed for transactions, the act may be performed on the next day that the public office or courthouse is open for transactions.

(b)   This section does not apply where the act required or permitted by law to be done is prescribed by Section 22 of Article II, or Section 5(11) of Article III, of the Constitution of North Carolina. (Code, ss. 3784, 3785, 3786; 1899, c. 733, s. 194; Rev., s. 2839; C.S., s. 3960; 1951, c. 1176, s. 1; 1995, c. 20, s. 16; 2003-337, s. 1.)

§ 103-6. Arbor Week.

The week in March of each year containing March 15 is hereby designated as Arbor Week in North Carolina. (1967, c. 39.)

§ 103-7. American Family Day.

The first Sunday in August of each year is designated as American Family Day in North Carolina. (1979, c. 457.)

§ 103-8. Indian solidarity week.

The last full week in September of each year is designated as Indian solidarity week in North Carolina. (1981, c. 769.)

§ 103-9. Prisoner of War Day.

The ninth of April of each year is designated as Prisoner of War Recognition Day. (1989, c. 428, s. 1.)

§ 103-10. Pearl Harbor Remembrance Day.

The seventh of December of each year is designated as Pearl Harbor Remembrance Day in North Carolina. (1991, c. 175, s. 1.)

§ 103-11. Disability History and Awareness Month.

The month of October of each year is designated as Disability History and Awareness Month in North Carolina. (2007-274, s. 1.)

§ 103-12. Organ Donation Awareness/Donate Life Month.

The month of April of each year is designated as Organ Donation Awareness/Donate Life Month in North Carolina. (2013-22, s. 1.)

§ 103-13. Fragile X Awareness Day.

The twenty-second of July of each year is designated as North Carolina Fragile X Awareness Day. (2013-238, s. 1.)

Chapter 104.

United States Lands.

Article 1.

Authority for Acquisition.

§ 104-1. Acquisition of lands for specified purposes authorized; concurrent jurisdiction reserved.

The United States is authorized, by purchase or otherwise, to acquire title to any tract or parcel of land in the State of North Carolina, not exceeding 25 acres, for the purpose of erecting thereon any customhouse, courthouse, post office, or other building, including lighthouses, lightkeepers' dwellings, lifesaving stations, buoys and local depots and buildings connected therewith, or for the establishment of a fish-cultural station and the erection thereon of such buildings and improvements as may be necessary for the successful operations of such fish-cultural station. The consent to acquisition by the United States is upon the express condition that the State of North Carolina shall so far retain a concurrent jurisdiction with the United States over such lands as that all civil and criminal process issued from the courts of the State of North Carolina may be executed thereon in like manner as if this authority had not been given, and that the State of North Carolina also retains authority to punish all violations of its criminal laws committed on any such tract of land. (1870-1, c. 44, s. 5; Code, ss. 3080, 3083; 1887, c. 136; 1899, c. 10; Rev., s. 5426; C.S., s. 8053.)

§ 104-2. Unused lands to revert to State.

The consent given in G.S. 104-1 is upon consideration of the United States building lighthouses, lighthouse keepers' dwellings, lifesaving stations, buoys, coal depots, fish stations, post offices, customhouses, and other buildings connected therewith, on the tracts or parcels of land so purchased, or that may be purchased; and that the title to land so conveyed to the United States shall revert to the State unless the construction of the aforementioned buildings be completed thereon within 10 years from the date of the conveyance from the grantor. (1870-1, c. 44, s. 5; Code, ss. 3080, 3083; 1887, c. 136; 1899, c. 10; Rev., s. 5426; C.S., s. 8054.)

§ 104-3. Exemption of such lands from taxation.

The lots, parcels, or tracts of land acquired under this Chapter, together with the tenements and appurtenances for the purpose mentioned in this Chapter, shall be exempt from taxation. (1870-1, c. 44, s. 3; Code, s. 3082; Rev., s. 5428; C.S., s. 8055.)

§ 104-4. Conveyances of such lands to be recorded.

All deeds, conveyances, or other title papers for the same shall be recorded, as in other cases, in the office of the register of deeds of the county in which the lands so conveyed may lie, in the same manner and under the same regulations as other deeds and conveyances are now recorded, and in like manner may be recorded a sufficient description by metes and bounds, courses and distances, of any tract or legal division of any public land belonging to the United States, which may be set apart by the general government for the purpose before mentioned, by an order, patent, or other official document or paper so describing such land. (1870-1, c. 44, s. 2; 1872-3, c. 201; Code, s. 3081; Rev., s. 5429; C.S., s. 8056.)

§ 104-5. Forest reserve in North Carolina authorized; powers conferred.

The United States is authorized to acquire by purchase, or by condemnation with adequate compensation, except as hereinafter provided, such lands in North Carolina as in the opinion of the federal government may be needed for the establishment of a national forest reserve in that region. This consent is given upon condition that the State of North Carolina shall retain a concurrent jurisdiction with the United States in and over such lands so far that civil process in all cases, and such criminal process as may issue under the authority of the State of North Carolina against any person charged with the commission of any crime without or within said jurisdiction, may be executed thereon in like manner as if this consent had not been given. Power is hereby conferred upon the Congress of the United States to pass such laws as it may deem necessary to the acquisition as hereinbefore provided, for incorporation in such national forest reserve such forest-covered lands lying in North Carolina as in the opinion of the federal government may be needed for this purpose, but as much as 200 acres of any tract of land occupied as a home by bona fide residents in this State on the eighteenth day of January, 1901, shall be exempt from the provisions of this section. Power is hereby conferred upon Congress to pass such laws and to make or provide for the making of such rules and regulations, of both civil and criminal nature, and to provide punishment therefor, as in its judgment may be necessary for the management, control, and protection of such lands as may be from time to time acquired by the United States under the provisions of this section. (1901, c. 17; Rev., s. 5430; C.S., s. 8057; 1929, c. 67, s. 1.)

§ 104-6. Acquisition of lands for river and harbor improvement; reservation of right to serve process.

The consent of the legislature of the State is hereby given to the acquisition by the United States of any tracts, pieces, or parcels of land within the limits of the State, by purchase or condemnation, for use as sites for locks and dams, or for any other purpose in connection with the improvement of rivers and harbors within and on the borders of the State. The consent hereby given is in accordance with the seventeenth clause of the eighth section of the first article of the Constitution of the United States, and with the acts of Congress in such cases made and provided; and this State retains concurrent jurisdiction with the United States over any lands acquired and held in pursuance of the provisions of this section, so far as that all civil and criminal process issued under authority of any law of this State may be executed in any part of the premises so acquired, or the buildings or structures thereon erected. (1907, c. 681; C.S., s. 8058.)

§ 104-7. Acquisition of lands by the United States for customhouses, courthouses, post offices, forts, arsenals, or armories; cession of jurisdiction; exemption from taxation.

(a)   The consent of the State is hereby given, in accordance with the seventeenth clause, eighth section, of the first article of the Constitution of the United States, to the acquisition by the United States, by purchase, condemnation, or otherwise, of any land in the State that either is:

(1)   Required for customhouses, courthouses, post offices, forts, arsenals, or armories; provided that the total land to be acquired for a particular facility does not exceed 25 acres; or

(2)   To be added to Fort Bragg, Pope Air Force Base, Camp Lejeune, New River Marine Corps Air Station, Seymour Johnson Air Force Base, Cherry Point Marine Corps Air Station, Military Ocean Terminal at Sunny Point, or the United States Coast Guard Air Station at Elizabeth City. Any of the land to be added to a military base named in this subdivision shall be contiguous to and within a 25-mile radius of the military base for which the property is acquired.

(a1)   Notwithstanding the provisions of subsection (a) above, the consent of the State is not given to the acquisition by the United States, by purchase, condemnation or otherwise, of any land in a county or counties which have no existing military base at which aircraft squadrons are stationed, for the purpose of establishing an outlying landing field to support training and operations of aircraft squadrons stationed at or transient to military bases or military stations located outside of the State. Exclusive jurisdiction in and over any land acquired by the United States without the consent of the State under this subsection is not ceded to the United States for any purpose.

(b)   Exclusive jurisdiction in and over any land acquired by the United States with the consent of the State under subsection (a) of this section is hereby ceded to the United States for all purposes for which the United States requests cession of jurisdiction except that jurisdiction in and over these lands with respect to: (i) the service of all civil and criminal process of the courts of this State, (ii) the concurrent power to enforce the criminal law, (iii) the power to enforce State laws for the protection of public health and the environment and for the conservation of natural resources, and (iv) the entire legislative jurisdiction of the State with respect to marriage, divorce, annulment, adoption, commitment of the mentally incompetent, and descent and distribution of property is reserved to the State. Cession of jurisdiction shall continue only so long as the United States owns the land.

(c)   The jurisdiction ceded shall not vest until the United States has acquired title to the land by purchase, condemnation, or otherwise; accepted the cession of jurisdiction in writing; and filed a certified copy of the acceptance in the office of the register of deeds in the county or counties in which the land is located.

(d)   So long as land acquired with the consent of the State under subsection (a) of this section remains the property of the United States, and no longer, the land shall be exempt and exonerated from all State, county, and municipal taxation, assessment, or other charges that may be levied or imposed under the authority of this State.

109

(e)   Persons residing on lands in the State for which any jurisdiction has been ceded under this section shall not be deprived of any civil or political rights, including the right of suffrage, by reason of the cession of jurisdiction to the United States. (1907, c. 25; C.S., s. 8059; 2005-69, s. 1; 2009-20, s. 1; 2012-18, s. 1.16.)

§ 104-8. Further authorization of acquisition of land.

The United States is hereby authorized to acquire lands by condemnation or otherwise in this State for the purpose of preserving the navigability of navigable streams and for holding and administering such lands for national park purposes: Provided, that this section and G.S. 104-9 shall in nowise affect the authority conferred upon the United States and reserved to the State in G.S. 104-5 and 104-6. (1925, c. 152, s. 1.)

§ 104-9. Condition of consent granted in preceding section.

This consent is given upon condition that the State of North Carolina shall retain a concurrent jurisdiction with the United States in and over such lands so far that civil process in all cases, and such criminal process as may issue under the authority of the State of North Carolina against any person charged with the commission of any crime, without or within said jurisdiction, may be executed thereon in like manner as if this consent had not been given. (1925, c. 152, s. 2.)

§ 104-10. Migratory bird sanctuaries or other wildlife refuges.

The United States is authorized to acquire by purchase, or by condemnation with adequate compensation, such lands in North Carolina as in the opinion of the federal government may be needed for the establishment of one or more migratory bird sanctuaries or other wildlife refuges. This consent is given upon condition that the State of North Carolina shall retain a concurrent jurisdiction with the United States in and over such lands so far that civil process in all cases, and such criminal process as may issue under the authority of the State of North Carolina against any person charged with the commission of any crime without or within said jurisdiction, may be executed therein in like manner as if this consent had not been given. Power is hereby conferred upon the Congress of the United States to pass such laws as it may deem necessary to the acquisition as hereinbefore provided, for incorporation in such sanctuaries or refuges such lands lying in North Carolina as in the opinion of the federal government may be suitable and needed for this purpose. Power is hereby conferred upon Congress to pass such laws and to make or provide for the making of such rules and regulations, of both civil and criminal nature, and to provide punishment therefor, as in its judgment may be necessary for the management, control and protection of such lands as may be from time to time acquired by the United States under the provisions of this section. (1929, c. 163, s. 1.)

§ 104-11. Utilities Commission to secure rights-of-way, etc., for waterway improvements by use of federal funds.

Hereafter whenever any waterway improvement in North Carolina by the use of federal funds is provided for upon condition that the State or locality shall furnish rights-of-way, permits for the dumping of dredged material, or furnish or do any other thing in connection with the proposed waterway improvement, the Utilities Commission is authorized and empowered to represent the State or locality in such matter of securing the rights-of-way, permits for the dumping of dredged material, or other things so required in connection with such waterway improvement; and in prosecuting such undertaking, the Utilities Commission may follow the same procedure provided in Article 2 for the acquisition of rights-of-way for the intercoastal waterway from the Cape Fear River to the South Carolina line: Provided, however, that said Utilities Commission is not hereby authorized to enter into obligation or contract for the payment of any money or proceeds through condemnation or otherwise without the express approval of the Governor and Council of State. (1935, c. 240; 1937, c. 434.)

§ 104-11.1. Governor may accept a retrocession of jurisdiction over federal areas.

Whenever a duly authorized official or agent of the United States, acting pursuant to authority conferred by the Congress, notifies the Governor or any other State official, department or agency, that the United States desires or is willing to relinquish to the State the jurisdiction, or a portion thereof, held by the United States over the lands designated in such notice, the Governor may, in his discretion, accept such relinquishment. Such acceptance may be made by sending a notice of acceptance to the official or agent designated by the United States to receive such notice of acceptance. The Governor shall send a signed copy of the notice of acceptance, together with the notice of relinquishment received from the United States, to the Secretary of State, who shall maintain a permanent file of said notices.

Upon the sending of said notice of acceptance to the designated official or agent of the United States, the State shall immediately have such jurisdiction over the lands designated in the notice of relinquishment as said notice shall specify.

The provisions of this section shall apply to the relinquishment of jurisdiction acquired by the United States under the provisions of this Chapter or any other provision of law. (1957, c. 1202.)

Article 2.

Inland Waterways.

§ 104-12. Acquisition of land for inland waterway from Cape Fear River; grant of State lands.

For the purpose of aiding in the construction of the proposed inland waterway by the United States from the Cape Fear River at Southport to the North Carolina-South Carolina State line, the Secretary of State is hereby authorized to issue to the United States of America a grant to the land located within said inland waterway, right-of-way, which is to be 1,000 feet to 1,750 feet wide insofar as such land is subject to grant by the State of North Carolina, the said grant to issue upon a certificate furnished to the Secretary of State by the Secretary of War, or by any authorized officer of the corps of engineers of the United States Army, or by any other authorized official, exercising control over the construction of the said waterway. Whenever in the construction of such inland waterway within this State, lands theretofore submerged shall be raised above the water by the deposit of excavated material, the land so formed shall become the property of the United States if within the limits of said inland waterway, right-of-way, herein set out 1,000 feet to 1,750 feet and the Secretary of State is hereby authorized to issue to the United States a grant to the land so formed within the limits above specified, the grant to issue upon a certificate furnished to the Secretary of State by some authorized official of the United States, as above provided. If said lands so required for the inland waterway right-of-way shall be marshlands, or sound lands, the title to which has heretofore been vested in the State Board of Education, the Governor of the State, as President thereof, and the Superintendent of Public Instruction as Secretary, are hereby authorized and required to execute proper conveyance to the United States of America for said marshlands or sound lands, free of cost, both to the State and to the United States government, upon a certificate furnished to said Board of Education by the Secretary of War, or by any authorized officer of the corps of engineers of the United States Army, or by any other authorized official exercising control over the construction of the said inland waterway. (1931, c. 2, s. 1; 2011-183, s. 127(b).)

§ 104-13. Utilities Commission to secure right-of-way over private lands; condemnation by United States.

If the title to any part of the lands acquired by the United States government for the construction of such inland waterway from the Cape Fear River at Southport to the North Carolina-South Carolina State line shall be in any private person, company or corporation, railroad company, street railway company, telephone or telegraph company, or other public service corporation or shall have been donated or condemned or any public use by any political subdivision of the State, or if it may be necessary, for the purpose of obtaining the proper title to any lands, the title to which has heretofore been vested in the State Board of Education, then the Utilities Commission, in the name of the State of North Carolina, is hereby authorized and empowered, acting for and in behalf of the State of North Carolina, to secure a right-of-way 1,000 to 1,750 feet wide for said inland waterway across and through such lands or any part thereof, by purchase, donation or otherwise, through agreement with the owner or owners where possible, and when any such property is thus acquired, the Governor and Secretary of State shall execute a deed for the same to the United States; and if for any reason the said Commission shall be unable to secure such right-of-way across any such property by voluntary donation by and/or with the owner or owners, the said Commission acting for and in behalf of the State of North Carolina is hereby vested with the power to condemn the same, and in so doing, the ways, means, methods and procedure of the Chapter of the General

Statutes of North Carolina, entitled "Eminent Domain," shall be used by it as near as the same is suitable for the purposes of this Article, and in all instances, the general and special benefits to the owner thereof shall be assessed as offsets against the damages to such property or lands.

As such condemnation proceedings might result in delay in the acquiring of title to all parts of the right-of-way and in the construction of the said inland waterway by the United States, said Utilities Commission is authorized to enter any of said lands and property and take possession of the same at the time hereinafter provided as needed for this use in behalf of the State or the United States government for the purposes herein set out, prior to the bringing of the proceeding for condemnation and prior to the payment of the money for such land or property under any judgment in condemnation. In the event the owner or owners shall appeal from the report of the commissioners appointed in any condemnation proceeding hereunder, it shall not be necessary for said Commission, acting in behalf of the State of North Carolina, or the United States government, to deposit the money assessed by said commissioners with the clerk.

Whenever proceedings in condemnation are instituted in pursuance of the provisions of this section, the said Commission upon the filing of the petition or petitions in such proceedings, shall have the right to take immediate possession, on behalf of the State, of such lands or property to the extent of the interest to be acquired and the order of the clerk of the superior court of the county where the action is instituted, shall be sufficient to vest the title and possession in the State through the Utilities Commission. The Governor and Secretary of State shall, upon vesting of the title and possession, execute a deed to the United States and said lands or property may then be appropriated and used by the United States for the purposes aforesaid: Provided, that in every case the proceedings in condemnation shall be diligently prosecuted to final judgment in order that the just compensation, if any, to which the owners of the property are entitled may be ascertained and when so ascertained and determined, such compensation, if any, shall be promptly paid as hereinafter in this Article provided.

If the United States government shall so determine, it is hereby authorized to condemn and use all lands and property which may be needed for the purposes herein set out and which is specifically described and set out in the paragraph next preceding, under the authority of said United States government, and according to the provisions existing in the federal statutes for condemning lands and property for the use of the United States government. In case the United

States government shall so condemn said land and property, the said Utilities Commission is hereby authorized to pay all expenses of the condemnation proceedings and any award that may be made thereunder, out of the money which may be appropriated for said purposes.

All sums which may be agreed upon between the said Utilities Commission and the owner of any property needed by the United States government for said inland waterway and all sums which may be assessed in favor of the owner of any property condemned hereunder, shall constitute and remain a fixed and valid claim against the State of North Carolina until paid and satisfied in full, but the order of the clerk when entered in any condemnation proceeding shall divest the owner of the land condemned of all right, title, interest and possession in and to such land and property. (1931, c. 2, s. 2; 1937, c. 434.)

§ 104-14. Use declared paramount public purpose.

In such condemnation proceedings the uses for which such land or property is condemned are hereby declared to be for a purpose paramount to all other public uses, and the fact that any portion of it has heretofore been condemned by a railroad company, a street railway company, telephone or telegraph company, or other public service corporation, or by any political subdivision of the State of North Carolina, for public uses, or has been conveyed by any person or corporation for any such public uses, or vested in the State Board of Education, or by any other act dedicated to any public use, shall in no way affect the right of the State of North Carolina, or the United States government, to proceed and condemn such land and property as hereinbefore provided. (1931, c. 2, s. 3.)

§ 104-15. Method of payment of expenses and awards.

Whenever said Commission has agreed with the owner of any such land or property as to the purchase price thereof, or the damage for the construction of the inland waterway has finally been determined in any condemnation proceeding necessary to secure such land or property, the said Commission is hereby authorized and directed to pay all of said sums and other expenses incident thereto by proper warrant upon the sum which may be appropriated for said purpose, and all such sums shall constitute and remain a fixed and valid claim against the State of North Carolina until paid and satisfied in full. (1931, c. 2, s. 4.)

§ 104-16. State and United States may enter upon lands for survey, etc.

For the purpose of determining the lands necessary for the uses herein set out, the Utilities Commission or the United States government, or the agents of either, shall have the right to enter upon any lands along the general line of the right-of-way in this Article specified, and make such surveys, and do such other acts as in their judgment may be necessary for the purpose of definitely locating the specific lines of said right-of-way and the lands required for said purposes, and there shall be no claim against the State of North Carolina or the United States for such acts as may be done in making said surveys. (1931, c. 2, s. 5; 1937, c. 434.)

§ 104-17. Construction, maintenance, etc., of bridges over waterway.

The Board of Transportation or the road governing body of any political subdivision of the State of North Carolina is hereby authorized and directed to construct, maintain and operate in perpetuity, all bridges over the waterway without cost to the United States. (1931, c. 2, s. 7; 1933, c. 172, s. 17; 1957, c. 65, s. 11; 1973, c. 507, s. 5.)

§ 104-18. Concurrent jurisdiction over waterway.

The State of North Carolina retains concurrent jurisdiction with the United States over any lands acquired and held in pursuance of the provisions of this Chapter, so far as that all civil and criminal process issued under authority of any law of this State may be executed in any part of the premises so acquired for such inland waterway, or for the buildings or constructions thereon erected for the purposes of such inland waterway. (1931, c. 2, s. 8.)

§ 104-19. Acquisition of land for inland waterway from Beaufort Inlet; grant of State lands.

For the purpose of aiding in the construction of the proposed inland waterway by the United States from Beaufort Inlet in the State of North Carolina to the Cape Fear River, the Secretary of State is hereby authorized to issue to the United States of America a grant to the land located within said inland waterway, right-of-way, which is to be 1,000 feet wide, insofar as such land is subject to grant by the State of North Carolina, the said grant to issue upon a certificate furnished to the Secretary of State by the Secretary of War, or by any authorized officer of the corps of engineers of the United States Army, or by any other authorized official, exercising control over the construction of the said waterway. Whenever in the construction of such inland waterway within this State, lands theretofore submerged shall be raised above the water by the deposit of excavated material, the land so formed shall become the property of the United States if within the limits of said inland waterway, right-of-way, herein set out 1,000 feet, and the Secretary of State is hereby authorized to issue to the United States a grant to the land so formed within the limits above specified, the grant to issue upon a certificate furnished to the Secretary of State by some authorized official of the United States, as above provided. If said lands so required for the inland waterway right-of-way shall be marshlands, the title to which has heretofore been vested in the State Board of Education, the Governor of the State, as President thereof, and the Superintendent of Public Instruction as Secretary, are hereby authorized and required to execute a proper conveyance to the United States of America for said marshlands, free of cost, both to the State and to the United States government, upon a certificate furnished, to said Board of Education by the Secretary of War, or by any authorized officer of the corps of engineers of the United States Army, or by any other authorized official exercising control over the construction of the said inland waterway. (1927, c. 44, s. 1; 2011-183, s. 127(b).)

§ 104-20. Utilities Commission to secure right-of-way; condemnation by United States.

If the title to any part of the lands required by the United States government for the construction of an inland waterway from Beaufort Inlet to the Cape Fear River is owned by a private person, company or corporation, railroad company, street railway company, telephone or telegraph company, or other public service corporation, or has been donated or condemned for any public use by any

117

political subdivision of the State or if it may be necessary, for the purpose of obtaining the proper title to any lands, the title to which has heretofore been vested in the State Board of Education, then the Utilities Commission, in the name of the State of North Carolina, may secure a right-of-way 1,000 feet wide for the inland waterway across and through the lands or any part thereof, if possible by purchase, donation or otherwise, through agreement with the owner or owners, and when any property is thus acquired, the Governor and Secretary of State shall execute a deed for the same to the United States; and if for any reason the Commission is unable to secure a right-of-way across the property by voluntary agreement with the owner or owners as aforesaid, the Commission acting for and in behalf of the State of North Carolina, is hereby vested with the power to condemn the same, and in so doing, the ways, means, methods and procedure of Chapter 40A of the General Statutes of North Carolina, entitled "Eminent Domain," shall be used by it as near as the same is suitable for the purposes of this law, and in all instances, the general and the special benefits to the owner thereof shall be assessed as offsets against the damages to the property or lands.

As condemnation proceedings might result in delay in the acquiring of title to all parts of the right-of-way and in the construction of the inland waterway by the United States, the Utilities Commission is authorized to enter any of the lands and property and take possession of the same at the time hereinafter provided as needed for this use in behalf of the State or the United States government for the purposes herein set out prior to the bringing of the proceeding for condemnation and prior to the payment of the money for the land or property under any judgment in condemnation. In the event the owner or owners shall appeal from the report of the commissioners appointed in the condemnation proceeding it shall not be necessary for the Commission, acting in behalf of the State of North Carolina, the State of North Carolina, or the United States government, to deposit the money assessed by the commissioners with the clerk.

Whenever proceedings in condemnation are instituted under the provisions of this section, the Commission upon the filing of the petition or petitions in the proceedings, may take immediate possession on behalf of the State of the lands or property to the extent of the interest to be acquired and the Governor and Secretary of State shall thereupon execute a deed to the United States and the lands or property may then be appropriated and used by the United States for the purposes described in this section. Provided, that in every case the proceedings in condemnation shall be diligently prosecuted to final judgment in order that the just compensation to which the owners of the property are entitled may be ascertained and when so ascertained and determined the compensation shall be promptly paid as hereinafter in this law provided.

If the United States government shall so determine, it is hereby authorized to condemn and use all lands and property that may be needed for the purposes herein set out and which is specifically described and set out in the preceding paragraphs, under the authority of the United States government, and according to the provisions existing in the federal statutes for condemning lands and property for the use of the United States government. In case the United States government shall so condemn the land and property, the Utilities Commission is hereby authorized to pay all expenses of the condemnation proceedings and any award that may be made thereunder, out of the money that may be appropriated for these purposes. (1927, c. 44, s. 2; 1929, c. 4; c. 7, s. 1; 1937, c. 434; 2001-487, s. 38(d).)

§ 104-21. Use declared paramount public purpose.

In such condemnation proceedings the uses for which such land or property is condemned are hereby declared to be for a purpose paramount to all other public uses, and the fact that any portion of it has heretofore been condemned by a railroad company, street railway company, telephone or telegraph company, or other public service corporation, or by any political subdivision of the State of North Carolina, for public uses, or has been conveyed by any person or corporation for any such public uses, or vested in the State Board of Education, shall in no way affect the right of the State of North Carolina, or the United States government, to proceed and condemn such land and property as hereinbefore provided. (1927, c. 44, s. 3.)

§ 104-22. Method of payment of expenses and awards.

Whenever said Commission has agreed with the owner of any such land or property as to the purchase price thereof, or the damage for the construction of the inland waterway has finally been determined in any condemnation proceeding necessary to secure such land or property, the said Commission is hereby authorized and directed to pay all of said sum and other expenses incident thereto by proper warrant upon the sum which may be appropriated for said purpose, and all such sums shall constitute and remain a fixed and valid claim against the State of North Carolina until paid and satisfied in full. (1927, c. 44, s. 4.)

§ 104-23. Maintenance and operation of bridges over waterway.

The Board of Transportation or the road governing body of any political subdivision of the State of North Carolina is hereby authorized and directed to take over and maintain and operate in perpetuity, by contract with the United States government, if necessary, or otherwise, any bridge or bridges which may be subject to their respective control and which the United States government may construct across said inland waterway. (1927, c. 44, s. 6; 1929, c. 4; c. 7, s. 2; 1957, c. 65, s. 11; 1973, c. 507, s. 5.)

§ 104-24. Concurrent jurisdiction over waterway.

The State of North Carolina retains concurrent jurisdiction with the United States over any lands acquired and held in pursuance of the provisions of this Chapter, so far as that all civil and criminal process issued under authority of any law of this State may be executed in any part of the premises so acquired for such inland waterway, or for the buildings or constructions thereon erected for the purposes of such inland waterway. (1927, c. 44, s. 7.)

§ 104-25. Lands conveyed to United States for inland waterway.

For the purpose of aiding in the construction of a proposed inland waterway by the United States from the City of Norfolk, in the State of Virginia, to Beaufort Inlet, in the State of North Carolina, the Secretary of State is hereby authorized to issue to the United States of America a grant to the land located within a distance of 1,000 feet on either side of the center of the said inland waterway, insofar as such land is subject to grant by the State of North Carolina, the said grant to issue upon a certificate furnished to the Secretary of State by the Secretary of War, or by any authorized officer of the corps of engineers of the United States Army, or by any other authorized official, exercising control of the construction of the said waterway.

Wherever, in the construction of the said inland waterway, lands theretofore submerged shall be raised above the water by deposit of excavated material, the lands so formed shall become the property of the United States for a distance of 1,000 feet on either side of the center of such canal or channel, and the Secretary of State is hereby authorized to issue to the United States a grant to the land so formed within the distance above mentioned, the grant to issue upon a certificate furnished to the Secretary of State by some authorized official of the United States as above provided. (1913, c. 197; C.S., s. 7583; 1937, c. 445; 2011-183, s. 127(b).)

§§ 104-26 through 104-30. Reserved for future codification purposes.

Article 3.

Jurisdiction over National Park System Lands.

§ 104-31. Governor authorized to cede jurisdiction.

(a) Whenever the United States shall desire to acquire legislative jurisdiction over any lands of the national park system within this State and shall make application for that purpose, the Governor is authorized to cede to the United States such measure of jurisdiction, not exceeding that requested by the United States, as he may deem proper over all or any part of such lands as to which a cession of legislative jurisdiction is requested, reserving to the State such concurrent or partial jurisdiction as he may deem proper.

(b) Said application on behalf of the United States shall state in particular the measure of jurisdiction desired and shall be accompanied by an accurate description of the lands of the national park system over which such jurisdiction is desired and information as to which of such lands are then owned or leased by the United States.

(c) Said cession of jurisdiction shall become effective when it is accepted on behalf of the United States, which acceptance shall be indicated, in writing upon the instrument of cession, by an authorized official of the United States and admitting it to record in the appropriate land records of the county in which lands are situated. (1979, c. 560, s. 1.)

§ 104-32. Jurisdiction reserved.

Notwithstanding any other provision of law, there are reserved over any lands as to which any legislative jurisdiction may be ceded to the United States pursuant to this Article, the State's entire legislative jurisdiction with respect to taxation and that of each State agency, county, city, political subdivision, and public district of the State; the State's entire legislative jurisdiction with respect to marriage, divorce, annulment, adoption, commitment of the mentally incompetent, and descent and distribution of property; concurrent power to enforce the criminal law; and the power to execute any process, civil or criminal, issued under the authority of the State; nor shall any persons residing on such lands be deprived of any civil or political rights, including the right of suffrage, by reason of the cession of such jurisdiction to the United States. (1979, c. 560, s. 1.)

§ 104-33. Applicability of Article.

The provisions of this Article shall not apply to any lands owned by the United States and held in trust for the Eastern Band of Cherokee Indians, located in Jackson, Swain, Graham, or Cherokee Counties. (1979, c. 560, s. 2.)
Chapter 104A.

Degrees of Kinship.

§ 104A-1. Degrees of kinship; how computed.

In all cases where degrees of kinship are to be computed, the same shall be computed in accordance with the civil law rule, as follows:

(1)   The degrees of lineal kinship of two persons is computed by counting one degree for each person in the line of ascent or descent, exclusive of the person from whom the computing begins; and

(2)   The degree of collateral kinship of two persons is computed by commencing with one of the persons and ascending from him to a common ancestor, descending from that ancestor to the other person, and counting one degree for each person in the line of ascent and in the line of descent, exclusive

of the person from whom the computation begins, the total to represent the degree of such kinship. (1951, c. 315; 1953, c. 1077, s. 2.)

Chapter 104B.

Hurricanes or Other Acts of Nature.

Article 1.

In General.

§ 104B-1. Removal of property deposited by hurricane or other act of nature.

Whenever the house, garage, building, or any part thereof, or other property of a person, firm or corporation shall be deposited on the land of another by any hurricane, tornado, tidal wave, flood or other act of nature and is not removed from said land within 30 days after the deposit, the owner of such land may notify in writing the owner of the house, garage, building, or other property of such deposit and may require owner to remove the property so deposited within 60 days after receipt of the notice. If the owner of the deposited property fails to remove it within 60 days after receipt of the notice, the owner of the land may remove the deposited property and destroy it or may use it as he sees fit without incurring liability to the owner of the deposited property, or may sell it and retain the proceeds for his own use; provided, the amount by which the proceeds of any such sale exceed the cost of removal and sale shall be paid to the owner of the deposited property or held for his account.

If the owner of the land is unable to notify the owner of the deposited property and, after diligent search, the owner of the deposited property cannot be located and notified, the owner of the land may, at any time after the expiration of 120 days from the date of the deposit of the property on his land, remove, use, or sell the deposited property in the same manner and under the same restrictions as provided above for removal, use, or sale after notice.

Sales made under this section may be either public or private sales. (1955, c. 643.)

Article 2.

123

Zoning of Potential Flood Areas.

§ 104B-2: Repealed by Session Laws 1965, c. 431, s. 1.

Article 3.

Protection of Sand Dunes along Outer Banks.

§§ 104B-3 through 104B-16: Repealed by Session Laws 1979, c. 141, s. 1.

Chapter 104C.

Atomic Energy, Radioactivity and Ionizing Radiation.

§§ 104C-1 through 104C-3: Repealed by Session Laws 1971, c. 882, s. 6.

§§ 104C-4 through 104C-5. Recodified as §§ 104E-1 to 104E-23.

Chapter 104D.

Southern States Energy Compact.

§ 104D-1. Compact entered into; form of compact.

The Southern States Energy Compact is hereby enacted into law and entered into with all other jurisdictions legally joining therein in the form substantially as follows:

SOUTHERN STATES ENERGY COMPACT

Article I. Policy and Purpose. The party states recognize that the proper employment and conservation of energy and employment of energy-related

124

facilities, materials, and products, within the context of a responsible regard for the environment, can assist substantially in the industrialization of the South and the development of a balanced economy for the region. They also recognize that optimum benefit from and acquisition of energy resources and facilities require systematic encouragement, guidance, and assistance from the party states on a cooperative basis. It is the policy of the party states to undertake such cooperation on a continuing basis; it is the purpose of this compact to provide the instruments and framework for such a cooperative effort to improve the economy of the South and contribute to the individual and community well-being of the region's people.

Article II. The Board. (a) There is hereby created an agency of the party states to be known as the "Southern States Energy Board" (hereinafter called the Board). The Board shall be composed of three members from each party state, one of whom shall be appointed or designated in each state to represent the Governor, the State Senate and the State House of Representatives, respectively. Each member shall be designated or appointed in accordance with the law of the state which he represents and shall serve and be subject to removal in accordance with such law. Any member of the Board may provide for the discharge of his duties and the performance of his functions thereon, either for the duration of his membership or for any lesser period of time, by a deputy or assistant, if the laws of his state make specific provision therefor. The federal government may be represented without vote if provision is made by federal law for such representation.

(b)   Each party state shall be entitled to one vote on the Board, to be determined by majority vote of each member or member's representative from the party state present and voting on any question. No action of the Board shall be binding unless taken at a meeting at which a majority of all party states are represented and unless a majority of the total number of votes on the Board are cast in favor thereof.

(c)   The Board shall have a seal.

(d)   The Board shall elect annually, from among its members, a chairman, a vice-chairman, and a treasurer. The Board shall appoint an Executive Director who shall serve at its pleasure and who shall also act as secretary, and who, together with the treasurer, shall be bonded in such amounts as the Board may require.

(e)   The Executive Director, with the approval of the Board, shall appoint and remove or discharge such personnel as may be necessary for the performance of the Board's functions irrespective of the civil service, personnel or other merit system laws of any of the party states.

(f)   The Board may establish and maintain, independently or in conjunction with any one or more of the party states, a suitable retirement system for its full-time employees. Employees of the Board shall be eligible for social security coverage in respect of old age and survivors insurance provided that the Board takes such steps as may be necessary pursuant to federal law to participate in such program of insurance as a governmental agency or unit. The Board may establish and maintain or participate in such additional programs of employee benefits as may be appropriate.

(g)   The Board may borrow, accept or contract for the services of personnel from any state or the United States or any subdivision or agency thereof, from any interstate agency, or from any institution, person, firm or corporation.

(h)   The Board may accept for any of its purposes and functions under this compact any and all donations, and grants of money, equipment, supplies, materials, and services (conditional or otherwise) from any state or the United States or any subdivision or agency thereof, or interstate agency, or from any institution, person, firm or corporation, and may receive, utilize, and dispose of the same.

(i)   The Board may establish and maintain such facilities as may be necessary for the transaction of its business. The Board may acquire, hold, and convey real and personal property and any interest therein.

(j)   The Board shall adopt bylaws, rules and regulations for the conduct of its business, and shall have the power to amend and rescind these bylaws, rules, and regulations. The Board shall publish its bylaws, rules, and regulations in convenient form and shall file a copy thereof, and shall also file a copy of any amendment thereto, with the appropriate agency or officer in each of the party states.

(k)   The Board annually shall make to the Governor of each party state, a report covering the activities of the Board for the preceding year, and embodying such recommendations as may have been adopted by the Board, which report shall be transmitted to the legislature of said state. The Board may issue such additional reports as it may deem desirable.

Article III. Finances. (a) The Board shall submit to the executive head or designated officer or officers of each party state a budget of its estimated expenditures for such period as may be required by the laws of that jurisdiction for presentation to the legislature thereof.

(b)   Each of the Board's budgets of estimated expenditures shall contain specific recommendations of the amount or amounts to be appropriated by each of the party states. One-half of the total amount of each budget of estimated expenditures shall be apportioned among the party states in equal shares; one quarter of each such budget shall be apportioned among the party states in accordance with the ratio of their populations to the total population of the entire group of party states based on the last decennial federal census; and one quarter of each such budget shall be apportioned among the party states on the basis of the relative average per capita income of the inhabitants in each of the party states based on the latest computations published by the federal census-taking agency. Subject to appropriations by their respective legislatures, the Board shall be provided with such funds by each of the party states as are necessary to provide the means of establishing and maintaining facilities, a staff of personnel, and such activities as may be necessary to fulfill the powers and duties imposed upon and entrusted to the Board.

(c)   The Board may meet any of its obligations in whole or in part with funds available to it under Article II(h) of this Compact, provided that the Board takes specific action setting aside such funds prior to the incurring of any obligation to be met in whole or in part in this manner. Except where the Board makes use of funds available to it under Article II(h) hereof, the Board shall not incur any obligation prior to the allotment of funds by the party jurisdictions adequate to meet the same.

(d)   The Board shall keep accurate accounts of all receipts and disbursements. The receipts and disbursements of the Board shall be subject to the audit and accounting procedures established under its bylaws. However, all receipts and disbursements of funds handled by the Board shall be audited yearly by a qualified public accountant and the report of the audit shall be included in and become a part of the annual report of the Board.

(e)   The accounts of the Board shall be open at any reasonable time for inspection.

Article IV. Advisory Committees. The Board may establish such advisory and technical committees as it may deem necessary, membership on which to include but not be limited to private citizens, expert and lay personnel, representatives of industry, labor, commerce, agriculture, civic associations, medicine, education, voluntary health agencies, and officials of local, state and federal government, and may cooperate with and use the services of any such committees and the organizations which they represent in furthering any of its activities under this Compact.

Article V. Powers. The Board shall have the power to:

(1)   Ascertain and analyze on a continuing basis the position of the South with respect to energy, energy-related industries, and environmental concerns.

(2)   Encourage the development, conservation and responsible use of energy and energy-related facilities, installations, and products as part of a balanced economy and healthy environment.

(3)   Collect, correlate, and disseminate information relating to civilian uses of energy and energy-related materials and products.

(4)   Conduct, or cooperate in conducting, programs of training for state and local personnel engaged in any aspect of:

a.   Energy, environment, and application of energy, environmental, and related concerns to industry, medicine, or education or the promotion or regulation thereof.

b.   The formulation or administration of measures designed to promote safety in any matter related to the development, use or disposal of energy and energy-related materials, products, installations, or wastes.

(5)   Organize and conduct, or assist and cooperate in organizing and conducting, demonstrations of energy product, material, or equipment use and disposal and of proper techniques or processes for the application of energy resources to the civilian economy or general welfare.

(6)   Undertake such nonregulatory functions with respect to sources of radiation as may promote the economic development and general welfare of the region.

(7)   Study industrial, health, safety, and other standards, laws, codes, rules, regulations, and administrative practices in or related to energy and environmental fields.

(8)   Recommend such changes in, or amendments or additions to, the laws, codes, rules, regulations, administrative procedures and practices or ordinances of the party states in any of the fields of its interest and competence as in its judgment may be appropriate. Any such recommendation shall be made through the appropriate state agency with due consideration of the desirability of uniformity but shall also give appropriate weight to any special circumstances which may justify variations to meet local conditions.

(9)   Prepare, publish and distribute, with or without charge, such reports, bulletins, newsletters or other material as it deems appropriate.

(10)   Cooperate with the United States Department of Energy or any agency successor thereto, any other officer or agency of the United States, and any other governmental unit or agency or officer thereof, and with any private persons or agencies in any of the fields of its interests.

(11)   Act as licensee of the United States Government or any party state with respect to the conduct of any research activity requiring such license and operate such research facility or undertake any program pursuant thereto.

(12)   a.   Ascertain from time to time such methods, practices, circumstances, and conditions as may bring about the prevention and control of energy and environmental incidents in the area comprising the party states, to coordinate the environmental and other energy-related incident prevention and control plans and the work relating thereto of the appropriate agencies of the party states and to facilitate the rendering of aid by the party states to each other in coping with energy and environmental incidents.

b.   The Board may formulate and, in accordance with need from time to time, revise a regional plan or regional plans for coping with energy and environmental incidents within the territory of the party states as a whole or within any subregion or subregions of the geographic area covered by this Compact.

Article VI. Supplementary Agreements. (a) To the extent that the Board has not undertaken an activity or project which would be within its power under the provisions of Article V of this Compact, any two or more of the party states (acting by their duly constituted administrative officials) may enter into supplementary agreements for the undertaking and continuance of such an activity or project. Any such agreement shall specify its purpose or purposes; its duration and the procedure for termination thereof or withdrawal therefrom; the method of financing and allocating the costs of the activity or project; and such other matters as may be necessary or appropriate. No such supplementary agreement entered into pursuant to this Article shall become effective prior to its submission to and approval by the Board. The Board shall give such approval unless it finds that the supplementary agreement or the activity or project contemplated thereby is inconsistent with the provisions of this Compact or a program or activity conducted by or participated in by the Board.

(b)   Unless all of the party states participate in a supplementary agreement, any cost or costs thereof shall be borne separately by the states party thereto. However, the Board may administer or otherwise assist in the operation of any supplementary agreement.

(c)   No party to a supplementary agreement entered into pursuant to this Article shall be relieved thereby of any obligation or duty assumed by said party state under or pursuant to this Compact, except that timely and proper performance of such obligation or duty by means of the supplementary agreement may be offered as performance pursuant to the Compact.

Article VII. Other Laws and Relationships. Nothing in this Compact shall be construed to:

(1)   Permit or require any person or other entity to avoid or refuse compliance with any law, rule, regulation, order or ordinance of a party state or subdivision thereof now or hereafter made, enacted or in force.

(2)   Limit, diminish or otherwise impair jurisdiction exercised by the United States Department of Energy, any agency successor thereto, or any other federal department, agency or officer pursuant to and in conformity with any valid and operative act of Congress.

(3)   Alter the relations between and respective internal responsibilities of the government of a party state and its subdivisions.

(4)   Permit or authorize the Board to exercise any regulatory authority or to own or operate any nuclear reactor for the generation of electric energy; nor shall the Board own or operate any facility or installation for industrial or commercial purposes.

Article VIII. Eligible Parties, Entry into Force and Withdrawal. (a) Any or all of the states of Alabama, Arkansas, Delaware, Florida, Georgia, Kentucky, Louisiana, Maryland, Mississippi, Missouri, North Carolina, Oklahoma, South Carolina, Tennessee, Texas, Virginia, West Virginia, the Commonwealth of Puerto Rico, and the United States Virgin Islands shall be eligible to become party to this Compact.

(b)   As to any eligible party state, this Compact shall become effective when its legislature shall have enacted the same into law: Provided that it shall not become initially effective until enacted into law by seven states.

(c)   Any party state may withdraw from this Compact by enacting a statute repealing the same, but no such withdrawal shall become effective until the Governor of the withdrawing state shall have sent formal notice in writing to the Governor of each other party state informing said Governors of the action of the legislature in repealing the Compact and declaring an intention to withdraw.

Article IX. Severability and Construction. The provisions of this Compact and of any supplementary agreement entered into hereunder shall be (severable) and if any phrase, clause, sentence or provision of this Compact or such supplementary agreement is declared to be contrary to the constitution of any participating state or of the United States or the applicability thereof to any government, agency, person, or circumstance is held invalid, the validity of the remainder of this Compact or such supplementary agreement and the applicability thereof to any government, agency, person or circumstance shall not be affected thereby. If this Compact or any supplementary agreement entered into hereunder shall be held contrary to the constitution of any state participating therein, the Compact or such supplementary agreement shall remain in full force and effect as to the remaining states and in full force and effect as to the state affected as to all severable matters. The provisions of this Compact and of any supplementary agreement entered into pursuant thereto shall be liberally construed to effectuate the purposes thereof. (1965, c. 858, s. 1; 1983, c. 282, s. 1.)

§ 104D-2. (For applicability see note) Appointment of North Carolina members and alternate members of Southern States Energy Board.

(a)   North Carolina members of the Southern States Energy Board shall be appointed as follows:

(1)   One member to be appointed by the Governor.

(2)   One member of the House of Representatives to be appointed by the Speaker of the House of Representatives.

(3)   One member of the Senate to be appointed by the President of the Senate.

(b)   Members shall serve at the pleasure of the original appointing authority and until their successors are appointed.

(c)   Each appointing authority is authorized to appoint an alternate member who may serve at and for such time as the regular member shall designate and shall have the same power and authority as the regular member when so serving. (1965, c. 858, s. 2; 1983, c. 282, s. 2.)

§ 104D-2. (For applicability see note) Appointment of North Carolina members and alternate members of Southern States Energy Board.

(a)   North Carolina members of the Southern States Energy Board shall be appointed as follows:

(1)   One member to be appointed by the Governor.

(2)   One member of the House of Representatives to be appointed by the Speaker of the House of Representatives.

(3)   One member of the Senate to be appointed by the President Pro Tempore of the Senate.

(b)   Members shall serve at the pleasure of the original appointing authority and until their successors are appointed.

(c)   Each appointing authority is authorized to appoint an alternate member who may serve at and for such time as the regular member shall designate and shall have the same power and authority as the regular member when so serving. (1965, c. 858, s. 2; 1983, c. 282, s. 2; 1991, c. 739, s. 9.)

§ 104D-3. Submission of budgets of Board.

Pursuant to Article III(a) of the compact, the Board shall submit its budgets of estimated expenditures to the Director of the Budget for presentation to the General Assembly. (1965, c. 858, s. 3.)

§ 104D-4. Supplementary agreements ineffective until funds appropriated.

Any supplementary agreement entered into pursuant to Article VI of the compact and requiring the expenditure of funds or the assumption of an obligation to expend funds in addition to those already appropriated shall not become effective as to this State until the required funds therefor are appropriated by the General Assembly. (1965, c. 858, s. 4.)

§ 104D-5. Cooperation with Board.

The departments, institutions and agencies of this State and its subdivisions are hereby authorized to cooperate with the Board in the furtherance of any of its activities pursuant to the Compact. (1965, c. 858, s. 5.)

§ 104D-6: Repealed by Session Laws 1983, c. 282, s. 3.

Chapter 104E.

North Carolina Radiation Protection Act.

§ 104E-1. Title.

This Chapter shall be known and may be cited as the "North Carolina Radiation Protection Act." (1975, c. 718, s. 1.)

§ 104E-2. Scope.

Except as otherwise specifically provided, this Chapter applies to all persons who receive, possess, use, transfer, own or acquire any source of radiation within the State of North Carolina; provided, however, that nothing in this Chapter shall apply to any person to the extent such person is subject to regulation by the United States Nuclear Regulatory Commission or its successors. (1975, c. 718, s. 1.)

§ 104E-3. Declaration of policy.

It is the policy of the State of North Carolina in furtherance of its responsibility to protect the public health and safety:

(1)   To institute and maintain a program to permit development and utilization of sources of radiation for purposes consistent with the health and safety of the public; and

(2)   To prevent any associated harmful effects of radiation upon the public through the institution and maintenance of a regulatory program for all sources of radiation, providing for:

a.   A single, effective system of regulation within the State;

b.   A system consonant insofar as possible with those of other states; and

c.   Compatibility with the standards and regulatory programs of the federal government for by-product, source and special nuclear materials. (1975, c. 718, s. 1.)

§ 104E-4. Purpose.

It is the purpose of this Chapter to effectuate the policies set forth in G.S. 104E-3 by providing for:

(1)   A program of effective regulation of sources of radiation for the protection of the occupational and public health and safety;

(2)   A program to promote an orderly regulatory pattern within the State, among the states and between the federal government and the State and facilitate intergovernmental cooperation with respect to use and regulation of sources of radiation to the end that duplication of regulation may be minimized; and

(3)   A program to establish procedures for assumption and performance of certain regulatory responsibilities with respect to sources of radiation. (1975, c. 718, s. 1.)

§ 104E-5. Definitions.

Unless a different meaning is required by the context, the following terms as used in this Chapter shall have the meanings hereinafter respectively ascribed to them:

(1)   "Agreement materials" means those materials licensed by the State under agreement with the United States Nuclear Regulatory Commission and which include by-product, source or special nuclear materials in a quantity not sufficient to form a critical mass, as defined by the Atomic Energy Act of 1954 as amended.

(2)   "Agreement state" means any state which has consummated an agreement with the United States Nuclear Regulatory Commission under the authority of section 274 of the Atomic Energy Act of 1954 as amended, as

authorized by compatible state legislation providing for acceptance by that state of licensing authority for agreement materials and the discontinuance of such licensing activities by the United States Nuclear Regulatory Commission.

(3)   "Atomic energy" means all forms of energy released in the course of nuclear fission or nuclear fusion or other atomic transformations.

(4)   "By-product material" means any radioactive material, except special nuclear material, yielded in or made radioactive by exposure to the radiation incident to the process of producing or utilizing special nuclear material.

(5)   "Commission" means the Radiation Protection Commission.

(6)   "Department" means the Department of Health and Human Services.

(7)   "Emergency" means any condition existing outside the bounds of nuclear operating sites owned or licensed by a federal agency, and further any condition existing within or outside of the jurisdictional confines of a facility licensed by the Department and arising from the presence of by-product material, source material, special nuclear materials, or other radioactive materials, which is endangering or could reasonably be expected to endanger the health and safety of the public, or to contaminate the environment.

(7a)   "Engineered barrier" means a man-made structure or device that is intended to improve a disposal facility's ability to meet (i) the performance objectives of Subpart C, Title 10, Code of Federal Regulations Part 61 in effect on 1 January 1987, (ii) other requirements set out in G.S. 104E-25, and (iii) requirements of rules adopted by the Commission under this Chapter.

(8)   "General license" means a license effective pursuant to regulations promulgated under the provisions of this Chapter without the filing of an application to transfer, acquire, own, possess, or use quantities of, or devices or equipment utilizing by-product, source, special nuclear materials, or other radioactive materials occurring naturally or produced artificially.

(9)   "Ionizing radiation" means gamma rays and x-rays, alpha and beta particles, high speed electrons, protons, neutrons, and other nuclear particles; but not sound or radio waves, or visible, infrared, or ultraviolet light.

(9a)   "Low-level radioactive waste" means low-level radioactive waste as defined in the Low-Level Radioactive Waste Policy Amendments Act of 1985,

Pub. L. 99-240, 99 Stat. 1842, 42 U.S.C. 2021b et seq. and other waste, including waste containing naturally occurring and accelerator produced radioactive material, which is not regulated by the United States Nuclear Regulatory Commission or other agency of the federal government and which is determined to be low-level radioactive waste by the North Carolina Radiation Protection Commission.

(9b)   "Low-level radioactive waste facility" means a facility for the storage, collection, processing, treatment, recycling, recovery, or disposal of low-level radioactive waste.

(9c)   "Low-level radioactive waste disposal facility" means any low-level radioactive waste facility or any portion of such facility, including land, buildings, and equipment, which is used or intended to be used for the disposal of low-level radioactive waste on or in land in accordance with rules promulgated under this Chapter.

(10)   "Nonionizing radiation" means radiation in any portion of the electromagnetic spectrum not defined as ionizing radiation, including, but not limited to, such sources as laser, maser or microwave devices.

(11)   "Person" means any individual, corporation, partnership, firm, association, trust, estate, public or private institution, group, agency, political subdivision of this State, any other state or political subdivision or agency thereof, and any legal successor, representative, agent, or agency of the foregoing, other than the United States Nuclear Regulatory Commission, or any successor thereto, and other than federal government agencies licensed by the United States Nuclear Regulatory Commission, or any successor thereto.

(12)   "Radiation" means gamma rays and x-rays, alpha and beta particles, high speed electrons, protons, neutrons, and other nuclear particles, and electromagnetic radiation consisting of associated and interacting electric and magnetic waves including those with frequencies between three times 10 to the eighth power cycles per second and three times 10 to the twenty-fourth power cycles per second and wavelengths between one times 10 to the minus fourteenth power centimeters and 100 centimeters.

(13)   "Radiation machine" means any device designed to produce or which produces radiation or nuclear particles when the associated control devices of the machine are operated.

137

(14)   "Radioactive material" means any solid, liquid, or gas which emits ionizing radiation spontaneously.

(14a)   "Shallow land burial" means disposal of low-level radioactive waste in subsurface trenches without the additional confinement of the waste as described in G.S. 104E-25.

(14b)   "Secretary" means the Secretary of Environment and Natural Resources.

(15)   "Source material" means (i) uranium, thorium, or any other material which the Department declares to be source material after the United States Nuclear Regulatory Commission, or any successor thereto has determined the material to be such; or (ii) ores containing one or more of the foregoing materials, in such concentration as the Department declares to be source material after the United States Nuclear Regulatory Commission, or any successor thereto, has determined the material in such concentration to be source material.

(16)   "Special nuclear material" means (i) plutonium, uranium 233, uranium 235, uranium enriched in the isotope 233 or in the isotope 235, and any other material which the Department declares to be special nuclear material after the United States Nuclear Regulatory Commission, or any successor thereto, has determined the material to be such, but does not include source material; or (ii) any material artificially enriched by any of the foregoing, but does not include source material.

(17)   "Specific license" means a license, issued after application, to use, manufacture, produce, transfer, receive, acquire, own or process quantities of, or devices or equipment utilizing by-product, source, special nuclear materials, or other radioactive materials occurring naturally or produced artificially. Nothing in this Chapter shall require the licensing of individual natural persons involved in the use of radiation machines or radioactive materials for medical diagnosis or treatment.

(18)   Repealed by Session Laws 1987, c. 850, s. 3. (1975, c. 718, s. 1; 1981, c. 704, s. 8; 1987, c. 633, ss. 1-4; c. 850, s. 3; 1989, c. 727, s. 219(16); 1993, c. 501, s. 2.1; 1995, c. 504, s. 4; 1997-443, s. 11A.119(a); 2011-145, s. 13.3(ccc).)

§ 104E-6. Designation of State radiation protection agency.

The Department is hereby designated the State agency to administer a statewide radiation protection program consistent with the provisions of this Chapter. (1975, c. 718, s. 1.)

§ 104E-6.1. Conveyance of land used for low-level radioactive waste disposal facility to State.

(a)   No land may be used as a low-level radioactive waste disposal facility until fee simple title to the land has been conveyed to the State of North Carolina. In consideration for such conveyance, the State shall enter into a lease agreement with the grantor for a term equal to the estimated life of the facility in which the State will be the lessor and the grantor the lessee. Such lease agreement shall specify that for an annual rent of fifty dollars ($50.00), the lessee shall be allowed to use the land for the development and operation of a low-level radioactive waste disposal facility. Such lease agreement shall provide that the lessor or any person authorized by the lessor shall have at all times the right to enter without a search warrant or permission of the lessee upon any and all parts of the premises for monitoring, inspection and all other purposes necessary to carry out the provisions of Chapter 104E. The lessee shall remain fully liable for all damages, losses, personal injury or property damage which may result or arise out of the lessee's operation of the facility, and for compliance with regulatory requirements concerning insurance, bonding for closure and post-closure costs, monitoring and other financial or health and safety requirements as required by applicable law and regulations. The State, as lessor, shall be immune from liability except as otherwise provided by statute. The lease shall be transferrable with the written consent of the lessor, which consent will not be unreasonably withheld. In the case of such a transfer of the lease, the transferee shall be subject to all terms and conditions that the State deems necessary to ensure compliance with applicable laws and regulations. If the lessee or any successor in interest fails in any material respect to comply with any applicable law, regulation, or license condition, or with any term or condition of the lease, the State may terminate the lease after giving the lessee written notice specifically describing the failure to comply and upon providing the lessee a reasonable time to comply. If the lessee does not effect compliance within the reasonable time allowed, the State may reenter and take possession of the premises.

139

(b)   Notwithstanding the termination of the lease by either the lessee or the lessor for any reason, the lessee shall remain liable for, and be obligated to perform all acts necessary or required by law, regulation, license conditions or the lease for the permanent closure of the site until the site has either been permanently closed or until a substitute operator has been secured and assumed the obligations of the lessee.

(c)   In the event of changes in laws or regulations applicable to the facility which make continued operation by the lessee impossible or economically infeasible, the lessee shall have the right to terminate the lease upon giving the State reasonable notice of not less than six months, in which case the lessor shall have the right to secure a substitute lessee and operator.

(d)   In the event of termination of the lease by the lessor as provided in subsection (a) of this section, or by the lessee as provided in subsection (c) of this section, the lessee shall be paid the fair market value of any improvements made to the leased premises less the costs to the lessor resulting from termination of the lease and securing a substituted lessee and operator; provided, that the lessor shall have no obligation to secure a substitute lessee or operator and may require the lessee to permanently close the facility. (1981, c. 704, s. 9; 1987, c. 633, s. 5; 1989 (Reg. Sess., 1990), c. 1004, s. 5; 2007-495, s. 9.)

§ 104E-6.2. Local ordinances prohibiting low-level radioactive waste facilities invalid; petition to preempt local ordinance.

(a)   It is the intent of the General Assembly to maintain a uniform system for the management of low-level radioactive waste and to place limitations upon the exercise by all units of local government in North Carolina of the power to regulate the management of low-level radioactive waste by means of special, local, or private acts or resolutions, ordinances, property restrictions, zoning regulations, or otherwise. Notwithstanding any authority granted to counties, municipalities, or other local authorities to adopt local ordinances, including but not limited to those imposing taxes, fees, or charges or regulating health, environment, or land use, any local ordinance that prohibits or has the effect of prohibiting the establishment or operation of a low-level radioactive waste facility that the Secretary has preempted pursuant to subsections (b) through (f) of this section, shall be invalid to the extent necessary to effectuate the purposes of this Chapter. To this end, all provisions of special, local, or private acts or resolutions are repealed that:

(1)   Prohibit the transportation, treatment, storage, or disposal of low-level radioactive waste within any county, city, or other political subdivision.

(2)   Prohibit the siting of a low-level radioactive waste facility within any county, city, or other political subdivision.

(3)   Place any restriction or condition not placed by this Chapter upon the transportation, treatment, storage, or disposal of low-level radioactive waste, or upon the siting of a low-level radioactive waste facility within any county, city, or other political subdivision.

(4)   In any manner are in conflict or inconsistent with the provisions of this Chapter.

(a1)   No special, local, or private acts or resolutions enacted or taking effect hereafter may be construed to modify, amend, or repeal any portion of this Chapter unless it expressly provides for such by specific references to the appropriate section of this Chapter. Further to this end, all provisions of local ordinances, including those regulating land use, adopted by counties, municipalities, or other local authorities that prohibit or have the effect of prohibiting the establishment or operation of a low-level radioactive waste facility are invalidated to the extent preempted by the Secretary pursuant to this Section.

(b)   When a low-level radioactive waste facility would be prevented from construction or operation by a county, municipal, or other local ordinance, the operator of the proposed facility may petition the Secretary to review the matter. After receipt of a petition, the Secretary shall hold a hearing in accordance with the procedures in subsection (c) of this section and shall determine whether or to what extent to preempt the local ordinance to allow for the establishment and operation of the facility.

(c)   When a petition described in subsection (b) of this section has been filed with the Secretary, the Secretary shall hold a public hearing to consider the petition. The public hearing shall be held in the affected locality within 60 days after receipt of the petition by the Secretary. The Secretary shall give notice of the public hearing by:

(1)   Publication in a newspaper or newspapers having general circulation in the county or counties where the facility is or is to be located or operated, once a week for three consecutive weeks, the first notice appearing at least 30 days prior to the scheduled date of the hearing; and

(2)   First class mail to persons who have requested notice. The Secretary shall maintain a mailing list of persons who request notice in advance of the hearing pursuant to this section. Notice by mail shall be complete upon deposit of a copy of the notice in a post-paid wrapper addressed to the person to be notified at the address that appears on the mailing list maintained by the Secretary, in a post office or official depository under the exclusive care and custody of the United States Postal Service.

(c1)   Any interested person may appear before the Secretary at the hearing to offer testimony. In addition to testimony before the Secretary, any interested person may submit written evidence to the Secretary for the Secretary's consideration. At least 20 days shall be allowed for receipt of written comment following the hearing.

(d)   The Secretary shall determine whether or to what extent to preempt local ordinances so as to allow the establishment and operation of the facility no later than 60 days after conclusion of the hearing. The Secretary shall preempt a local ordinance only if the Secretary makes all five of the following findings:

(1)   That there is a local ordinance that would prohibit or have the effect of prohibiting the establishment or operation of a low-level radioactive waste facility.

(2)   That the proposed facility is needed in order to establish adequate capability to meet the current or projected low-level radioactive waste management needs of this State or to comply with the terms of any interstate agreement for the management of low-level radioactive waste to which the State is a party and therefore serves the interests of the citizens of the State as a whole.

(3)   That all legally required State and federal permits or approvals have been issued by the appropriate State and federal agencies or that all State and federal permit requirements have been satisfied and that the permits or approvals have been denied or withheld only because of the local ordinance.

142

(4)   That local citizens and elected officials have had adequate opportunity to participate in the siting process.

(5)   That the construction and operation of the facility will not pose an unreasonable health or environmental risk to the surrounding locality and that the facility operator has taken or consented to take reasonable measures to avoid or manage foreseeable risks and to comply to the maximum feasible extent with applicable local ordinances.

(d1)   If the Secretary does not make all five findings set out above, the Secretary shall not preempt the challenged local ordinance. The Secretary's decision shall be in writing and shall identify the evidence submitted to the Secretary plus any additional evidence used in arriving at the decision.

(e)   The decision of the Secretary shall be final unless a party to the action files a written appeal under Article 4 of Chapter 150B of the General Statutes, as modified by G.S. 7A-29 and this section, within 30 days of the date of the decision. The record on appeal shall consist of all materials and information submitted to or considered by the Secretary, the Secretary's written decision, a complete transcript of the hearing, all written material presented to the Secretary regarding the location of the facility, the specific findings required by subsection (d) of this section, and any minority positions on the specific findings required by subsection (d) of this section. The scope of judicial review shall be that the court may affirm the decision of the Secretary, or may remand the matter for further proceedings, or may reverse or modify the decision if the substantial rights of the parties may have been prejudiced because the agency findings, inferences, conclusions, or decisions are:

(1)   In violation of constitutional provisions;

(2)   In excess of the statutory authority or jurisdiction of the agency;

(3)   Made upon unlawful procedure;

(4)   Affected by other error of law;

(5)   Unsupported by substantial evidence admissible under G.S. 150B-29(a) or G.S. 150B-30 in view of the entire record as submitted; or

(6)   Arbitrary or capricious.

(e1)   If the court reverses or modifies the decision of the agency, the judge shall set out in writing, which writing shall become part of the record, the reasons for the reversal or modification.

(f)   In computing any period of time prescribed or allowed by this procedure, the provisions of Rule 6(a) of the Rules of Civil Procedure, G.S. 1A-1, shall apply. (1981, c. 704, s. 9; 1987, c. 633, s. 6; c. 850, s. 4; 1987 (Reg. Sess., 1988), c. 993, s. 24; c. 1082, s. 10; c. 1100, s. 40.5; 1989, c. 168, s. 14; 1993, c. 501, s. 3; 2001-474, s. 16.)

§ 104E-7. Radiation Protection Commission - Creation and powers.

(a)   There is hereby created the North Carolina Radiation Protection Commission of the Department of Environment and Natural Resources with the power to promulgate rules and regulations to be followed in the administration of a radiation protection program. All rules and regulations for radiation protection that were adopted by the Commission for Public Health and are not inconsistent with the provisions of this Chapter shall remain in full force and effect unless and until repealed or superseded by action of the Radiation Protection Commission. The Radiation Protection Commission is authorized:

(1)   To advise the Department in the development of comprehensive policies and programs for the evaluation, determination, and reduction of hazards associated with the use of radiation;

(2)   To adopt, promulgate, amend and repeal such rules, regulations and standards relating to the manufacture, production, transportation, use, handling, servicing, installation, storage, sale, lease, or other disposition of radioactive material and radiation machines as may be necessary to carry out the policy, purpose and provisions of this Chapter. To this end, the Commission is authorized to require licensing or registration of all persons who manufacture, produce, transport, use, handle, service, install, store, sell, lease, or otherwise dispose of radioactive material and radiation machines, as the Commission deems necessary to provide an adequate protection and supervisory program: provided, that prior to adoption of any regulation or standard, or amendment or repeal thereof, the Commission shall afford interested parties the opportunity, at a public hearing, as provided in G.S. 104E-13, to submit data or views orally or in writing. The recommendations of nationally recognized bodies in the field of

144

radiation protection shall be taken into consideration in such standards relative to permissible dosage of radiation;

(3)   To require all sources of ionizing radiation to be shielded, transported, handled, used, stored, or disposed of in such a manner to provide compliance with the provisions of this Chapter and rules, regulations and standards adopted hereunder;

(4)   To require, on prescribed forms furnished by the Department, registration, periodic reregistration, licensing, or periodic relicensing of persons to use, manufacture, produce, transport, transfer, install, service, receive, acquire, own, or possess radiation machines and other sources of radiation;

(5)   To exempt certain sources of radiation or kinds of uses or users from the licensing or registration requirements set forth in this Chapter when the Commission determines that the exemption of such sources of radiation or kinds of uses or users will not constitute a significant risk to the health and safety of the public;

(6)   To promulgate rules and regulations pursuant to this Chapter which may provide for recognition of other state and federal licenses as the Commission shall deem desirable, subject to such registration requirements as it may prescribe; and exercise all incidental powers necessary to carry out the provisions of this Chapter;

(7)   To provide by rule and regulation for an electronic product safety program to protect the public health and safety, which program may authorize regulation and inspection of sources of nonionizing radiation throughout the State. The product safety program may include the establishment of minimum qualifications for the operators of these products or sources.

(8)   To adopt, amend, repeal or promulgate such rules, regulations, and standards relating to the nonradioactive, toxic and hazardous aspects of radioactive waste disposal, as may be necessary to protect the public health and safety.

(9)   To adopt regulations establishing financial responsibility requirements for maintenance, operation and long-term care of low-level radioactive waste facilities, including insurance during the operation of the facility and adequate assurance of availability of funds for facility closure and post-closure monitoring and corrective measures.

(10)   To adopt rules which exempt a generator of low-level radioactive waste who operates a low-level radioactive waste facility solely for the management of wastes he produces, from any requirement, made applicable by this Chapter or rules adopted pursuant to this Chapter to low-level radioactive waste facilities generally where, because of the low volume or activity of the wastes involved, such exemption would not endanger the public health or safety, or the environment.

(b)   No license for a low-level radioactive waste facility that would accept low-level radioactive waste from the public, or from another person for a fee, shall be issued other than for a facility authorized by the General Assembly. (1975, c. 718, s. 1; 1979, c. 694, s. 3; 1981, c. 704, s. 10; 1987, c. 850, s. 5; 1989, c. 727, s. 219(17); 1991, c. 735, s. 3; 1997-443, s. 11A.119(a); 2001-474, s. 2; 2007-182, s. 2.)

§ 104E-8. Radiation Protection Commission - Members; selections; removal; compensation; quorum; services.

(a)   The Commission shall consist of 11 voting public members and 10 nonvoting ex officio members. The 11 voting public members of the Commission shall be appointed by the Governor as follows:

(1)   One member who shall be actively involved in the field of environmental protection;

(2)   One member who shall be an employee of one of the licensed public utilities involved in the generation of power by atomic energy;

(3)   One member who shall have experience in the field of atomic energy other than power generation;

(4)   One member who shall be a scientist or engineer from the faculty of one of the institutions of higher learning in the State;

(5)   One member who shall have recognized knowledge in the field of radiation and its biological effects from the North Carolina Medical Society;

(6)   One member who shall have recognized knowledge in the field of radiation and its biological effects from the North Carolina Dental Society;

(7)   One member who shall have recognized knowledge in the field of radiation and its biological effects from the State at large;

(8)   One member who shall have recognized knowledge in the field of radiation and its biological effects and who shall be a practicing hospital administrator from the North Carolina Hospital Association;

(9)   One member who shall have recognized knowledge in the field of radiation and its biological effects from the North Carolina Chiropractic Association;

(10)   One member who shall have recognized knowledge in the clinical application of radiation, shall be a practicing radiologic technologist from the North Carolina Society of Radiologic Technologists, and shall be certified by the American Registry of Radiologic Technologists;

(11)   One member who shall have recognized knowledge in the clinical application of radiation and shall be a practicing podiatrist licensed by the North Carolina State Board of Podiatry Examiners.

(b)   Public members so appointed shall serve terms of office of four years. Four of the initial members shall be appointed for two years, three members for three years, and three members for four years. Any appointment to fill a vacancy on the Commission created by the resignation, dismissal, death or disability of a public member shall be for the balance of the unexpired term. At the expiration of each public member's term, the Governor shall reappoint or replace the member with a member of like qualifications. At its first meeting on or after July first of each year, the Commission shall designate by election one of its public members as chairman and one of its public members as vice-chairman to serve through June thirtieth of the following year.

(c)   The 10 ex officio members shall be appointed by the Governor, shall be members or employees of the following State agencies or their successors, and shall serve at the Governor's pleasure:

(1)   The Utilities Commission.

(2)   The Commission for Public Health.

(3)   The Environmental Management Commission.

(4)   The Board of Transportation.

(5)   The Division of Emergency Management of the Department of Public Safety.

(6)   The Division of Health Service Regulation of the Department.

(7)   The Department of Labor.

(8)   The Industrial Commission.

(9)   The Department of Insurance.

(10)   The Medical Care Commission.

(d)   The Governor shall have the power to remove any member from the Commission for misfeasance, malfeasance, or nonfeasance in accordance with G.S. 143B-13.

(e)   The members of the Commission shall receive per diem and necessary travel and subsistence expenses in accordance with the provisions of G.S. 138-5.

(f)   A majority of the public members of the Commission shall constitute a quorum for the transaction of business.

(g)   All clerical and other services required by the Commission shall be supplied by the Secretary. (1975, c. 718, s. 1; 1989, c. 727, s. 219(18); 1989 (Reg. Sess., 1990), c. 1004, ss. 19(b), 41; 1991, c. 342, ss. 2, 3; 2002-70, s. 2; 2007-182, s. 2; 2011-145, ss. 13.3(ddd), 19.1(g); 2011-391, s. 27(c).)

§ 104E-9. Powers and functions of Department of Health and Human Services.

(a)   The Department of Health and Human Services is authorized:

(1)   To advise, consult and cooperate with other public agencies and with affected groups and industries.

(2)   To encourage, participate in, or conduct studies, investigations, public hearings, training, research, and demonstrations relating to the control of sources of radiation, the measurement of radiation, the effect upon public health and safety of exposure to radiation and related problems.

(3)   To require the submission of plans, specifications, and reports for new construction and material alterations on (i) the design and protective shielding of installations for radioactive material and radiation machines and (ii) systems for the disposal of radioactive waste materials, for the determination of any radiation hazard and may render opinions, approve or disapprove such plans and specifications.

(4)   To collect and disseminate information relating to the sources of radiation, including but not limited to: (i) maintenance of a record of all license applications, issuances, denials, amendments, transfers, renewals, modifications, suspensions, and revocations; and (ii) maintenance of a record of registrants and licensees possessing sources of radiation requiring registration or licensure under the provisions of this Chapter, and regulations hereunder, and any administrative or judicial action pertaining thereto; and to develop and implement a responsible data management program for the purpose of collecting and analyzing statistical information necessary to protect the public health and safety. The Department may refuse to make public dissemination of information relating to the source of radiation within this State after the Department first determines that the disclosure of such information will contravene the stated policy and purposes of this Chapter and such disclosure would be against the health, welfare and safety of the public.

(5)   To respond to any emergency which involves possible or actual release of radioactive material; and to perform or supervise decontamination and otherwise protect the public health and safety in any manner deemed necessary. This section does not in any way alter or change the provisions of Chapter 166 of the North Carolina General Statutes concerning response during an emergency by the Department of Military and Veterans Affairs or its successor.

(6)   To develop and maintain a statewide environmental radiation program for monitoring the radioactivity levels in air, water, soil, vegetation, animal life, milk, and food as necessary to ensure protection of the public and the environment from radiation hazards.

(7)   To implement the provisions of this Chapter and the regulations duly promulgated under the Chapter.

(8)   To establish fees in accordance with G.S. 104E-19.

(9)   To enter upon any lands and structures upon lands to make surveys, borings, soundings, and examinations as may be necessary to determine the suitability of a site for a low-level radioactive waste facility or low-level radioactive disposal facility. The Department shall give 30 days' notice of the intended entry authorized by this section in the manner prescribed for service of process by G.S. 1A-1, Rule 4. Entry under this section shall not be deemed a trespass or taking; provided, however, that the Department shall make reimbursement for any damage to such land or structures caused by such activities.

(10)   To encourage research and development and disseminate information on state-of-the-art means of handling and disposing of low-level radioactive waste.

(11)   To promote public education and public involvement in the decision-making process for the siting and permitting of proposed low-level radioactive waste facilities. The Department shall assist localities in which facilities are proposed in collecting and receiving information relating to the suitability of the proposed site. At the request of a local government in which facilities are proposed, the Department shall direct the appropriate agencies of State government to develop such relevant data as that locality shall reasonably request.

(b)   The Division of Health Service Regulation of the Department shall develop a training program for tanning equipment operators that meets the training rules adopted by the Commission. If the training program is provided by the Department, the Department may charge each person trained a reasonable fee to recover the actual cost of the training program. (1975, c. 718, s. 1; 1979, c. 694, s. 4; 1981, c. 704, s. 10.1; 1987, c. 633, s. 7; 1987 (Reg. Sess., 1988), c. 993, s. 25; 1989, c. 727, s. 219(19); 1991, c. 735, s. 2; 1993, c. 501, s. 4; 1995, c. 509, s. 49; 1997-443, s. 11A.119(a); 2001-474, s. 3; 2002-70, s. 3; 2009-451, s. 13.3(b); 2011-145, s. 13.3(eee); 2011-391, s. 27(d).)

§ 104E-9.1. Restrictions on use and operation of tanning equipment.

(a)   Operators of tanning equipment and owners of tanning facilities subject to rules adopted pursuant to this Chapter shall comply with or ensure compliance with the following:

(1)   The operator shall provide to each consumer a warning statement that defines the potential hazards and consequences of exposure to ultraviolet radiation. Before allowing the consumer's initial use of the tanning equipment, the operator shall obtain the signature of the consumer on the warning statement acknowledging receipt of the warning.

(2)   The operator shall not allow a person 13 years and younger to use tanning equipment without a written prescription from the person's medical physician specifying the nature of the medical condition requiring the treatment, the number of visits, and the time of exposure for each visit.

(3)   Neither an operator nor an owner shall claim or distribute promotional materials that claim that using tanning equipment is safe or free from risk or that using tanning equipment will result in medical or health benefits.

(b)   The Commission may adopt, and the Department shall enforce, rules to implement this section. The requirements of this section are in addition to other rules adopted pursuant to this Chapter that are applicable to tanning facilities and do not conflict with this section.

(c)   As used in this section, unless the context requires otherwise, the term:

(1)   "Consumer" means any individual who is provided access to a tanning facility that is subject to registration and regulation under this Chapter.

(2)   "Tanning equipment" means ultraviolet or other lamps and equipment containing such lamps intended to induce skin tanning through the irradiation of any part of the living human body with ultraviolet radiation.

(3)   "Tanning facility" means any location, place, area, structure, or business that provides consumers access to tanning equipment. For the purpose of this definition, tanning equipment registered to different persons at the same location and tanning equipment registered to the same person, but at separate locations, shall constitute separate tanning facilities. (2004-157, s. 1.)

§ 104E-10. Licensing of by-product, source, and special nuclear materials and other sources of ionizing radiation.

(a)   The Governor, on behalf of this State, is authorized to enter into agreements with the federal government providing for discontinuance of certain of the responsibilities of the federal government with respect to sources of ionizing radiation and the assumption thereof by this State.

(b)   Upon the signing of an agreement with the Nuclear Regulatory Commission or its successor as provided in subsection (a) above, the Commission shall provide by rule or regulation for general or specific licensing of persons to use, manufacture, produce, transport, transfer, receive, acquire, own, or possess by-product, source, or special nuclear materials or devices, installations, or equipment utilizing such materials. Such rule or regulation shall provide for amendment, suspension, renewal or revocation of licenses. Each application for a specific license shall be in writing on forms prescribed by the Commission and furnished by the Department and shall state, and be accompanied by, such information or documents, including, but not limited to plans, specifications and reports for new construction or material alterations as the Commission may determine to be reasonable and necessary to decide the qualifications of the applicant to protect the public health and safety. The Commission may require all applications or statements to be made under oath or affirmation. Each license shall be in such form and contain such terms and conditions as the Commission may deem necessary. No license issued under the authority of this Chapter and no right to possess or utilize sources of radiation granted by any license shall be assigned or in any manner disposed of; and the terms and conditions of all licenses shall be subject to amendment, revision, or modification by rules, regulations, or orders issued in accordance with the provisions of this Chapter.

(c)   Any person who, on the effective date of an agreement under subsection (a) above, possesses a license issued by the federal government shall be deemed to possess the same pursuant to a license issued under this Chapter, which shall expire either 90 days after receipt from the Department of a notice of expiration of such license, or on the date of expiration specified in the federal license, whichever is earlier.

(d)   Repealed by Session Laws 1987, c. 850, s. 6. (1975, c. 718, s. 1; 1979, c. 694, s. 1; 1981, c. 704, s. 11.1; 1987, c. 850, s. 6.)

§ 104E-10.1. Additional requirements for low-level radioactive waste facilities.

(a)   An applicant for a license for a low-level radioactive facility shall satisfy the Department that:

(1)   Any low-level radioactive waste facility heretofore constructed or operated by the applicant (or any parent or subsidiary corporation if the applicant is a corporation) has been operated in accordance with sound waste management practices and in substantial compliance with federal and state laws and regulations; and

(2)   The applicant (or any parent or subsidiary corporation if the applicant is a corporation) is financially qualified to operate the subject low-level radioactive waste facility.

(a1)   The approval of a license shall be contingent upon the applicant first satisfying the Department that the applicant has met the above two requirements. In order to continue to hold a license under this Chapter, a licensee must remain financially qualified, and must provide any information requested by the Department to show that the licensee continues to be financially qualified.

(b)   Each license applicant or license holder or any parent or subsidiary corporation if the license applicant or license holder is a corporation, as a condition of receiving or holding a license, shall have an independent annual audit by a firm of duly licensed certified public accountants carrying a minimum of five million dollars ($5,000,000) professional liability insurance coverage, proof of which coverage shall be provided with the issuance of the audit report. Each license applicant or license holder referred to above shall also provide the Department with a copy of the report and shall submit a copy of the report to the State Auditor for approval regarding its adequacy and completeness. As a minimum, the required report shall include the financial statements prepared in accordance with generally accepted accounting principles, all disclosures in the public interest required by law, and the auditor's opinion and comments relating to the financial statements. The audit shall be performed in conformity with generally accepted auditing standards.

(c)   Within 10 days of receiving an application for a license or an amendment to a license to operate a low-level radioactive waste facility, the Department shall notify the clerk of the board of commissioners of the county or counties in which the facility is proposed to be located or is located, and, if the

153

facility is to be located or is located within a city, the clerk of the governing board of the city, that the application has been filed, and shall file a copy of the application with the clerk. Prior to issuing a license or an amendment to an existing license the Secretary or the Secretary's designee shall conduct a public hearing in the county, or in one of the counties, in which a person proposes to operate a low-level radioactive waste facility or to enlarge an existing facility. The Secretary shall give notice of the hearing at least 30 days prior to the date thereof by:

(1)   Publication in a newspaper or newspapers having general circulation in the county or counties where the facility is to be located for three consecutive weeks beginning 30 days prior to the scheduled date of the hearing; and

(2)   First class mail to persons who have requested such notice. The Department shall maintain a mailing list of persons who request notice pursuant to this subsection. (1981, c. 704, s. 11; 1985, c. 529; 1987, c. 24, ss. 1-3; c. 850, ss. 7, 8; 1989, c. 727, s. 219(20); 1997-443, s. 11A.119(a); 2007-495, s. 10.)

§ 104E-10.2. Conveyance of property used for radioactive material disposal.

A license to dispose of radioactive waste materials on land shall include a legal description of the disposal site that would be sufficient as a description in an instrument of conveyance. The license to dispose of radioactive waste materials shall not be effective unless the owner of the disposal site files a certified copy of the license in the register of deeds' office in the county or counties in which the site is located. The register of deeds shall record the certified copy of the license and index it in the grantor index under the name of the owner of the land. When any such site is sold, leased, conveyed or transferred in any manner, the deed or other instrument of transfer shall contain in the description section in no smaller type than that used in the body of the deed or instrument a statement that the property has been used as a disposal site for radioactive waste materials and a reference by book and page to the recordation of the license. (1981, c. 480, s. 1.)

§ 104E-10.3. Low-level radioactive waste facility access licenses.

The Commission shall provide by regulation for the licensing of access to any low-level radioactive waste facility located in the State. No person shall send waste to a low-level radioactive waste facility unless licensed or otherwise authorized to do so by the Department. No low-level radioactive waste facility shall receive waste from any source not licensed by the Department except as may be otherwise specifically authorized by the Department. Such regulations shall provide, at a minimum, for amendment, suspension, or revocation of licenses, and for authorization for access to a low-level radioactive waste facility by the Department on a temporary or emergency basis. Each application for a license or amendment shall be in writing and shall include such information as may be required by regulation, and such additional information as the Department deems necessary. The application for a license shall set forth the manner in which the applicant plans to comply with the requirements of this Chapter and regulations promulgated thereunder. Upon receipt of an application under this section the Department shall review the application and shall issue a license only if it finds that the applicant is fully qualified under all applicable laws and regulation. (1987, c. 850, s. 9.)

§ 104E-11. Inspections, agreements, and educational programs.

(a)   Authorized representatives of the Department shall have the authority to enter upon any public or private property, other than a private dwelling, at all reasonable times for the purpose of determining compliance with the provisions of this Chapter and rules, regulations and standards adopted hereunder.

(b)   After approval by the Commission, the Governor is authorized to enter into agreements with the federal government, other states, or interstate agencies, whereby this State will perform on a cooperative basis with the federal government, other states, or interstate agencies, inspections, emergency response to radiation accidents, and other functions related to the control of radiation.

(c)   The Department is authorized to institute educational programs for the purpose of training or educating persons who may possess, use, handle, transport, or service radioactive materials or radiation machines. (1975, c. 718, s. 1.)

155

§ 104E-12. Records.

(a)   The Commission is authorized to require each person who possesses or uses a source of radiation:

(1)   To maintain appropriate records relating to its receipt, storage, use, transfer, or disposal and maintain such other records as the Commission may require, subject to such exemptions as may be provided by the rules and regulations promulgated by the Commission; and

(2)   To maintain appropriate records showing the radiation exposure of all individuals for whom personnel monitoring may be required by the Commission, subject to such exemptions as may be provided by the rules and regulations promulgated by the Commission.

Copies of all records required to be kept by this subsection shall be submitted to the Department or its duly authorized agents upon request.

(b)   The Commission is authorized to require that any person possessing or using a source of radiation furnish to each employee for whom personnel monitoring is required a copy of such employee's personal exposure record upon the request of such employee, at any time such employee has received radiation exposure in excess of limits established in the rules and regulations promulgated by the Commission, and upon termination of employment. (1975, c. 718, s. 1.)

§ 104E-13. Administrative procedures and judicial review.

(a)   The Department may refuse to grant a license as provided in G.S. 104E-7 or 104E-10 to any applicant who does not possess the requirements or qualifications which the Commission may prescribe in rules and regulations. The Department may suspend, revoke, or amend any license in the event that the person to whom such license was granted violates any of the rules and regulations of the Commission, or ceases, or fails to have the reasonable facilities prescribed by the Commission: Provided, that before any order is entered denying an application for a license or suspending, revoking, or amending a license previously granted, the applicant or person to whom such license was granted shall be given notice and granted a hearing as provided in Chapter 150B of the North Carolina General Statutes.

(b)   Whenever the Department in its opinion determines that an emergency exists requiring immediate action to protect the public health and safety the Department may, without notice or hearing, issue an order reciting the existence of such emergency and requiring that such action be taken as is necessary to meet the emergency. Notwithstanding any provision of this Chapter, such order shall be effective immediately. Any person to whom such order is directed shall comply therewith immediately, and on application to the Department shall be afforded a hearing within 10 days. On the basis of such hearing, the emergency order shall be continued, modified, or revoked within 30 days after such hearing, as the Department may deem appropriate under the evidence.

(c)   Any applicant or person to whom a license was granted who shall be aggrieved by any order of the Department or its duly authorized agent denying such application or suspending, revoking, or amending such license may appeal directly to the superior court as provided in Chapter 150B of the North Carolina General Statutes. (1975, c. 718, s. 1; 1987, c. 850, s. 10.)

§ 104E-14. Impounding of materials.

(a)   Authorized representatives of the Department shall have the authority in the event of an emergency to impound or order the impounding of sources of radiation in the possession of any person who is not equipped to observe or fails to observe the provisions of this Chapter or any rules or regulations promulgated by the Commission.

(b)   The Department may release such sources of radiation to the owner thereof upon terms and conditions in accordance with the provisions of this Chapter and rules and regulations adopted hereunder or may bring an action in the appropriate superior court for an order condemning such sources of radiation and providing for the destruction or other disposition so as to protect the public health and safety. (1975, c. 718, s. 1.)

§ 104E-15. Transportation of radioactive materials.

(a)   The Radiation Protection Commission is authorized to adopt, promulgate, amend, and repeal rules and regulations governing the transportation of radioactive materials in North Carolina, which, in the judgment

157

of the Commission, shall promote the public health, safety, or welfare and protect the environment.

(1)   Such rules and regulations may include, but shall not be limited to, provisions for the use of signs designating radioactive material cargo; for the packing, marking, loading, and handling of radioactive materials, and the precautions necessary to determine whether the material when offered is in proper condition for transport, and may include designation of routes in this State which are to be used for the transportation of radioactive materials.

(2)   Such rules and regulations shall not include the carrier vehicle or its equipment, the licensing of packages, nor shall they apply to the handling or transportation of radioactive material within the confines of a facility licensed by or owned by a federal agency.

(3)   The Commission is authorized to adopt by reference, in whole or in part, such federal rules and regulations governing the transportation of radioactive material which are established by the United States Nuclear Regulatory Commission, the United States Department of Transportation, or the United States Postal Service (or any federal agency which is a successor to any of the foregoing agencies), as such federal rules may be amended from time to time.

(b)   The Department is authorized to enter into agreements with the respective federal agencies designed to avoid duplication of effort and/or conflict in enforcement and inspection activities so that:

(1)   Rules and regulations adopted by the Commission pursuant to this section of this Chapter may be enforced, within their respective jurisdictions, by any authorized representatives of the Department of Environment and Natural Resources and the Department of Transportation, according to mutual understandings between such departments of their respective responsibilities and authorities.

(2)   The Department, through any authorized representative, is authorized to inspect any records of persons engaged in the transportation of radioactive materials during the hours of business operation when such records reasonably relate to the method or contents of packing, marking, loading, handling, or shipping of radioactive materials within the State.

(3)   The Department, through any authorized representative, may enter upon and inspect the premises or vehicles of any person engaged in the

transportation of radioactive materials during hours of business operation, with or without a warrant, for the purpose of determining compliance with the provisions of this Chapter and the rules and regulations promulgated by the Commission.

(c)   Upon a determination by the Department that any provision of this section, or the rules and regulations promulgated by the Commission are being violated or that any practice in the transportation of radioactive materials constitutes a clear and imminent danger to the public health, property, or safety, it shall issue an order requiring correction as provided in G.S. 104E-13(b). (1975, c. 716, s. 7; c. 718, s. 1; 1989, c. 727, s. 219(22); 1997-443, s. 11A.119(a).)

§ 104E-16. Nonreverting Radiation Protection Fund.

(a)   There is hereby established under the control and direction of the Department a Nonreverting Radiation Protection Fund which shall be used to defray the expenses of any project or activity for:

(1)   Emergency response to and decontamination of radiation accidents as provided in G.S. 104E-9(a)(5), or

(2)   Perpetual maintenance and custody of radioactive materials as the Department may undertake.

In addition to any moneys that shall be appropriated or otherwise made available to it, the Fund may be maintained by fees, charges, or other moneys paid to or recovered by or on behalf of the Department under the provisions of this Chapter, except for the clear proceeds of penalties. Any moneys paid to or recovered by or on behalf of the Department as fees, charges, or other payments authorized by this Chapter, except for the clear proceeds of penalties, shall be paid to the Radiation Protection Fund in an amount equal to the sum expended for the projects or activities in subdivisions (1) and (2) above.

(b)   Repealed by Session Laws 1987, c. 850, s. 11. (1975, c. 718, s. 1; 1981, c. 704, s. 11.2; 1987, c. 633, s. 8; c. 850, s. 11; 1998-215, s. 47(b).)

§ 104E-17. Payments to State and local agencies.

Upon completion of any project or activity stated in G.S. 104E-16(a)(1), and from time to time during any project or activity stated in G.S. 104E-16(a)(2), each State and local agency that has participated by furnishing personnel, equipment or material shall deliver to the Department a record of the expenses incurred by the agency. The amount of incurred expenses shall be disbursed by the Secretary of Environment and Natural Resources to each such agency from the Radiation Protection Fund. Upon completion of any project or activity stated in G.S. 104E-16(a)(1), and from time to time during any project or activity stated in G.S. 104E-16(a)(2), the Secretary of Environment and Natural Resources shall prepare a statement of all expenses and costs of the project or activity expended by the State and shall make demand for payment upon the person having control over the radioactive materials or the release thereof which necessitated said project or activity. Any person having control over the radioactive materials or the release thereof and any other person causing or contributing to an incident necessitating any project or activity stated in G.S. 104E-16 shall be directly liable to the State for the necessary expenses incurred thereby and the State shall have a cause of action to recover from any or all such persons. If the person having control over the radioactive materials or the release thereof shall fail or refuse to pay the sum expended by the State, the Secretary of Environment and Natural Resources shall refer the matter to the Attorney General of North Carolina, who shall institute an action in the name of the State in the Superior Court of Wake County, or in his discretion, in the superior court of the county in which the project or activity was undertaken by the State, to recover such cost and expenses.

In any action instituted by the Attorney General under this section, a verified and itemized statement of the expenses incurred by the State in any project or activity stated in G.S. 104E-16 shall be filed with the complaint and shall constitute prima facie the amount due the State; and any judgment for the State thereon shall be for such amount in the absence of allegation and proof on the part of the defendant or defendants that the statement of expenses incurred by and the amount due the State is not correct because of an error in:

(1)   Calculating the amount due, or

(2)   Not properly crediting the account with any cash payment or payments or other satisfaction which may have been made thereon. (1975, c. 718, s. 1; 1989, c. 727, s. 219(23); 1997-443, s. 11A.119(a).)

§ 104E-18. Security for emergency response and perpetual maintenance costs.

(a)   No person shall use, manufacture, produce, transport, transfer, receive, acquire, own, possess or dispose of radioactive material until that person shall have procured and filed with the Department such bond, insurance or other security as the Commission may by regulation require. Such bond, insurance or other security shall:

(1)   Run in favor of the Radiation Protection Fund in the amount of the estimated total cost as established by the Commission that may be incurred by the State in any project or activity stated in G.S. 104E-16, and

(2)   Have as indemnitor on such bond or insurance an insurance company licensed to do business in the State of North Carolina.

(b)   The Commission may from time to time:

(1)   Cause an audit to be made of any person that insures itself by means of other security as provided for in subsection (a) above;

(2)   Amend or modify the estimated total cost for security established pursuant to this section; and

(3)   Provide by regulation for the discontinuance of indemnification by one insurer and the assumption thereof by another insurer, as the Commission deems necessary to carry out the provisions of this Chapter and rules and regulations adopted and promulgated hereunder.

(c)   Repealed by Session Laws 2001-474, s. 4. (1975, c. 718, s. 1; 1981, c. 704, s. 12; 1987, c. 850, s. 12; 1987 (Reg. Sess., 1988), c. 1082, s. 11; 2001-474, s. 4.)

§ 104E-19. (See Editor's notes) Fees.

(a)   An annual fee in the amount set by the Department is imposed on a person who is required to be registered or licensed under this Chapter. The Department must set the fees at amounts that provide revenue to offset its costs in performing its duties under this Chapter.

(b)   Repealed by Session Laws 1987, c. 850, s. 13.

(c)   The annual fees under subsection (a) of this section shall not exceed the maximum amounts as follows:

(1)   For tanning facilities: two hundred dollars ($200.00) for the first piece of tanning equipment and thirty dollars ($30.00) for each additional piece of tanning equipment.

(2)   For the following categories of facilities registered to use X-ray tubes or X-ray equipment: clinics, chiropractors, dentists, educational, government, podiatrists, industrial, physicians, veterinarians, and other; two hundred dollars ($200.00) for the first X-ray tube or piece of X-ray equipment and thirty dollars ($30.00) for each additional X-ray tube or piece of X-ray equipment.

(3)   For the following categories of facilities registered to use X-ray tubes or X-ray equipment: industrial medical, health departments, and service; three hundred dollars ($300.00) for the first X-ray tube or piece of X-ray equipment and forty dollars ($40.00) for each additional X-ray tube or piece of X-ray equipment.

(4)   For the following categories of facilities registered to use X-ray tubes or X-ray equipment: hospitals and industrial radiography; four hundred dollars ($400.00) for the first X-ray tube or piece of X-ray equipment and fifty dollars ($50.00) for each additional X-ray tube or piece of X-ray equipment. (1975, c. 718, s. 1; 1981, c. 704, s. 13; 1987, c. 633, s. 9; c. 850, s. 13; 1987 (Reg. Sess., 1988), c. 993, s. 26; 2001-474, s. 5; 2009-451, s. 13.3(a).)

§ 104E-20. Prohibited uses and facilities.

(a)   It shall be unlawful for any person to use, manufacture, produce, transport, transfer, receive, acquire, own or possess any source of radiation unless licensed, registered or exempted by the Department in accordance with the provisions of this Chapter and the rules and regulations adopted and promulgated hereunder.

(b)   Shallow land burial is prohibited. (1975, c. 718, s. 1; 1987, c. 633, s. 10.)

§ 104E-21. Conflicting laws.

(a)   Ordinances, resolutions or regulations, now or hereafter in effect, of the governing body of a municipality or county or board of health relating to by-product, source and special nuclear materials shall not be superseded by this Chapter. Provided, that such ordinances or regulations are and continue to be consistent and compatible with the provisions of this Chapter, as amended, and rules and regulations promulgated by the Commission.

(b)   It is the intent of the General Assembly to prescribe a uniform system for the management of low-level radioactive waste and to place limitations upon the exercise by all units of local government in North Carolina of the power to regulate the management of low-level radioactive waste by special, local or private acts or resolutions as provided in G.S. 143B-216.10(b). (1975, c. 718, s. 1; 1981, c. 704, s. 25.)

§ 104E-22. Tort claims against persons rendering emergency assistance.

Any and all tort claims against any person which arise while that person is rendering assistance during an emergency (i) at the request of any authorized representative of the State of North Carolina or (ii) pursuant to a mutual radiological assistance agreement as provided for in G.S. 104E-11(b), shall constitute claims against this State; and the disposition thereof shall be governed by the provisions of Article 31 of Chapter 143 of the General Statutes. In any civil action brought against said person, the provisions of Article 31A of Chapter 143 of the General Statutes shall apply as if such person were an employee of this State. (1975, c. 718, s. 1.)

§ 104E-23. Penalties; injunctive relief.

(a)   Any person who violates the provisions of G.S. 104E-15 or 104E-20, or who hinders, obstructs, or otherwise interferes with any authorized representative of the Department in the discharge of his official duties in making inspections as provided in G.S. 104E-11, or in impounding materials as provided in G.S. 104E-14, shall be guilty of a Class 1 misdemeanor and, upon conviction thereof, shall be punished as provided by law. Any person who willfully violates the provisions of G.S. 104E-10.2 shall be guilty of a Class 1 misdemeanor and, upon conviction, shall be punished as provided by law.

(b)   The Secretary may, either before or after the institution of any other action or proceedings authorized by law, institute a civil action in the superior court of the county in which the defendant in said action resides for injunctive relief to prevent a threatened or continued violation of any provision of this Chapter or any order or regulation issued pursuant to this Chapter. (1975, c. 718, s. 1; 1979, c. 694, s. 5; 1981, c. 480, s. 2; 1993, c. 539, s. 685; 1994, Ex. Sess., c. 24, s. 14(c).)

§ 104E-24. Administrative penalties.

(a)   The Department may impose an administrative penalty on any person:

(1)   Who fails to comply with this Chapter, any order issued hereunder, or any rules adopted pursuant to this Chapter;

(2)   Who refuses to allow an authorized representative of the Radiation Protection Commission or the Department of Environment and Natural Resources a right of entry as provided for in G.S. 104E-11 or impounding materials as provided for in G.S. 104E-14.

(b)   Each day of a continuing violation shall constitute a separate violation. Such penalty shall not exceed ten thousand dollars ($10,000) per day. In determining the amount of the penalty, the Department shall consider the degree and extent of the harm caused by the violation. Any person assessed a penalty shall be notified of the assessment by registered or certified mail, and the notice shall specify the reasons for the assessment.

(c)   Any person wishing to contest a penalty or order issued under this section shall be entitled to an administrative hearing and judicial review in accordance with the procedures outlined in Articles 3, 3A, and 4 of Chapter 150B of the General Statutes.

(d)   The Secretary may bring a civil action in the superior court of the county in which such violation is alleged to have occurred to recover the amount of administrative penalty whenever a person:

(1)   Who has not requested an administrative hearing fails to pay the penalty within 60 days after being notified of such penalty, or

(2)   Who has requested an administrative hearing fails to pay the penalty within 60 days after service of a written copy of the decision as provided in G.S. 150B-36.

(e)   The clear proceeds of penalties imposed pursuant to this section shall be remitted to the Civil Penalty and Forfeiture Fund in accordance with G.S. 115C-457.2. (1981, c. 704, s. 14; 1987, c. 850, s. 14; 1989, c. 727, s. 219(24); 1997-443, s. 11A.119(a); 1998-215, s. 47(a).)

§ 104E-25. Performance objectives, technical requirements and design criteria applicable to low-level radioactive waste disposal facilities; engineered barriers.

(a)   As used in this section, the term "Part 61" means Title 10, Code of Federal Regulations Part 61 in effect on 1 January 1987. Unless a different meaning is required by definitions generally applicable to this Chapter or by the context, terms defined or used in Part 61 shall have the same meaning in this section as in Part 61.

(b)   The Commission shall adopt rules for low-level radioactive waste disposal facilities which incorporate and are consistent with the performance objectives and technical requirements set out in Subparts C and D of Part 61. In the event that Part 61 is amended, the Commission shall amend its rules at least to the extent necessary to maintain the State's status as an agreement state. The Commission may adopt rules which exceed the requirements of applicable federal statutes and regulations.

(c)   Low-level radioactive waste disposal facilities shall incorporate engineered barriers for all waste classifications. The Commission shall specify minimum design criteria for engineered barriers. Different engineered barrier design criteria may be specified for different waste classifications. In the event that a single disposal unit is used for the disposal of wastes having more than one waste classification, the engineered barrier employed shall be that specified for the highest waste classification in the disposal unit.

(d)   Engineered barriers shall be designed and constructed to complement and, where appropriate, improve the ability of the disposal facility to meet the

165

performance objectives of this section. The site for a low-level radioactive waste disposal facility shall meet all hydrogeological and other criteria and standards applicable to disposal site suitability as though engineered barriers were not required. Engineered barriers shall not substitute for a suitable site or compensate for any deficiency in a site.

(e)   Engineered barriers shall be designed and constructed of materials having physical and chemical properties so as to provide reasonable assurance that the barriers will maintain their functional integrity under all reasonably foreseeable conditions for at least the institutional control period. To the maximum extent possible, engineered barriers shall be chemically nonreactive with waste, waste containers and surrounding soil. Engineered barriers shall not detract from the ability of the disposal facility to meet the performance objectives adopted by the Commission under this Chapter. The Commission shall determine the appropriate design life of engineered barriers, which may exceed the institutional control period; however no reliance may be placed on engineered barriers beyond the end of the institutional control period.

(f)   Disposal units and the incorporated engineered barriers shall be designed and constructed to meet the following objectives:

(1)   Prevention of the migration of water into the disposal unit.

(2)   Prevention of the migration of waste or waste contaminated water out of the disposal unit.

(3)   Detection of water and other fluids in the disposal unit.

(4)   Temporary collection and retention of water and other liquids for a time sufficient to allow for their detection and removal or other remedial measures without contamination of groundwater or surrounding soil.

(5)   Facilitation of remedial measures without disturbing other disposal units.

(6)   Facilitation of recovery of waste, other than Class A waste, in the packing or container in which the waste was placed for disposal.

(7)   Reasonable assurance that waste will be isolated for at least the institutional control period.

166

(8)   Prevention of contact between waste and the surrounding earth, except for earth that may be used as fill within the disposal unit.

(g)   The term "container" means any portable device into which waste is placed for storage, transportation, treatment, disposal, or other handling and includes the first enclosure which encompasses the waste. All waste shall be packed in containers for disposal. The Commission shall adopt standards for the design and construction of containers for disposal which are consistent with applicable federal standards. Standards for containers may vary for different types and classifications of waste. The standards for disposal containers may supplement or duplicate any of the requirements for engineered barriers set out in this section; however the requirements for engineered barriers are separate and cumulative, and engineered barriers and containers may not substitute for or replace one another.

(h)   Waste shall be converted into a form for disposal which is as chemically stable, nonreactive, and physically stable as can be reasonably achieved, as determined by the Commission, taking into consideration costs and available technology. All liquid waste shall be solidified prior to disposal.

(i)   In adopting rules specifying performance objectives, technical requirements, and design criteria and standards for a low-level radioactive waste disposal facility, the Commission shall consider the possibility of unforeseen differences between expected and actual performance of the facility. The Commission shall consider best available technology and costs.

(j)   The Commission shall require that the bottom of a low-level radioactive waste disposal facility shall be at least seven feet above the seasonal high water table. The Commission shall require additional separation wherever necessary to adequately protect the public health and the environment. (1987, c. 633, s. 11.)

§ 104E-26. Standards and criteria for licensing low-level radioactive waste facilities.

Standards and criteria for licensing low-level radioactive waste facilities shall be developed by the Commission. Such standards and criteria shall be developed with public participation and shall be incorporated into rules adopted by the Commission for the licensing of such facilities. Standards and criteria shall be

167

consistent with all applicable federal and State law, including statutes, regulations and rules; shall be developed and revised in light of the best available scientific data; and shall be based on consideration of at least the following factors:

(1)   Hydrological and geological factors, including flood plains, depth to water table, groundwater travel time, soil pH, soil cation exchange capacity, soil composition and permeability, cavernous bedrock, seismic activity, slope, mines, climate and earthquake faults;

(2)   Environmental and public health factors, including air quality, quality of surface and groundwater, and proximity to public water supply watersheds;

(3)   Natural and cultural resources, including wetlands, gamelands, endangered species habitats, proximity to parks, forests, wilderness areas, nature preserves, and historic sites;

(4)   Local land uses;

(5)   Transportation factors, including proximity to waste generators, route safety, and method of transportation;

(6)   Aesthetic factors, including the visibility, appearance, and noise level of the facility. (1987, c. 850, s. 15.)

§ 104E-27. Volume reduction required.

(a)   The Commission shall develop and adopt rules that require generators of low-level radioactive waste to implement best management practices, including prevention, minimization, reduction, segregation, and hold-for-decay storage, as a condition of access to any low-level radioactive waste disposal facility located in this State.

(b)   Repealed by Session Laws 2001-474, s. 6.

(c)   The Department shall periodically review the State's comprehensive low-level radioactive waste management system and make recommendations to the Governor, cognizant State agencies, and the General Assembly on ways to improve waste management; reduce the amount of waste generated; and minimize the amount of low-level radioactive waste that must be disposed of. (1987, c. 850, s. 15.1; 1993, c. 501, s. 5; 2001-474, s. 6.)

§ 104E-28. Limited liability for volunteers in low-level radioactive waste abatement.

Part 5 of Article 21A of Chapter 143 of the General Statutes shall apply to civil liability and penalties pursuant to this Chapter. (1987, c. 269, s. 4.)

§ 104E-29. Confidential information protected.

(a)   The following information received or prepared by the Department in the course of carrying out its duties and responsibilities under this Chapter is confidential information and shall not be subject to disclosure under G.S. 132-6:

(1)   Information which the Secretary determines is entitled to confidential treatment pursuant to G.S. 132-1.2. If the Secretary determines that information received by the Department is not entitled to confidential treatment, the Secretary shall inform the person who provided the information of that determination at the time such determination is made. The Secretary may refuse to accept or may return any information that is claimed to be confidential that the Secretary determines is not entitled to confidential treatment.

(2)   Information that is confidential under any provision of federal or state law.

(3)   Information compiled in anticipation of enforcement or criminal proceedings, but only to the extent disclosure could reasonably be expected to interfere with the institution of such proceedings.

(b)   Confidential information may be disclosed to officers, employees, or authorized representatives of federal or state agencies if such disclosure is necessary to carry out a proper function of the Department or the requesting agency or when relevant in any proceeding under this Chapter.

(c)   Except as provided in subsection (b) of this section or as otherwise provided by law, any officer or employee of the State who knowingly discloses information designated as confidential under this section shall be guilty of a Class 1 misdemeanor and shall be removed from office or discharged from employment. (1991, c. 745, s. 1; 1993, c. 539, s. 686; 1994, Ex. Sess., c. 24, s. 14(c).)

Chapter 104F

Southeast Interstate Low-Level Radioactive Waste Management Compact.

§§ 104F-1 through 104F-5: Repealed by Session Laws 1999-357, s. 2.

Chapter 104G.

North Carolina Low-Level Radioactive Waste Management Authority Act of 1987.

§§ 104G-1 through 104G-23: Repealed by Session Laws 1999-357, s. 4.

Chapter 105.

Taxation.

SUBCHAPTER I. LEVY OF TAXES.

§ 105-1. Title and purpose of Subchapter.

The title of this Subchapter shall be "The Revenue Act." The purpose of this Subchapter shall be to raise and provide revenue for the necessary uses and purposes of the government and State of North Carolina during the next biennium and each biennium thereafter, and the provisions of this Subchapter shall be and remain in full force and effect until changed by law. It is the policy of this State that as many State taxes as possible be structured so that they are deductible for federal income tax purposes under the Internal Revenue Code. (1939, c. 158, ss. A, B; 1941, c. 50, s. 1; 1983 (Reg. Sess., 1984), c. 1097, s. 1.)

§ 105-1.1. Supremacy of State Constitution.

The State's power of taxation is vested in the General Assembly. Under Article V, Section 2(1), of the North Carolina Constitution, this power cannot be surrendered, suspended, or contracted away. In the exercise of this power, the General Assembly may amend or repeal any provision of this Subchapter in its discretion. No provision of this Subchapter constitutes a contract that the provision will remain in effect in future years, and any representation made to the contrary is of no effect. (2003-416, s. 12.)

Article 1.

Inheritance Tax.

§§ 105-2 through 105-32: Repealed by Session Laws 1998-212, s. 29A.2(a), effective January 1, 1999, and applicable to the estates of decedents dying on or after that date.

Article 1A.

Estate Taxes.

§ 105-32.1. (Repealed effective January 1, 2013, and applicable to the estates of decedents dying on or after that date.) Definitions.

The following definitions apply in this Article:

(1)   Code. - Defined in G.S. 105-228.90.

(2)   Personal representative. - The person appointed by the clerk of superior court under Chapter 28A of the General Statutes to administer the estate of a decedent or, if no one is appointed under that Chapter, the person required to file a federal estate tax return for the estate of the decedent.

(3)   Secretary. - Defined in G.S. 105-228.90. (1998-212, s. 29A.2(b); 2013-316, s. 7(a).)

Article 2.

Privilege Taxes.

§ 105-33. Taxes under this Article.

(a)   General. - Taxes in this Article are imposed for the privilege of carrying on the business, exercising the privilege, or doing the act named.

(b)   License Taxes. - A license tax imposed by this Article is an annual tax. The tax is due by July 1 of each year. The tax is imposed for the privilege of engaging in a specified activity during the fiscal year that begins on the July 1 due date of the tax. The full amount of a license tax applies to a person who, during a fiscal year, begins to engage in an activity for which this Article requires a license. Before a person engages in an activity for which this Article requires a license, the person must obtain the required license.

(c)   Other Taxes. - The taxes imposed by this Article on a percentage basis or another basis are due as specified in this Article.

(d)   Repealed by Session Laws 1998-95, s. 2.

(e)   Repealed by Session Laws 1989, c. 584, s. 1.

(f), (g) Repealed by Session Laws 1998-95, s. 2.

(h)   Liability Upon Transfer. - A grantee, transferee, or purchaser of any business or property subject to the State taxes imposed in this Article must make diligent inquiry as to whether the State tax has been paid. If the business or property has been granted, sold, transferred, or conveyed to an innocent purchaser for value and without notice that the vendor owed or is liable for any of the State taxes imposed under this Article, the property, while in the possession of the innocent purchaser, is not subject to any lien for the taxes.

(i), (j) Repealed by Session Laws 1998-95, s. 2.

(k)   Repealed by Session Laws 1987, c. 190. (1939, c. 158, s. 100; 1943, c. 400, s. 2; 1951, c. 643, s. 2; 1953, c. 981, s. 1; 1963, c. 294, s. 3; 1973, c. 476, s. 193; 1977, c. 657, s. 1; 1981, c. 83, ss. 1, 2; 1985, c. 114, s. 10; 1985 (Reg. Sess., 1986), c. 826, ss. 1, 2; c. 934, s. 3; 1987, c. 190; 1989, c. 584, s. 1; 1989 (Reg. Sess., 1990), c. 814, s. 1; 1991 (Reg. Sess., 1992), c. 981, s. 1; 1993, c.

539, s. 688; 1994, Ex. Sess., c. 24, s. 14(c); 1996, 2nd Ex. Sess., c. 14, ss. 18, 19; 1998-95, ss. 1, 2.)

§ 105-33.1. Definitions.

The following definitions apply in this Article:

(1)   City. - Defined in G.S. 105-228.90.

(1a)   Code. - Defined in G.S. 105-228.90.

(2)   Repealed by Session Laws 1998-95, s. 3.

(3)   Person. - Defined in G.S. 105-228.90.

(4)   Secretary. - Defined in G.S. 105-228.90. (1991, c. 45, s. 1; 1991 (Reg. Sess., 1992), c. 922, s. 2; 1993, c. 12, s. 3; c. 354, s. 6; 1998-95, s. 3.)

§ 105-34: Repealed by Session Laws 1979, c. 63.

§ 105-35: Repealed by Session Laws 1979, c. 72.

§§ 105-36 through 105-37: Repealed by Session Laws 1996, Second Extra Session, c. 14, s. 17.

§ 105-37.1. (Repealed effective January 1, 2014, and applicable to admissions purchased on or after that date.) Live entertainment and ticket resales.

(a)   Scope. - A privilege tax is imposed on the following:

(1)   The gross admissions receipts of a person who is engaged in providing admission to live entertainment of any kind. Gross admissions receipts under this subdivision do not include charges for amenities. If charges for amenities are not separately stated on the face of an admission ticket, then the charge for admission is considered to be equal to the admission charge for a ticket to the same event that does not include amenities and is for a seat located directly in front of or closest to a seat that includes amenities.

173

(2)   The gross admissions receipts of a person who is engaged in the business of reselling on the Internet under G.S. 14-344.1 an admission ticket that is taxable under subdivision (1) of this subsection. If the price of an admission ticket is printed on the face of the ticket, gross receipts under this subdivision exclude the face price. If the price of an admission ticket is not printed on the face of the ticket, the tax under this subdivision applies to the difference between the amount the reseller paid for the ticket and the amount the reseller charges for the ticket.

(3)   Repealed by Session Laws 2010-31, s. 31.7(a), effective June 30, 2010.

(b)   Rate and Payment. - The rate of the privilege tax imposed by this section is three percent (3%). The tax is due when a return is due. A return is due by the 10th day after the end of each month and covers the gross receipts received during the previous month.

(c)   Advance Report. - A person who owns or controls a live entertainment performance subject to the tax imposed by this section and who plans to bring the performance to this State from outside the State must file a statement with the Secretary that lists the dates, times, and places of the performance. The statement must be filed no less than five days before the first performance in this State.

(d)   Local Taxes. - Cities may levy a license tax on a person taxed under subdivision (a)(1) of this section; however, the tax may not exceed twenty-five dollars ($25.00). Cities may not levy a license tax on a person taxed under subdivision (a)(2) of this section. Counties may not levy a license tax on a person taxed under this section. (1939, c. 158, ss. 105, 106; 1943, c. 400, s. 2; 1945, c. 708, s. 2; 1947, c. 501, s. 2; 1963, c. 1231; 1967, c. 865; 1973, c. 476, s. 193; c. 476, s. 193; 1977, c. 657, s. 1; 1981, c. 2; c. 83, s. 3; c. 977; 1985, c. 376; 1985 (Reg. Sess., 1986), c. 819, s. 3; 1987 (Reg. Sess., 1988), c. 1082, s. 1.1; 1989, c. 584, ss. 5, 6; 1989 (Reg. Sess., 1990), c. 814, s. 2; 1991, c. 45, s. 2; 1996, 2nd Ex. Sess., c. 14, s. 20; 1998-95, ss. 4, 5; 1999-337, s. 14(a); 1999-456, s. 26; 2010-31, s. 31.7(a); 2011-330, s. 1; 2013-316, s. 5(a).)

§ 105-37.2: Repealed by Session Law 1998-96, s. 3.

§ 105-38: Repealed by Session Laws 1999-337, s. 14(b).

§ 105-38.1. (Repealed effective January 1, 2014, and applicable to admissions purchased on or after that date.) Motion picture shows.

(a)   A privilege tax at the rate of one percent (1%) is imposed on the gross receipts of a person who is engaged in the business of operating a motion picture show for which an admission is charged. The tax is due when a return is due. A return is due by the 10th day after the end of each month and covers the gross receipts received during the previous month. If a person offers an entertainment or amusement that includes both a motion picture taxable under this section and an entertainment or amusement taxable under G.S. 105-37.1, the tax in that statute applies to the entire gross receipts and the tax levied in this section does not apply.

(b)   Repealed by Session Laws 1999-337, s. 15(a). (1998-95, s. 5.1; 1999-337, s. 15(a); 2013-316, s. 5(a).)

§ 105-39. Repealed by Session Laws 1987 (Reg. Sess., 1988), c. 1082, s. 1.)

§ 105-40. (Repealed effective January 1, 2014, and applicable to admissions purchased on or after that date.) Amusements - Certain exhibitions, performances, and entertainments exempt from tax.

The following forms of amusement are exempt from the taxes imposed under this Article:

(1)   All exhibitions, performances, and entertainments, except as in this Article expressly mentioned as not exempt, produced by local talent exclusively, for the benefit of religious, charitable, benevolent or educational purposes, as long as no compensation is paid to the local talent.

(2)   The North Carolina Symphony Society, Incorporated, as specified in G.S. 140-10.1.

(3)   All exhibits, shows, attractions, and amusements operated by a society or association organized under the provisions of Chapter 106 of the General Statutes where the society or association has obtained a permit from the Secretary to operate without the payment of taxes under this Article.

(4)   All outdoor historical dramas, as specified in Article 19C of Chapter 143 of the General Statutes.

(5)   All elementary and secondary school athletic contests, dances, and other amusements.

(6)   The first one thousand dollars ($1,000) of gross receipts derived from dances and other amusements actually promoted and managed by civic organizations when the entire proceeds of the dances or other amusements are used exclusively for civic and charitable purposes of the organizations and not to defray the expenses of the organization conducting the dance or amusement. The mere sponsorship of a dance or another amusement by a civic or fraternal organization does not exempt the dance or other amusement, because the exemption applies only when the dance or amusement is actually managed and conducted by the civic or fraternal organization.

(6a)   A youth athletic contest with an admissions price that does not exceed ten dollars ($10.00) sponsored by a person exempt from income tax under Article 4 of this Chapter. For the purpose of this subdivision, a youth athletic contest means a contest in which each participating athlete is less than 20 years of age.

(7)   All dances, motion picture shows, and other amusements promoted and managed by a qualifying corporation that operates a center for the performing and visual arts if the dance or other amusement is held at the center. "Qualifying corporation" means a corporation that is exempt from income tax under G.S. 105-130.11(a)(3). "Center for the performing and visual arts" means a facility, having a fixed location, that provides space for dramatic performances, studios, classrooms, and similar accommodations to organized arts groups and individual artists. This exemption does not apply to athletic events.

(7a)   All exhibitions, performances, and entertainments promoted and managed by "a nonprofit arts organization." This exemption does not apply to athletic events. A "nonprofit arts organization" is an organization that meets both of the following requirements:

a.   It is exempt from income tax under G.S. 105-130.11(a)(3).

b.   Its primary purpose is to create, produce, present, or support music, dance, theatre, literature, or visual arts.

(8)   A person that is exempt from income tax under Article 4 of this Chapter and is engaged in the business of operating a teen center. A "teen center" is a

fixed facility whose primary purpose is to provide recreational activities, dramatic performances, dances, and other amusements exclusively for teenagers.

(9)   All entertainments or amusements offered or given on the Cherokee Indian reservation when the person giving, offering, or managing the entertainment or amusement is authorized to do business on the reservation and pays the tribal gross receipts levy to the tribal council.

(10)   Arts festivals held by a person that is exempt from income tax under Article 4 of this Chapter and that meets the following conditions:

a.   The person holds no more than two arts festivals during a calendar year.

b.   Each of the person's arts festivals last no more than seven consecutive days.

c.   The arts festivals are held outdoors on public property and involve a variety of exhibitions, entertainments, and activities.

(11)   Community festivals held by a person who is exempt from income tax under Article 4 of this Chapter and that meets all of the following conditions:

a.   The person holds no more than one community festival during a calendar year.

b.   The community festival lasts no more than seven consecutive days.

c.   The community festival involves a variety of exhibitions, entertainments, and activities, the majority of which are held outdoors and are open to the public.

(12)   All farm-related exhibitions, shows, attractions, or amusements offered on land used for bona fide farm purposes as defined in G.S. 153A-340. (1939, c. 158, s. 108; 1998-95, ss. 5.1, 6; 1998-96, s. 2; 1999-337, s. 15(b); 2000-140, s. 61; 2004-84, s. 1; 2006-216, s. 1; 2007-527, ss. 2, 3(a), (b); 2009-550, s. 5.1; 2013-316, s. 5(a).)

§ 105-41. Attorneys-at-law and other professionals.

(a)   Every individual in this State who practices a profession or engages in a business and is included in the list below must obtain from the Secretary a statewide license for the privilege of practicing the profession or engaging in the business. A license required by this section is not transferable to another person. The tax for each license is fifty dollars ($50.00).

(1)   An attorney-at-law.

(2)   A physician, a veterinarian, a surgeon, an osteopath, a chiropractor, a chiropodist, a dentist, an ophthalmologist, an optician, an optometrist, or another person who practices a professional art of healing.

(3)   A professional engineer, as defined in G.S. 89C-3.

(4)   A registered land surveyor, as defined in G.S. 89C-3.

(5)   An architect.

(6)   A landscape architect.

(7)   A photographer, a canvasser for any photographer, or an agent of a photographer in transmitting photographs to be copied, enlarged, or colored.

(8)   A real estate broker as defined in G.S. 93A-2. A real estate broker who is also a real estate appraiser is required to obtain only one license under this section to cover both activities.

(9)   A real estate appraiser, as defined in G.S. 93E-1-4. A real estate appraiser who is also a real estate broker is required to obtain only one license under this section to cover both activities.

(10)   A person who solicits or negotiates loans on real estate as agent for another for a commission, brokerage, or other compensation.

(11)   A mortician or embalmer licensed under G.S. 90-210.25.

(12)   An individual licensed under Article 9F of Chapter 143 of the General Statutes, the Home Inspector Licensure Act.

(b)   The following persons are exempt from the tax:

(1)   A person who is at least 75 years old.

(2)   A person practicing the professional art of healing for a fee or reward, if the person is an adherent of an established church or religious organization and confines the healing practice to prayer or spiritual means.

(3)   A blind person engaging in a trade or profession as a sole proprietor. A "blind person" means any person who is totally blind or whose central visual acuity does not exceed 20/200 in the better eye with correcting lenses, or where the widest diameter of visual field subtends an angle no greater than 20 degrees. This exemption shall not extend to any sole proprietor who permits more than one person other than the proprietor to work regularly in connection with the trade or profession for remuneration or recompense of any kind, unless the other person in excess of one so remunerated is a blind person.

(c)   Every person engaged in the public practice of accounting as a principal, or as a manager of the business of public accountant, shall pay for such license fifty dollars ($50.00), and in addition shall pay a license of twelve dollars and fifty cents ($12.50) for each person employed who is engaged in the capacity of supervising or handling the work of auditing, devising or installing systems of accounts.

(d)   Repealed by Session Laws 1998-95, s. 7, effective July 1, 1999.

(e)   Licenses issued under this section are issued as personal privilege licenses and shall not be issued in the name of a firm or corporation. A licensed photographer having a located place of business in this State is liable for a license tax on each agent or solicitor employed by the photographer for soliciting business. If any person engages in more than one of the activities for which a privilege tax is levied by this section, the person is liable for a privilege tax with respect to each activity engaged in.

(f)   Repealed by Session Laws 1981, c. 17.

(g)   Repealed by Session Laws 1998-95, s. 7, effective July 1, 1999.

(h)   Counties and cities may not levy any license tax on the business or professions taxed under this section.

(i)   Obtaining a license required by this Article does not of itself authorize the practice of a profession, business, or trade for which a State qualification

179

license is required. (1939, c. 158, s. 109; 1941, c. 50, s. 3; 1943, c. 400, s. 2; 1949, c. 683; 1953, c. 1306; 1957, c. 1064; 1973, c. 476, s. 193; 1981, c. 17; c. 83, ss. 4, 5; 1989, c. 584, s. 7; 1991 (Reg. Sess., 1992), c. 974, s. 1; 1993, c. 419, s. 13.2; 1998-95, s. 7; 2002-158, s. 3; 2005-276, s. 23A.1(b); 2008-206, s. 1; 2009-445, s. 1; 2011-330, s. 6.)

§ 105-41.1. Repealed by Session Laws 1975, c. 619, s. 2, effective October 1, 1975.

§ 105-42: Repealed by Session Laws 1996, Second Extra Session, c. 14, s. 17.

§ 105-43. Repealed by Session Laws 1973, c. 1195, s. 8.

§ 105-44: Repealed by Session Laws 1981 (Regular Session, 1982), c. 1228.

§§ 105-45 through 46: Repealed by Session Laws 1996, Second Extra Session, c.14, s. 17.

§ 105-47: Repealed by Session Laws 1979, c. 69.

§ 105-48: Repealed by Session Laws 1979, c. 67.

§ 105-48.1: Repealed by Session Laws 1981, c. 7.

§ 105-49: Repealed by Session Laws 1989, c. 584, s. 10.

§ 105-50: Repealed by Session Laws 1996, Second Extra Session, c. 14, s. 17.

§ 105-51: Repealed by Session Laws 1989, c. 584, s. 12.

§ 105-51.1: Repealed by Session Laws 1996, Second Extra Session, c. 14, s. 17.

§ 105-52: Repealed by Session Laws 1979, c. 16, s. 1.

§§ 105-53 through 105-55: Repealed by Session Laws 1996, Second Extra Session, c. 14, s. 17.

§ 105-56: Repealed by Session Laws 1981, c. 5.

§ 105-57: Repealed by Session Laws 1987 (Reg. Sess., 1988), c. 1081, s. 1.

§ 105-58: Repealed by Session Laws 1996, Second Extra Session, c. 14, s. 17.

§ 105-59: Repealed by Session Laws 1981 (Regular Session, 1982), c. 1282, s. 44.

§§ 105-60 through 105-61: Repealed by Session Laws 1996, Second Extra Session, c. 14, s. 17.

§ 105-61.1: Repealed by Session Laws 1989, c. 584, s. 17.

§ 105-62: Repealed by Session Laws 1996, Second Extra Session, c. 14, s. 17.

§ 105-63: Repealed by Session Laws 1979, c. 65.

§ 105-64: Repealed by Session Laws 1989, c. 584, s. 19.

§ 105-64.1: Repealed by Session Laws 1989, c. 584, s. 19.

§§ 105-65 through 105-65.1: Repealed by Session Laws 1996, Second Extra Session, c. 14, s.17.

§ 105-65.2: Repealed by Session Laws 1989, c. 584, s. 19.

§ 105-66: Repealed by Session Laws 1989, c. 584, s. 19.

§ 105-66.1: Repealed by Session Laws 1996, Second Extra Session, c. 14, s. 17.

§ 105-67: Repealed by Session Laws 1991 (Regular Session, 1992), c. 965, s. 1.

§ 105-68: Repealed by Session Laws 1981 (Regular Session, 1982), c. 1229.

§ 105-69: Repealed by Session Laws 1973, c. 1200, s. 1.

§ 105-70: Repealed by Session Laws 1996, Second Extra Session, c. 14, s. 17.

§ 105-71: Repealed by Session Laws 1979, c. 70.

§ 105-72: Repealed by Session Laws 1996, Second Extra Session, c. 14, s. 17.

§ 105-73. Repealed by Session Laws 1957, c. 1340, ss. 2, 9.

§ 105-74: Repealed by Session Laws 1996, Second Extra Session, c. 14, s. 17.

§ 105-75: Repealed by Session Laws 1979, 2nd Session, c. 1304, s. 1.

§ 105-75.1: Repealed by Session Laws 1996, Second Extra Session, c. 14, s. 17.

§ 105-76: Repealed by Session Laws 1979, c. 62.

§ 105-77: Repealed by Session Laws 1996, Second Extra Session, c. 14, s. 17.

§ 105-78: Repealed by Session Laws 1979, c. 66.

§ 105-79: Repealed by Session Laws 1979, c. 150, s. 4.

§ 105-80: Repealed by Session Laws 1996, Second Extra Session, c. 14, s. 17.

§ 105-81. Repealed by Session Laws 1947, c. 501, s. 2.

§ 105-82: Repealed by Session Laws 1989, c. 584, s. 24.

§ 105-83. Installment paper dealers.

(a)   Every person engaged in the business of dealing in, buying, or discounting installment paper, notes, bonds, contracts, or evidences of debt for which, at the time of or in connection with the execution of the instruments, a lien is reserved or taken upon personal property located in this State to secure the payment of the obligations, shall submit to the Secretary quarterly no later than the twentieth day of January, April, July, and October of each year, upon forms prescribed by the Secretary, a full, accurate, and complete statement, verified by the officer, agent, or person making the statement, of the total face value of the obligations dealt in, bought, or discounted within the preceding three calendar months and, at the same time, shall pay a tax of two hundred seventy-seven thousandths of one percent (.277%) of the face value of these obligations.

(b)   Repealed by Session Laws 1998-95, s. 9.

(c)   If any person deals in, buys, or discounts any obligations described in this section without paying a tax imposed by this section, the person may not bring an action in a State court to enforce collection of an obligation dealt in, bought, or discounted during the period of noncompliance with this section until the person pays the amount of tax, penalties, and interest due.

(d)   This section does not apply to corporations liable for the tax levied under G.S. 105-102.3 or to savings and loan associations.

(e)   Counties and cities shall not levy any license tax on the business taxed under this section. (1939, c. 158, s. 148; 1957, c. 1340, s. 2; 1973, c. 476, s. 193; 1981, c. 83, ss. 8, 9; 1991, c. 45, s. 3; 1991 (Reg. Sess., 1992), c. 965, s. 3; 1998-95, s. 9; 1998-98, s. 1(f).)

§ 105-84: Repealed by Session Laws 1979, c. 150, s. 5.

§§ 105-85 through 105-86: Repealed by Session Laws 1996, Second Extra Session, c. 14, s. 17.

§ 105-87: Repealed by Session Laws 1981, c. 6.

§ 105-88. Loan agencies.

(a)   Every person, firm, or corporation engaged in any of the following businesses must pay for the privilege of engaging in that business an annual tax of two hundred fifty dollars ($250.00) for each location at which the business is conducted:

(1)   The business of making loans or lending money, accepting liens on, or contracts of assignments of, salaries or wages, or any part thereof, or other

183

security or evidence of debt for repayment of such loans in installment payment or otherwise.

(2)   The business of check cashing regulated under Article 22 of Chapter 53 of the General Statutes.

(3)   The business of pawnbroker regulated under Part 1 of Article 45 of Chapter 66 of the General Statutes.

(b)   This section does not apply to banks, industrial banks, trust companies, savings and loan associations, cooperative credit unions, the business of negotiating loans on real estate as described in G.S. 105-41, or insurance premium finance companies licensed under Article 35 of Chapter 58 of the General Statutes. This section applies to those persons or concerns operating what are commonly known as loan companies or finance companies and whose business is as hereinbefore described, and those persons, firms, or corporations pursuing the business of lending money and taking as security for the payment of the loan and interest an assignment of wages or an assignment of wages with power of attorney to collect the amount due, or other order or chattel mortgage or bill of sale upon household or kitchen furniture. No real estate mortgage broker is required to obtain a privilege license under this section merely because the broker advances the broker's own funds and takes a security interest in real estate to secure the advances and when, at the time of the advance, the broker has already made arrangements with others for the sale or discount of the obligation at a later date and does so sell or discount the obligation within the period specified in the arrangement or extensions thereof; or when, at the time of the advance the broker intends to sell the obligation to others at a later date and does, within 12 months from date of initial advance, make arrangements with others for the sale of the obligation and does sell the obligation within the period specified in the arrangement or extensions thereof; or because the broker advances the broker's own funds in temporary financing directly involved in the production of permanent-type loans for sale to others; and no real estate mortgage broker whose mortgage lending operations are essentially as described above is required to obtain a privilege license under this section.

(c)   At the time of making any such loan, the person, or officer of the firm or corporation making the loan, shall give to the borrower in writing in convenient form a statement showing the amount received by the borrower, the amount to be paid back by the borrower, the time in which the amount is to be paid, and the rate of interest and discount agreed upon.

(d)   A loan made by a person who does not comply with this section is not collectible at law under G.S. 105-269.13.

(e)   Counties, cities, and towns may levy a license tax on the business taxed under this section. Except as provided in G.S. 160A-211 and G.S. 153A-152, the tax may not exceed one hundred dollars ($100.00). (1939, c. 158, s. 152; 1967, c. 1080; c. 1232, s. 2; 1973, c. 476, s. 193; 1991, c. 45, s. 4; 1993, c. 539, s. 695; 1994, Ex. Sess., c. 24, s. 14(c); 1998-98, s. 1(g); 1999-438, s. 2; 2000-120, s. 3; 2000-173, s. 2; 2012-46, s. 25.)

§§ 105-89 through 105-90: Repealed by Session Laws 1996, Second Extra Session, c. 14, s. 17.

§ 105-90.1: Repealed by Session Laws 1989 (Regular Session, 1990), c. 814, s. 4.

§ 105-91: Repealed by Session Laws 1996, Second Extra Session, c. 14, s. 17.

§ 105-92: Repealed by Session Laws 1981 (Regular Session, 1982), c. 1227.

§ 105-93: Repealed by Session Laws 1979, c. 68.

§ 105-94. Repealed by Session Laws 1947, c. 501, s. 2.

§ 105-95. Repealed by Session Laws 1947, c. 831, s. 2.

§ 105-96: Repealed by Session Laws 1981 (Regular Session, 1982), c. 1231.

§§ 105-97 through 105-99: Repealed by Session Laws 1996, Second Extra Session, c. 14, s. 17.

§ 105-100: Repealed by Session Laws 1979, c. 64.

§ 105-101: Repealed by Session Laws 1979, c. 85, s. 1.

§ 105-102: Repealed by Session Laws 1981 (Regular Session, 1982), c. 1230.

§ 105-102.1: Repealed by Session Laws 1996, Second Extra Session, c. 14, s. 17.

§ 105-102.2: Repealed by Session Laws 1981 (Regular Session, 1982), c. 1213.

§ 105-102.3. Banks.

There is imposed upon every bank or banking association, including each national banking association, that is operating in this State as a commercial bank, an industrial bank, a savings bank created other than under Chapter 54B or 54C of the General Statutes or the Home Owners' Loan Act of 1933 (12 U.S.C. §§ 1461-68), a trust company, or any combination of such facilities or services, and whether such bank or banking association, hereinafter to be referred to as a bank or banks, is organized, under the laws of the United States or the laws of North Carolina, in the corporate form or in some other form of business organization, an annual privilege tax. A report and the privilege tax are due by the first day of July of each year on forms provided by the Secretary. The tax rate is thirty dollars ($30.00) for each one million dollars ($1,000,000) or fractional part thereof of total assets held as provided in this section. The assets upon which the tax is levied shall be determined by averaging the total assets shown in the four quarterly call reports of condition (consolidating domestic subsidiaries) for the preceding calendar year as required by bank regulatory authorities. If a bank has been in operation less than a calendar year, then the assets upon which the tax is levied shall be determined by multiplying the average of the total assets by a fraction, the denominator of which is 365 and the numerator of which is the number of days of operation. If a bank operates an international banking facility, as defined in G.S. 105-130.5(b)(13), the assets upon which the tax is levied shall be reduced by the average amount for the taxable year of all assets of the international banking facility which are employed outside the United States, as computed pursuant to G.S. 105-130.5(b)(13)c. For an out-of-state bank with one or more branches in this State, or for an in-state bank with one or more branches outside this State, the assets of the out-of-state bank or of the in-state bank upon which the tax is levied shall be reduced by the average amount for the taxable year of all assets of the out-of-state bank or of the in-state bank which are employed outside this State. The tax imposed in this section shall be for the privilege of carrying on the businesses herein defined on a statewide basis regardless of the number of places or locations of business within the State. Counties and cities may not levy a license or privilege tax on the businesses taxed under this section, nor on the business of an international banking facility as defined in subdivision (b)(13) of G.S. 105-130.5. (1973, c. 1053, s. 7; 1981, c. 855, s. 2; 1985 (Reg. Sess., 1986), c. 985, s. 4; 1995, c. 322, s. 2; 1998-95, s. 10; 1998-98, s. 1(h).)

§ 105-102.4: Repealed by Session Laws 1989, c. 584, s. 35.

§ 105-102.5: Repealed by Session Laws 1996, Second Extra Session, c. 14, s. 17.

§ 105-102.6. Publishers of newsprint publications.

(a)   Purpose. - The purpose of this section is to provide incentives for the recycling of newsprint and magazines and for the use of newsprint that contains recycled content.

(b)   Definitions. - The following definitions apply in this section:

(1)   Gross tonnage of newsprint consumed. - The weight in metric tons of all newsprint consumed by a publisher.

(2)   Newsprint. - Uncoated paper, whether supercalendered or machine finished, made primarily from mechanical wood pulp combined with some chemical wood pulp, weighing between 24.5 and 35 pounds for 500 sheets of paper two feet by three feet in size, and having a brightness of less than 60.

(2a)   Nonvirgin newsprint. - Newsprint that contains recycled postconsumer recovered paper.

(3)   Postconsumer recovered paper. - Paper products, generated by a business or consumer, that have served their intended end uses and have been separated or diverted from solid waste.

(4)   Publisher. - A person engaged in the business of producing publications printed on newsprint who acquires and uses newsprint for this business.

(5)   Recycled content percentage. - The percentage by weight of the total gross tonnage of newsprint consumed by the publisher that is recycled postconsumer recovered paper. For example, if a publisher consumes 10 tons of virgin newsprint, 10 tons of nonvirgin newsprint that contains fifty percent (50%) recycled postconsumer recovered paper, and 10 tons of nonvirgin newsprint that contains ten percent (10%) recycled postconsumer recovered paper, the publisher's recycled content percentage is 6/30 or twenty percent (20%).

(6)   Recycled content tonnage. - The weight in metric tons of the total gross tonnage of newsprint consumed by the publisher that is recycled postconsumer recovered paper.

(7)   Recycling. - Any process by which solid waste, or materials that would otherwise become solid waste, are collected, separated, or processed, and reused or returned to use in the form of raw materials or products.

(8)   Recycling tonnage. - The weight in metric tons of newsprint and magazines recycled or diverted to recycling by a publisher.

(9)   Virgin newsprint. - Newsprint that does not contain recycled postconsumer recovered paper.

(c)   Minimum Recycled Content Percentage. - The recycled content percentage of newsprint consumed by a publisher shall equal or exceed the following minimum recycled content percentages:

During 1991 and 1992, twelve percent (12%).

During 1993, fifteen percent (15%).

During 1994, twenty percent (20%).

During 1995 and 1996, twenty-five percent (25%).

During 1997 and 1998, thirty percent (30%).

During 1999 through 2004, thirty-five percent (35%).

After 2004, forty percent (40%).

A publisher who has developed and operates or contracts for the operation of a newspaper or magazine recycling program shall receive partial credit toward the recycled content percentage goals established in this subsection on the basis of one ton of credit toward its total recycled content tonnage for each ton of recycling tonnage.

(d)   Tax. - Every publisher shall apply for and obtain from the Secretary a newsprint publisher tax reporting number and shall file an annual report with the

Secretary by January 31 of each year. The report shall include the following information for the preceding calendar year:

(1)   Tonnage of virgin newsprint consumed.

(2)   Tonnage of nonvirgin newsprint consumed.

(3)   Gross tonnage of newsprint consumed.

(4)   Itemized percentages of recycled postconsumer recovered paper contained in tonnage of nonvirgin newsprint consumed.

(5)   Recycled content tonnage.

(6)   Recycled content percentage.

(7)   Recycling tonnage.

In addition, each publisher whose recycled content percentage for a calendar year is less than the applicable minimum recycled content percentage provided in subsection (c) shall pay a tax of fifteen dollars ($15.00) on each ton by which the publisher's recycled content tonnage falls short of the tonnage of recycled postconsumer recovered paper needed to achieve the applicable minimum recycled content percentage provided in subsection (c). This tax is due when the report is filed. No county or city may impose a license tax on the business taxed under this section.

(e)   Exemption. - The tax levied in this section does not apply to an amount calculated pursuant to subsection (d) to the extent the amount is attributable solely to the publisher's inability to obtain sufficient recycled content newsprint because (i) recycled content newsprint was not available at a price comparable to the price of virgin newsprint; (ii) recycled content newsprint of a quality comparable to virgin newsprint was not available; or (iii) recycled content newsprint was not available within a reasonable period of time during the reporting period. In order to claim the exemption provided in this subsection, a publisher must certify to the Secretary:

(1)   The amount of virgin newsprint consumed by the publisher during the reporting period solely for one of the reasons listed above.

(2)   That the publisher attempted to obtain recycled content newsprint from every manufacturer of recycled content newsprint that offered to sell recycled content newsprint to the publisher within the preceding calendar year.

(3)   The name, address, and telephone number of each recycled content newsprint manufacturer contacted, including the company name and the name of the company's individual representative or employee.

(f)   Use of Proceeds. - The Secretary shall, on or before April 15 of each year, credit the net proceeds of the tax imposed by this section to the Solid Waste Management Trust Fund created in G.S. 130A-309.12. (1991, c. 539, s. 2; c. 761, s. 18; 1991 (Reg. Sess., 1992), c. 1007, s. 1; 1995, c. 459, s. 1; 1997-456, s. 27; 1998-95, s. 11; 1999-346, s. 1.)

§ 105-103. Unlawful to operate without license.

When a license tax is required by law, and whenever the General Assembly shall levy a license tax on any business, trade, employment, or profession, or for doing any act, it shall be unlawful for any person, firm, or corporation without a license to engage in such business, trade, employment, profession, or do the act; and when such tax is imposed it shall be lawful to grant a license for the business, trade, employment, or for doing the act; and no person, firm, or corporation shall be allowed the privilege of exercising any business, trade, employment, profession, or the doing of any act taxed in this schedule throughout the State under one license, except under a statewide license. (1939, c. 158, s. 181; 1998-98, s. 41.)

§ 105-104: Repealed by Session Laws 2007-491, s. 2, effective January 1, 2008.

§ 105-105. Persons, firms, and corporations engaged in more than one business to pay tax on each.

Where any person, firm, or corporation is engaged in more than one business, trade, employment, or profession which is made under the provisions of this

Article subject to State license taxes, such persons, firms, or corporations shall pay the license tax prescribed in this Article for each separate business, trade, employment, or profession. (1939, c. 158, s. 183.)

§ 105-106. Effect of change in name of firm.

No change in the name of a firm, partnership, or corporation, nor the taking in of a new partner, nor the withdrawal of one or more of the firm, shall be considered as commencing business; but if any one or more of the partners remain in the firm, or if there is change in ownership of less than a majority of the stock, if a corporation, the business shall be regarded as continuing. (1939, c. 158, s. 184.)

§ 105-107: Repealed by Session Laws 1998-95, s. 12, effective July 1, 1999.

§ 105-108. Property used in a licensed business not exempt from taxation.

A State license, issued under any of the provisions of this Article shall not be construed to exempt from other forms of taxation the property employed in such licensed business, trade, employment, or profession. (1939, c. 158, s. 186.)

§ 105-109. Obtaining license and paying tax.

(a)   Repealed by Session Laws 1998-95, s. 13, effective July 1, 1999.

(b)   License Required. - Before a person may engage in a business, trade, or profession for which a license is required under this Article, the person must be licensed by the Department. To obtain a license, a person must submit an application to the Department for the license and pay the required tax. An application for a license is considered a return.

The Department must issue a license to a person who files a completed application and pays the required tax. A license must be displayed conspicuously at the location of the licensed business, trade, or profession.

191

(c)   Repealed by Session Laws 1998-212, s. 29A.14(a), effective January 1, 1999.

(d)   Penalties. - The penalties in G.S. 105-236 apply to this Article. The Secretary may collect a tax due under this Article in any manner allowed under Article 9 of this Chapter.

(e)   Local License Taxes. - The penalty and collection provisions of this section apply to taxes levied by counties of the State under the authority of this Article in the same manner and to the same extent as they apply to taxes levied by the State. The provisions of this section for the collection of delinquent license taxes apply to license taxes levied by the cities and towns of this State under authority of this Article, or any other provision of law, in the same manner and to the same extent as they apply to taxes levied by the State. (1939, c. 158, s. 187; 1957, c. 859; 1963, c. 294, s. 5; 1973, c. 108, s. 51; c. 476, s. 193; 1993, c. 539, ss. 698, 699; 1994, Ex. Sess., c. 24, s. 14(c); 1998-95, s. 13; 1998-212, s. 29A.14(a); 2007-491, s. 7.)

§ 105-109.1. Repealed by Session Laws 1999-337, s. 16..

§ 105-110: Repealed by Session Laws 1998-212, s. 29A.14(b).

§ 105-111: Repealed by Session Laws 2001-414, s. 2.

§ 105-112: Repealed by Session Laws 1998-212, s. 29A.14(c).

§ 105-113. Repealed by Session Laws 1999-337, s. 17.

§ 105-113.1: Deleted.

Article 2A.

Tobacco Products Tax.

Part 1. General Provisions.

§ 105-113.2. Short title.

This Article may be cited as the "Tobacco Products Tax Act" or "Tobacco Products Tax Article." (1969, c. 1075, s. 2; 1991, c. 689, s. 266; 1998-98, s. 56.)

§ 105-113.3. Scope of tax; administration.

(a)   Scope. - The taxes imposed by this Article shall be collected only once on the same tobacco product. Except as permitted by Article 2 of this Chapter, a city or county may not levy a privilege license tax on the sale of tobacco products.

(b)   Administration. - Article 9 of this Chapter applies to this Article. (1969, c. 1075, s. 2; 1991, c. 689, s. 268; 1998-212, s. 29A.14(d).)

§ 105-113.4. Definitions.

The following definitions apply in this Article:

(1)   Affiliate. - A person who directly or indirectly controls, is controlled by, or is under common control with another person.

(1a)   Affiliated manufacturer. - A manufacturer licensed under G.S. 105-113.12 who is an affiliate of a manufacturer licensed under G.S. 105-113.12.

(1b)   Cigar. - A roll of tobacco wrapped in a substance that contains tobacco, other than a cigarette.

(1c)   Cigarette. - Any of the following:

a.   A roll of tobacco wrapped in paper or in a substance that does not contain tobacco.

b.   A roll of tobacco wrapped in a substance that contains tobacco and that, because of its appearance, the type of tobacco used in the filler, or its packaging and labeling, is likely to be offered to or purchased by a consumer as a cigarette described in subpart a. of this subdivision.

(2)   Cost price. - The price a person liable for the tax on tobacco products imposed by Part 3 of this Article paid for the products, before any discount, rebate, or allowance or the tax imposed by that Part.

(3)   Distributor. - Either of the following:

a.   A person, wherever resident or located, who purchases non-tax-paid cigarettes directly from the manufacturer of the cigarettes and stores, sells, or otherwise disposes of the cigarettes.

b.   A manufacturer of cigarettes.

(4)   Repealed by Session Laws 1991, c. 689, s. 267.

(4a)   Integrated wholesale dealer. - A wholesale dealer who is an affiliate of a manufacturer of tobacco products, other than cigarettes, and is not a retail dealer.

(5)   Licensed distributor. - A distributor licensed under Part 2 of this Article.

(6)   Manufacturer. - A person who produces tobacco products or a person who contracts with another person to produce tobacco products and is the exclusive purchaser of the products under the contract.

(7)   Package. - The individual packet, can, box, or other container used to contain and to convey tobacco products to the consumer.

(8)   Person. - Defined in G.S. 105-228.90.

(9)   Retail dealer. - A person who sells a tobacco product to the ultimate consumer of the product.

(10)   Sale. - A transfer, a trade, an exchange, or a barter, in any manner or by any means, with or without consideration.

(10a)   Secretary. - The Secretary of Revenue.

(11)   Repealed by Session Laws 1993, c. 442, s. 1, effective January 1, 1994.

(11a)   Tobacco product. - A cigarette, a cigar, or any other product that contains tobacco and is intended for inhalation or oral use.

(12)   Repealed by Session Laws 1993, c. 442, s. 1, effective January 1, 1994.

(13)   Use. - The exercise of any right or power over cigarettes, incident to the ownership or possession thereof, other than the making of a sale thereof in the course of engaging in a business of selling cigarettes. The term includes the keeping or retention of cigarettes for use.

(14)   Wholesale dealer. - Either of the following:

a.   A person who acquires tobacco products other than cigarettes for sale to another wholesale dealer or to a retail dealer.

b.   A manufacturer of tobacco products other than cigarettes. (1969, c. 1075, s. 2; 1973, c. 476, s. 193; 1991, c. 689, s. 267; 1993, c. 354, s. 7; c. 442, s. 1; 2007-435, s. 2; 2009-559, s. 1; 2011-330, s. 2(a).)

§ 105-113.4A. Licenses.

(a)   General. - To obtain a license required by this Article, an applicant must file an application with the Secretary on a form provided by the Secretary and pay the tax due for the license. An application must include the applicant's name, address, federal employer identification number, and any other information required by the Secretary. A license is not transferable or assignable and must be displayed at the place of business for which it is issued.

(b)   Requirements. - An applicant for a license must meet the following requirements:

(1)   If the applicant is a corporation, the applicant must either be incorporated in this State or be authorized to transact business in this State.

(2)   If the applicant for a license is a limited liability company, the applicant must either be organized in this State or be authorized to transact business in this State.

(3)   If the applicant for a license is a limited partnership, the applicant must either be formed in this State or be authorized to transact business in this State.

(4)   If the applicant for a license is an individual or a general partnership, the applicant must designate an agent for service of process and give the agent's name and address.

(c)   Denial. - The Secretary may investigate an applicant for a license required under this Article to determine if the information the applicant submits with the application is accurate and if the applicant is eligible to be licensed under this Article. The Secretary may refuse to issue a license to an applicant that has done any of the following:

(1)   Submitted false or misleading information on its application.

(2)   Had a license issued under this Article cancelled by the Secretary for cause.

(3)   Had a tobacco products license or registration issued by another state cancelled for cause.

(4)   Been convicted of fraud or misrepresentation.

(5)   Been convicted of any other offense that indicates the applicant may not comply with this Article if issued a license.

(6)   Failed to remit payment for a tax debt under this Chapter. The term "tax debt" has the same meaning as defined in G.S. 105-243.1.

(7)   Failed to file a return due under this Chapter.

(d)   Refund. - A refund of a license tax is allowed only when the tax was collected or paid in error. No refund is allowed when a license holder surrenders a license or the Secretary revokes a license.

(e)   Duplicate or Amended License. - Upon application to the Secretary, a license holder may obtain without charge a duplicate or amended license as provided in this subsection. A duplicate or amended license must state that it is a duplicate or amended license, as appropriate:

(1)   A duplicate license, if the license holder establishes that the original license has been lost, destroyed, or defaced.

(2)   An amended license, if the license holder establishes that the location of the place of business for which the license was issued has changed.

(f)   Information on License. - The Secretary must include the following information on each license required by this Article:

(1)   The legal name of the license holder.

(2)   The name under which the license holder conducts business.

(3)   The physical address of the place of business of the license holder.

(4)   The account number assigned to the license by the Department.

(g)   Records. - The Secretary must keep a record of the following:

(1)   Applicants for a license under this Article.

(2)   Persons to whom a license has been issued under this Article.

(3)   Persons that hold a current license issued under this Article, by license category.

(h)   Lists. - The Secretary must provide the list required under subsection (g) of this section upon request of a manufacturer that is a license holder under this Article. The list must state the name, account number, and business address of each license holder on the list. (1991 (Reg. Sess., 1992), c. 955, s. 3; 2013-414, s. 22(a).)

§ 105-113.4B. Reasons why the Secretary can cancel a license.

(a)   Reasons. - The Secretary may cancel a license issued under this Article upon the written request of the license holder. The Secretary may summarily cancel the license of a license holder when the Secretary finds that the license holder is incurring liability for the tax imposed under this Article after failing to pay a tax when due under this Article. In addition, the Secretary may cancel the license of a license holder that commits one or more of the following acts after holding a hearing on whether the license should be cancelled:

(1)   Fails to obtain a license required by this Article.

(2)   Willfully fails to file a return required by this Article.

(3)   Willfully fails to pay a tax when due under this Article.

(4)   Makes a false statement in an application or return required under this Article.

(5)   Fails to keep records as required by this Article.

(6)   Refuses to allow the Secretary or a representative of the Secretary to examine the person's books, accounts, and records concerning tobacco product.

(7)   Fails to disclose the correct amount of tobacco product taxable in this State.

(8)   Fails to file a replacement bond or an additional bond if required by the Secretary under this Article.

(9)   Violates G.S. 14-401.18.

(b)   Procedure. - The Secretary must send a person whose license is summarily cancelled a notice of the cancellation and must give the person an opportunity to have a hearing on the cancellation within 10 days after the cancellation. The Secretary must give a person whose license may be cancelled after a hearing at least 10 days' written notice of the date, time, and place of the hearing. A notice of a summary license cancellation and a notice of hearing must be sent by registered mail to the last known address of the license holder.

(c)   Release of Bond. - When the Secretary cancels a license and the license holder has paid all taxes and penalties due under this Article, the Secretary must take one of the following actions concerning a bond or an irrevocable letter of credit filed by the license holder:

(1)   Return an irrevocable letter of credit to the license holder.

(2)   Return a bond to the license holder or notify the person liable on the bond and the license holder that the person is released from liability on the bond. (1999-333, s. 6; 2013-414, s. 22(b).)

§ 105-113.4C. Enforcement of Master Settlement Agreement Provisions.

The Master Settlement Agreement between the states and the tobacco product manufacturers, incorporated by reference into the consent decree referred to in S.L. 1999-2, requires each state to diligently enforce Article 37 of Chapter 66 of the General Statutes. The Office of the Attorney General and the Secretary of Revenue shall perform the following responsibilities in enforcing Article 37:

(1)   The Office of the Attorney General must give to the Secretary of Revenue a list of the nonparticipating manufacturers under the Master Settlement Agreement and the brand names of the products of the nonparticipating manufacturers.

(2)   The Office of the Attorney General must update the list provided under subdivision (1) of this section when a nonparticipating manufacturer becomes a participating manufacturer, another nonparticipating manufacturer is identified, or more brands or products of nonparticipating manufacturers are identified.

(3)   The Secretary of Revenue must require the taxpayers of the tobacco excise tax to identify the amount of tobacco products of nonparticipating manufacturers sold by the taxpayers, and may impose this requirement as provided in G.S. 66-290(10).

(4)   The Secretary of Revenue must determine the amount of State tobacco excise taxes attributable to the products of nonparticipating manufacturers, based on the information provided by the taxpayers, and must report this information to the Office of the Attorney General. (1999-311, s. 2.)

§ 105-113.4D. Tax with respect to inventory on effective date of tax increase.

Every person subject to the taxes levied in this Article who, on the effective date of a tax increase under this Article, has on hand any tobacco products must file a complete inventory of the tobacco products within 20 days after the effective date of the increase, and must pay an additional tax to the Secretary when filing the inventory. The amount of tax due is the amount due based on the difference between the former tax rate and the increased tax rate. (1969, c. 1075, s. 2; 1973, c. 476, s. 193; 1991, c. 689, s. 263; 2009-451, s. 27A.5(b).)

Part 2. Cigarette Tax.

§ 105-113.5. Tax on cigarettes.

A tax is levied on the sale or possession for sale in this State, by a distributor, of all cigarettes at the rate of two and one-fourth cents (2.25¢) per individual cigarette. (1969, c. 1075, s. 2; c. 1246, s. 1; 1991, c. 689, s. 262; 2004-170, s. 5; 2005-276, s. 34.1(a), (b); 2009-451, s. 27A.5(a).)

§ 105-113.6. Use tax levied.

A tax is levied upon the sale or possession for sale by a person other than a distributor, and upon the use, consumption, and possession for use or consumption of cigarettes within this State at the rate set in G.S. 105-113.5. This tax does not apply, however, to cigarettes upon which the tax levied in G.S. 105-113.5 has been paid. (1969, c. 1075, s. 2; 1993, c. 442, s. 2.)

§ 105-113.7: Recodified as G.S. 105-113.4D by Session Laws 2009-451, s. 27A.5(b), effective September 1, 2009.

§ 105-113.8. Federal Constitution and statutes.

Any activities which this Article may purport to tax in violation of the Constitution of the United States or any federal statute are hereby expressly exempted from taxation under this Article. (1969, c. 1075, s. 2.)

§ 105-113.9. Out-of-state shipments.

Any distributor engaged in interstate business shall be permitted to set aside part of the stock as necessary to conduct interstate business without paying the tax otherwise required by this Part, but only if the distributor complies with the requirements prescribed by the Secretary concerning keeping of records, making of reports, posting of bond, and other matters for administration of this Part.

"Interstate business" as used in this section means:

(1)   The sale of cigarettes to a nonresident where the cigarettes are delivered by the distributor to the business location of the nonresident purchaser in another state; and

(2)   The sale of cigarettes to a nonresident wholesaler or retailer registered through the Secretary who has no place of business in North Carolina and who purchases the cigarettes for the purposes of resale not within this State and where the cigarettes are delivered to the purchaser at the business location in North Carolina of the distributor who is also licensed as a distributor under the laws of the state of the nonresident purchaser. (1969, c. 1075, s. 2; 1973, c. 476, s. 193; 1977, c. 874; 1993, c. 442, s. 3.)

§ 105-113.10. Manufacturers exempt from paying tax.

(a)   Shipping to Other Distributors. - Any manufacturer shipping cigarettes to other distributors who are licensed under G.S. 105-113.12 may, upon application to the Secretary and upon compliance with requirements prescribed by the Secretary, be relieved of paying the taxes levied in this Part. No manufacturer may be relieved of the requirement to be licensed as a distributor in order to make shipments, including drop shipments, to a retail dealer or ultimate user.

(b)   Shipping for Affiliated Manufacturer. - A manufacturer may, upon application to the Secretary and upon compliance with requirements prescribed by the Secretary, be relieved of paying the taxes levied in this Part on cigarettes that are manufactured by an affiliated manufacturer and temporarily stored at and shipped from its facilities. (1969, c. 1075, s. 2; c. 1246, s. 2; 1973, c. 476, s. 193; 1975, c. 275, s. 2; 1993, c. 442, s. 4; 2011-330, s. 2(b).)

§ 105-113.11. Licenses required.

After the effective date of this Article, no person shall engage in business as a distributor in this State, without having first obtained from the Secretary the appropriate license for that purpose as prescribed herein. Any license required by this Article shall be in addition to any and all other licenses which may be required by law. (1969, c. 1075, s. 2; 1973, c. 476, s. 193.)

§ 105-113.12. Distributor must obtain license.

(a)   A distributor shall obtain for each place of business a continuing distributor's license and shall pay a tax of twenty-five dollars ($25.00) for the license.

(b)   For the purposes of this section, a "place of business" is a place where a distributor receives or stores non-tax-paid cigarettes.

(c)   An out-of-state distributor may obtain a distributor's license upon compliance with the provisions of G.S. 105-113.24 and payment of a tax of twenty-five dollars ($25.00). (1969, c. 1075, s. 2; 1991 (Reg. Sess., 1992), c. 955, s. 4; 1993, c. 442, s. 5.)

§ 105-113.13. Secretary may require a bond or irrevocable letter of credit.

(a)   Repealed by Session Laws 2013-414, s. 22(c), effective September 1, 2013.

(b)   The Secretary may require a distributor to furnish a bond in an amount that adequately protects the State from loss if the distributor fails to pay taxes due under this Part. A bond shall be conditioned on compliance with this Part, shall be payable to the State, and shall be in the form required by the Secretary. The Secretary shall set the bond amount based on the anticipated tax liability of the distributor. The Secretary shall periodically review the sufficiency of bonds required of the distributor and shall increase the amount of a required bond if the bond amount no longer covers the anticipated tax liability of the distributor. The Secretary shall decrease the amount of a required bond if the Secretary finds that a lower bond amount will protect the State adequately from loss. For purposes of this section, a bond may also include an irrevocable letter of credit. (1969, c. 1075, s. 2; 1973, c. 476, s. 193; 1991 (Reg. Sess., 1992), c. 955, s. 5; 1993, c. 442, s. 6; 2013-414, s. 22(c).)

§§ 105-113.14 through 105-113.15: Repealed by Session Laws 1991 (Regular Session, 1992), c. 955, s. 6, effective July 15, 1992.

§ 105-113.16. Repealed by Session Laws 1999-333, s. 7.

§ 105-113.17. Identification of dispensers.

Each vending machine that dispenses cigarettes must be marked to identify its owner in the manner required by the Secretary. (1969, c. 1075, s. 2; 1973, c. 476, s. 193; 1991 (Reg. Sess., 1992), c. 955, s. 8.)

§ 105-113.18. Payment of tax; reports.

The taxes levied in this Part are payable when a report is required to be filed. The following reports are required to be filed with the Secretary:

(1)   Distributor's Report. - A distributor shall file a monthly report in the form prescribed by the Secretary. The report covers sales and other activities occurring in a calendar month and is due within 20 days after the end of the month covered by the report. The report shall state the amount of tax due and shall identify any transactions to which the tax does not apply.

(1a)   Report of Free Cigarettes. - A manufacturer who distributes cigarettes without charge shall file a monthly report in the form prescribed by the Secretary. The report covers cigarettes distributed without charge in a calendar month and is due within 20 days after the end of the month covered by the report. The report shall state the number of cigarettes distributed without charge and the amount of tax due.

(2)   Use Tax Report. - Every other person who has acquired non-tax-paid cigarettes for sale, use, or consumption subject to the tax imposed by this Part shall, within 96 hours after receipt of the cigarettes, file a report in the form prescribed by the Secretary showing the amount of cigarettes so received and any other information required by the Secretary. The report shall be accompanied by payment of the full amount of the tax.

(3)   Shipping Report. - Any person, except a licensed distributor, who transports cigarettes upon the public highways, roads, or streets of this State, upon notice from the Secretary, shall file a report in the form prescribed by the Secretary and containing the information required by the Secretary.

(4)   Repealed by Session Laws 1981 (Regular Session, 1982), c. 1209, s. 1. (1969, c. 1075, s. 2; 1973, c. 476, s. 193; 1981 (Reg. Sess., 1982), c. 1209, s. 1; 1993, c. 442, s. 7; 1993 (Reg. Sess., 1994), c. 745, s. 2.)

§§ 105-113.19 through 105-113.20: Repealed by Session Laws 1993, c. 442, s. 8.

§ 105-113.21. Discount; refund.

(a)   Repealed by Session Laws 2003-284, s. 45A.1(a), effective for reporting periods beginning on or after August 1, 2003.

(a1)   Discount. - A distributor who files a timely report under G.S. 105-113.18 and who sends a timely payment may deduct from the amount due with the report a discount of two percent (2%). This discount covers expenses incurred in preparing the records and reports required by this Part, and the expense of furnishing a bond.

(b)   Refund. - A distributor in possession of packages of stale or otherwise unsalable cigarettes upon which the tax has been paid may return the cigarettes to the manufacturer as provided in this subsection and apply to the Secretary for refund of the tax. The application shall be in the form prescribed by the Secretary and shall be accompanied by an affidavit from the manufacturer stating the number of cigarettes returned to the manufacturer by the applicant. The Secretary shall refund the tax paid, less the discount allowed, on the unsalable cigarettes. The distributor must return the cigarettes to the manufacturer of the cigarettes or to the affiliated manufacturer who is contracted by the manufacturer of the cigarettes to serve as the manufacturer's agent for the purposes of validating quantities and disposing of unsalable cigarettes. (1969, c. 1075, s. 2; cc. 1222, 1238; 1973, c. 476, s. 193; 1993, c. 442, s. 9; 2001-414, s. 3; 2003-284, s. 45A.1(a); 2004-84, s. 2(a); 2011-330, s. 2(c).)

§§ 105-113.22 through 105-113.23: Repealed by Session Laws 1993, c. 442, s. 8.

§ 105-113.24. Out-of-State distributors to register and remit tax.

(a)   The Secretary may authorize any distributor outside this State engaged in the business of selling and shipping cigarettes into the State to obtain a license and report and pay taxes required by this Part.

(b)   A nonresident distributor must agree to submit the distributor's books, accounts, and records to reasonable examination by the Secretary or the Secretary's duly authorized agents. The Secretary may require a nonresident distributor to file a bond in accordance with G.S. 105-113.13.

(c)   Each such nonresident distributor, other than a foreign corporation which has qualified with the Secretary of State as doing business in this State shall, by a duly executed instrument filed in the office of the Secretary of State, constitute and appoint the Secretary of State his lawful attorney in fact upon whom any original process in any action or legal proceeding against such nonresident distributor arising out of any matter relating to this Article may be served, and therein agree that any original process against him so served shall be of the same force and effect as if served on him within this State, and that the authority thereof shall continue in force irrevocably so long as any such nonresident distributor shall remain liable for any taxes, interest and penalties under this Article.

(d)   Any nonresident distributor who shall comply with the provisions of this section may be licensed as a distributor. (1969, c. 1075, s. 2; 1973, c. 476, s. 193; 1991 (Reg. Sess., 1992), c. 955, s. 9; 1993, c. 442, ss. 9.1(a), 9.1(b).)

§ 105-113.25: Repealed by Session Laws 1993, c. 442, s. 8.

§ 105-113.26. Records to be kept.

Every person required to be licensed under this Article and every person required to make reports under this Article shall keep complete and accurate records of all sales and other information as required under this Article. The records shall be in the form prescribed by the Secretary.

These records shall be safely preserved for a period of three years in a manner to ensure their security and accessibility for inspection by the Department. The Secretary may consent to the destruction of any records at any time within this three-year period. (1969, c. 1075, s. 2; 1973, c. 476, s. 193; 1993, c. 442, s. 10.)

§ 105-113.27. Non-tax-paid cigarettes.

(a)   Except as otherwise provided in this Article, licensed distributors shall not sell, borrow, loan, or exchange non-tax-paid cigarettes to, from, or with other licensed distributors.

(b)   No person shall sell or offer for sale non-tax-paid cigarettes.

(c)   The possession of more than six hundred cigarettes on which tax has been paid to another state or country, by any person other than a licensed distributor, is prima facie evidence that the cigarettes are possessed in violation of this Part. (1969, c. 1075, s. 2; 1993, c. 442, s. 11; 1999-337, s. 18.)

§ 105-113.28: Repealed by Session Laws 1993, c. 442, s. 8.

§ 105-113.29. Unlicensed place of business.

It shall be unlawful for any person to maintain a place of business within this State required by this Article to be licensed to engaged in the business of selling or offering for sale cigarettes without first obtaining such licenses. (1969, c. 1075, s. 2.)

§ 105-113.30. Records and reports.

It shall be unlawful for any person who is required under the provisions of this Article to keep records or make reports, to fail to keep such records, refuse to keep such reports, make false entries in such records, fail to produce such records for inspection by the Secretary or his duly authorized agents, fail to file a report, or make a false or fraudulent report or statement. (1969, c. 1075, s. 2; 1973, c. 476, s. 193.)

§ 105-113.31. Possession and transportation of non-tax-paid cigarettes; seizure and confiscation of vehicle or vessel.

(a)   It shall be unlawful for any person to transport non-tax-paid cigarettes in violation of this Part. The Secretary may adopt rules allowing quantities of non-tax-paid cigarettes, not exceeding six hundred, to be brought into this State by a transient, a tourist, or a person returning to this State after traveling outside this State, for their own use. The possession or transportation of these cigarettes is not subject to the penalties imposed by this section.

(b)　(1)　Every person who transports non-tax-paid cigarettes on the public highways, roads, streets, or waterways of this State must transport with the cigarettes invoices or delivery tickets for the cigarettes showing the true name and complete and exact address of the consignee or purchaser, the quantity and brands of the cigarettes transported, and the true name and complete and exact address of the person who has paid or who will pay the tax imposed by this Part or the tax, if any, of the state or foreign country at the point of ultimate destination.

(2)　A common carrier that has issued a bill of lading for a shipment of cigarettes and is without notice to itself or to any of its agents or employees that the cigarettes are non-tax-paid in violation of this Part is considered to have complied with this Part and the vehicle or vessel in which the cigarettes are being transported is not subject to confiscation under this section. In the absence of the required invoices, delivery tickets, or bills of lading, the cigarettes so transported, the vehicle or vessel in which the cigarettes are being transported, and any paraphernalia or devices used in connection with the non-tax-paid cigarettes are declared to be contraband goods and may be seized by any officer of the law, who shall take possession of the vehicle or vessel and cigarettes and shall arrest any person in charge of the vehicle or vessel and cigarettes.

(3)　The officer shall at once proceed against the person arrested, under the provisions of this Part, in any court having competent jurisdiction; but the vehicle or vessel shall be returned to the owner upon execution by the owner of a good and valid bond, with sufficient sureties, in a sum double the value of the property, which bond shall be approved by the officer and shall be conditioned to return the property to the custody of the officer on the day of trial to abide the judgment of the court. All non-tax-paid cigarettes seized under this section shall be held and shall, upon the acquittal of the person so charged, be returned to the established owner.

(4)　Unless the claimant can show that the non-tax-paid cigarettes seized were not transported in violation of this Part and that the property seized belongs to the claimant or that in the case of property other than cigarettes, the property was used in transporting non-tax-paid cigarettes in violation of this Part without the claimant's knowledge or consent, with the right on the part of the claimant to have a jury pass upon this claim, the court shall order a sale by public auction of the property seized, and the officer making the sale, after deducting the cost of the tax due, which the officer shall pay upon sale, expenses of keeping the property, the fee for the seizure, and the costs of the sale, shall pay all liens according to their priorities, which are established, by intervention or otherwise, at the hearing or in another proceeding brought for the purpose as being bona fide and as having been created without the lien or having any notice that the vehicle or vessel was being used for the unlawful transportation of non-tax-paid cigarettes, and shall pay the balance of the proceeds to the State Treasurer for the General Fund.

(5)   All liens against property sold under the provisions of this section shall be transferred from the property to the proceeds of the sale of the property. If, however, no one is found claiming the cigarettes, or the vehicle or vessel, then the taking of the cigarettes, vehicle, or vessel, along with a description, shall be advertised in a newspaper having circulation in the county where the items were taken, once a week for two weeks and by notices posted in three public places near the place of seizure, and if no claimant appears within ten days after the last publication of the advertisement, the property shall be sold, and the proceeds, after deducting the expenses and costs, shall be paid to the State Treasurer for the General Fund.

(6)   This section does not authorize an officer to search any vehicle or vessel or baggage of any person without a search warrant duly issued, except where the officer has knowledge that there are non-tax-paid cigarettes in the vehicle or vessel. (1969, c. 1075, s. 2; 1973, c. 476, s. 193; 1993, c. 442, s. 12.)

§ 105-113.32. Non-tax-paid cigarettes subject to confiscation.

All non-tax-paid cigarettes subject to the tax imposed by this Part, together with any container in which they are stored or displayed for sale (including but not limited to vending machines), are declared to be contraband goods and may be seized by any officer of the law. The officer shall arrest any person in charge of the contraband goods and shall at once proceed against the person arrested, under the provisions of this Part, in any court having competent jurisdiction. The disposition of the seized cigarettes and container shall be governed by the provisions of G.S. 105-113.31. (1969, c. 1075, s. 2; 1993, c. 442, s. 13.)

§ 105-113.33. Criminal penalties.

Any person who violates any of the provisions of this Article for which no other punishment is specifically prescribed shall be guilty of a Class 1 misdemeanor. (1969, c. 1075, s. 2; 1993, c. 539, s. 700; 1994, Ex. Sess., c. 24, s. 14(c).)

§ 105-113.34: Repealed by Session Laws 1993, c. 442, s. 8.

Part 3. Tax on Other Tobacco Products.

§ 105-113.35. Tax on tobacco products other than cigarettes.

(a)   Tax. - An excise tax is levied on tobacco products other than cigarettes at the rate of twelve and eight-tenths percent (12.8%) of the cost price of the products. This tax does not apply to the following:

(1)   A tobacco product sold outside the State.

(2)   A tobacco product sold to the federal government.

(3)   A sample tobacco product distributed without charge.

(b)   Primary Liability. - The wholesale dealer or retail dealer who first acquires or otherwise handles tobacco products subject to the tax imposed by this section is liable for the tax imposed by this section. A wholesale dealer or retail dealer who brings into this State a tobacco product made outside the State is the first person to handle the tobacco product in this State. A wholesale dealer or retail dealer who is the original consignee of a tobacco product that is made outside the State and is shipped into the State is the first person to handle the tobacco product in this State.

(c)   Secondary Liability. - A retail dealer who acquires non-tax-paid tobacco products subject to the tax imposed by this section from a wholesale dealer is liable for any tax due on the tobacco products. A retail dealer who is liable for tax under this subsection may not deduct a discount from the amount of tax due when reporting the tax.

(d)   Manufacturer's Option. - A manufacturer who is not a retail dealer and who ships tobacco products other than cigarettes to either a wholesale dealer or retail dealer licensed under this Part may apply to the Secretary to be relieved of paying the tax imposed by this section on the tobacco products. Once granted permission, a manufacturer may choose not to pay the tax until otherwise notified by the Secretary. To be relieved of payment of the tax imposed by this section, a manufacturer must comply with the requirements set by the Secretary.

Permission granted under this subsection to a manufacturer to be relieved of paying the tax imposed by this section applies to an integrated wholesale dealer with whom the manufacturer is an affiliate. A manufacturer must notify the Secretary of any integrated wholesale dealer with whom it is an affiliate when the manufacturer applies to the Secretary for permission to be relieved of paying the tax and when an integrated wholesale dealer becomes an affiliate of the manufacturer after the Secretary has given the manufacturer permission to be relieved of paying the tax.

If a person is both a manufacturer of cigarettes and a wholesale dealer of tobacco products other than cigarettes and the person is granted permission under G.S. 105-113.10 to be relieved of paying the cigarette excise tax, the permission applies to the tax imposed by this section on tobacco products other than cigarettes. A cigarette manufacturer who becomes a wholesale dealer after receiving permission to be relieved of the cigarette excise tax must notify the Secretary of the permission received under G.S. 105-113.10 when applying for a license as a wholesale dealer.

(d1)   Limitation. - Except as otherwise provided in this Article, integrated wholesale dealers may not sell, borrow, loan, or exchange non-tax-paid tobacco products other than cigarettes to, from, or with other integrated wholesale dealers.

(e)   Repealed by Session Laws 2009-451, s. 27A.5(c), effective September 1, 2009. (1969, c. 1075, s. 2; 1977, c. 1114, s. 4; 1991, c. 689, s. 269; 1991 (Reg. Sess., 1992), c. 955, s. 10; 2003-284, s. 45A.1(b); 2004-84, s. 2(b); 2005-276, s. 34.1(c); 2007-323, s. 6.23(a); 2007-435, s. 3; 2009-451, s. 27A.5(c); 2009-559, s. 2.)

§ 105-113.36. Wholesale dealer and retail dealer must obtain license.

A wholesale dealer shall obtain for each place of business a continuing tobacco products license and shall pay a tax of twenty-five dollars ($25.00) for the license. A retail dealer shall obtain for each place of business a continuing tobacco products license and shall pay a tax of ten dollars ($10.00) for the license. A "place of business" is a place where a wholesale dealer or where a retail dealer makes tobacco products other than cigarettes or a wholesale dealer or a retail dealer receives or stores non-tax-paid tobacco products other than cigarettes. (1969, c. 1075, s. 2; 1973, c. 476, s. 193; 1991, c. 689, s. 270; 1991 (Reg. Sess., 1992), c. 955, s. 11.)

§ 105-113.37. Payment of tax.

(a)   Monthly Report. - Except for tax on a designated sale under subsection (b), the taxes levied by this Article are payable when a report is required to be filed. A report is due on a monthly basis. A monthly report covers sales and other activities occurring in a calendar month and is due within 20 days after the end of the month covered by the report. A report shall be filed on a form provided by the Secretary and shall contain the information required by the Secretary.

(b)   Designation of Exempt Sale. - A wholesale dealer who sells a tobacco product to a person who has notified the wholesale dealer in writing that the person intends to resell the item in a transaction that is exempt from tax under G.S. 105-113.35(a)(1) or (2) may, when filing a monthly report under subsection (a), designate the quantity of tobacco products sold to the person for resale. A wholesale dealer shall report a designated sale on a form provided by the Secretary.

A wholesale dealer is not required to pay tax on a designated sale when filing a monthly report. The wholesale dealer shall pay the tax due on all other sales in accordance with this section. A wholesale dealer or a customer of a wholesale dealer may not delay payment of the tax due on a tobacco product by failing to pay tax on a sale that is not a designated sale or by overstating the quantity of tobacco products that will be resold in a transaction exempt under G.S. 105-113.35(a)(1) or (2).

A person who does not sell a tobacco product in a transaction exempt under G.S. 105-113.35(a)(1) or (2) after a wholesale dealer has failed to pay the tax due on the sale of the item to the person in reliance on the person's written

211

notification of intent is liable for the tax and any penalties and interest due on the designated sale. If the Secretary determines that a tobacco product reported as a designated sale is not sold as reported, the Secretary shall assess the person who notified the wholesale dealer of an intention to resell the item in an exempt transaction for the tax due on the sale and any applicable penalties and interest. A wholesale dealer who does not pay tax on a tobacco product in reliance on a person's written notification of intent to resell the item in an exempt transaction is not liable for any tax assessed on the item.

(c)   Repealed by Session Laws 1991 (Regular Session, 1992), c. 955, s. 12.

(d)   Shipping Report. - Any person who transports other tobacco products upon the public highways, roads, or streets of this State must, upon notice from the Secretary, file a report in a form prescribed by and containing the information required by the Secretary. (1969, c. 1075, s. 2; 1973, c. 476, s. 193; 1991, c. 689, s. 271; 1991 (Reg. Sess., 1992), c. 955, s. 12; 2009-559, s. 3.)

§ 105-113.38. Bond or irrevocable letter of credit.

The Secretary may require a wholesale dealer or a retail dealer to furnish a bond in an amount that adequately protects the State from loss if the dealer fails to pay taxes due under this Part. A bond shall be conditioned on compliance with this Part, shall be payable to the State, and shall be in the form required by the Secretary. The Secretary shall proportion a bond amount to the anticipated tax liability of the wholesale dealer or retail dealer. The Secretary shall periodically review the sufficiency of bonds required of dealers, and shall increase the amount of a required bond when the amount of the bond furnished no longer covers the anticipated tax liability of the wholesale dealer or retail dealer. The Secretary shall decrease the amount of a required bond when the Secretary determines that a smaller bond amount will adequately protect the State from loss. For purposes of this section, a bond may also include an irrevocable letter of credit. (1969, c. 1075, s. 2; 1991, c. 689, s. 272; 2012-79, s. 2.1.)

§ 105-113.39. Discount; refund.

(a)   Discount. - A wholesale dealer or a retail dealer who is primarily liable under G.S. 105-113.35(b) for the excise taxes imposed by this Part, who files a timely report under G.S. 105-113.37, and who sends a timely payment may deduct from the amount due with the report a discount of two percent (2%). This discount covers expenses incurred in preparing the records and reports required by this Part and the expense of furnishing a bond.

(b)   Refund. - A wholesale dealer or retail dealer who is primarily liable under G.S. 105-113.35(b) for the excise taxes imposed by this Part and is in possession of stale or otherwise unsalable tobacco products upon which the tax has been paid may return the tobacco products to the manufacturer and apply to the Secretary for refund of the tax. The application shall be in the form prescribed by the Secretary and shall be accompanied by an affidavit from the manufacturer listing the tobacco products returned to the manufacturer by the applicant. The Secretary shall refund the tax paid, less the discount allowed, on the listed products. (1969, c. 1075, s. 2; 1991, c. 689, s. 273; 2001-414, s. 4; 2003-284, s. 45A.1(c); 2004-84, s. 2(c); 2005-406, s. 2; 2008-207, s. 4.)

§ 105-113.40. Records of sales, inventories, and purchases to be kept.

Every wholesale dealer and retail dealer shall keep accurate records of the dealer's purchases, inventories, and sales of tobacco products. These records shall be open at all times for inspection by the Secretary or an authorized representative of the Secretary. (1969, c. 1075, s. 2; 1973, c. 476, s. 193; 1991, c. 689, s. 274.)

§ 105-113.40A. Use of tax proceeds.

The Secretary must credit the net proceeds of the tax collected under this Part as follows:

(1)   An amount equal to three percent (3%) of the cost price of the products to the General Fund.

(2)   The remainder to the University Cancer Research Fund established under G.S. 116-29.1. (2009-451, s. 27A.5(d); 2010-95, s. 1.)

213

Article 2B.

Soft Drink Tax.

§§ 105-113.41 through 105-113.67: Repealed by Session Laws 1996, Second Extra Session, c. 13, s. 4.2, effective July 1, 1999.

Article 2C.

Alcoholic Beverage License And Excise Taxes.

Part 1. General Provisions.

§ 105-113.68. Definitions; scope.

(a)   Definitions. - The following definitions apply in this Article:

(1)   ABC Commission. - The North Carolina Alcoholic Beverage Control Commission established under G.S. 18B-200.

(2)   Repealed by Session Laws 2004-170, s. 6, effective August 2, 2004.

(3)   ABC permit. - Defined in G.S. 18B-101.

(4)   Alcoholic beverage. - Defined in G.S. 18B-101.

(5)   Fortified wine. - Defined in G.S. 18B-101.

(6)   License. - A certificate, issued pursuant to this Article by a city or county, that authorizes a person to engage in a phase of the alcoholic beverage industry.

(7)   Malt beverage. - Defined in G.S. 18B-101.

(8)   Person. - Defined in G.S. 105-228.90.

(9)   Sale. - Defined in G.S. 18B-101.

(10)   Secretary. - The Secretary of Revenue.

(11)   Spirituous liquor or liquor. - Defined in G.S. 18B-101.

(12)   Unfortified wine. - Defined in G.S. 18B-101.

(13)   Wholesaler or importer. - When used with reference to wholesalers or importers of wine or malt beverages, the term includes resident wineries that sell their wines at retail and resident breweries that produce fewer than 25,000 barrels of malt beverages per year.

(14)   Wine. - Unfortified and fortified wine.

(15)   Wine shipper permittee. - A winery that holds a wine shipper permit issued by the ABC Commission under G.S. 18B-1001.1.

(b)   Scope. - All alcoholic beverages shall be taxed as provided in this Article regardless whether they meet all criteria of these definitions. (1971, c. 872, s. 2; 1973, c. 476, s. 193; 1975, c. 411, s. 1; 1981, c. 747, s. 2; 1985, c. 114, s. 1; c. 596, s. 3; 1993, c. 354, s. 9; c. 415, s. 26; 1995, c. 466, s. 16; 1998-95, s. 14; 1998-98, s. 58; 2003-402, s. 8; 2004-135, s. 3; 2004-170, s. 6; 2005-277, s. 2; 2005-435, s. 25(b).)

§ 105-113.69. License tax; effect of license.

The taxes imposed in Part 3 of this Article are license taxes on the privilege of engaging in the activity authorized by the license. Licenses issued under this Article authorize the licensee to engage in only those activities that are authorized by the corresponding ABC permit. The activities authorized by each retail ABC permit are described in Article 10 of Chapter 18B of the General Statutes and the activities authorized by each commercial ABC permit are described in Article 11 of that Chapter. (1949, c. 974, s. 6; 1951, c. 378, s. 4; 1963, c. 426, s. 12; 1971, c. 872, s. 2; 1981, c. 747, s. 3; 1985, c. 114, s. 1; 1998-95, s. 15.)

§ 105-113.70. Issuance, duration, transfer of license.

(a)   Issuance, Qualifications. - Each person who receives an ABC permit shall obtain the corresponding local license, if any, under this Article. All local licenses are issued by the city or county where the establishment for which the license is sought is located. The information required to be provided and the qualifications for a local license are the same as the information and qualifications required for the corresponding ABC permit. Upon proper application and payment of the prescribed tax, issuance of a local license is mandatory if the applicant holds the corresponding ABC permit. No local license may be issued under this Article until the applicant has received from the ABC Commission the applicable permit for that activity, and no county license may be issued for an establishment located in a city in that county until the applicant has received from the city the applicable license for that activity.

(b)   Duration. - All licenses issued under this section are annual licenses for the period from May 1 to April 30.

(c)   Transfer. - A license may not be transferred from one person to another or from one location to another.

(d)   License Exclusive. - A local government may not require a license for activities related to the manufacture or sale of alcoholic beverages other than the licenses stated in this Article. (1985, c. 114, s. 1; 1998-95, s. 16.)

§ 105-113.71. Local government may refuse to issue license.

(a)   Refusal to Issue. - Notwithstanding G.S. 105-113.70, the governing board of a city or county may refuse to issue a license if it finds that the applicant committed any act or permitted any activity in the preceding year that would be grounds for suspension or revocation of his permit under G.S. 18B-104. Before denying the license, the governing board shall give the applicant an opportunity to appear at a hearing before the board and to offer evidence. The applicant shall be given at least 10 days' notice of the hearing. At the conclusion of the hearing the board shall make written findings of fact based on the evidence at the hearing. The applicant may appeal the denial of a license to the superior court for that county, if notice of appeal is given within 10 days of the denial.

(b)   Local Exceptions. - The governing bodies of the following counties and cities in their discretion may decline to issue on-premises unfortified wine licenses: the counties of Alamance, Alexander, Ashe, Avery, Chatham, Clay, Duplin, Granville, Greene, Haywood, Jackson, Macon, Madison, McDowell, Montgomery, Nash, Pender, Randolph, Robeson, Sampson, Transylvania, Vance, Watauga, Wilkes, Yadkin; any city within any of those counties; and the cities of Greensboro, Aulander, Pink Hill, and Zebulon. (1985, c. 114, s. 1.)

§ 105-113.72: Repealed by Session Laws 1998-95, s. 17.

§ 105-113.73. Misdemeanor.

Except as otherwise expressly provided, violation of a provision of this Article is a Class 1 misdemeanor. (1939, c. 158, s. 525; 1971, c. 872, s. 2; 1981, c. 747, s. 32; 1985, c. 114, s. 1; 1993, c. 539, s. 701; 1994, Ex. Sess., c. 24, s. 14(c); 2003-402, s. 9.)

Part 2. State Licenses.

§ 105-113.74: Repealed by Session Laws 1998-95, s. 18.

§ 105-113.75: Repealed by Session Laws 1998-95, s. 19.

§ 105-113.76: Repealed by Session Laws 1998-95, s. 20.

Part 3. Local Licenses.

§ 105-113.77. City beer and wine retail licenses.

(a)   License and Tax. - A person holding any of the following retail ABC permits for an establishment located in a city shall obtain from the city a city license for that activity. The annual tax for each license is as stated.

ABC Permit   Tax for
Corresponding License

On-premises malt
beverage... $15.00

217

Off-premises malt
beverage.. 5.00

On-premises unfortified wine,

  on-premises fortified wine, or
both... 15.00

Off-premises unfortified wine,

  off-premises fortified wine, or
both... 10.00

(b)   Tax on Additional License. - The tax stated in subsection (a) is the tax for the first license issued to a person. The tax for each additional license of the same type issued to that person for the same year is one hundred ten percent (110%) of the base license tax, that increase to apply progressively for each additional license. (1985, c. 114, s. 1.)

§ 105-113.78. County beer and wine retail licenses.

A person holding any of the following retail ABC permits for an establishment located in a county shall obtain from the county a county license for that activity. The annual tax for each license is as stated.

ABC Permit   Tax for
Corresponding License

On-premises malt
beverage.. $25.00

Off-premises malt
beverage.. 5.00

On-premises unfortified wine,

    on-premises fortified wine, or
both.. 25.00

Off-premises unfortified wine,

off-premises fortified wine, or
both.. 25.00

(1985, c. 114, s. 1.)

§ 105-113.79. City wholesaler license.

A city may require city malt beverage and wine wholesaler licenses for businesses located inside the city, but may not require a license for a business located outside the city, regardless whether that business sells or delivers malt beverages or wine inside the city. The city may charge an annual tax of not more than thirty-seven dollars and fifty cents ($37.50) for a city malt beverage wholesaler or a city wine wholesaler license. (1985, c. 114, s. 1; 1998-95, s. 21.)

Part 4. Excise Taxes, Distribution of Tax Revenue.

§ 105-113.80. Excise taxes on beer, wine, and liquor.

(a)   Beer. - An excise tax of sixty-one and seventy-one hundredths cents (61.71¢) per gallon is levied on the sale of malt beverages.

(b)   Wine. - An excise tax of twenty-six and thirty-four hundredths cents (26.34¢) per liter is levied on the sale of unfortified wine, and an excise tax of twenty-nine and thirty-four hundredths cents (29.34¢) per liter is levied on the sale of fortified wine.

(c)   Liquor. - An excise tax of thirty percent (30%) is levied on liquor sold in ABC stores. Pursuant to G.S. 18B-804(b), the price of liquor on which this tax is computed is the distiller's price plus (i) the State ABC warehouse freight and bailment charges, and (ii) a markup for local ABC boards. (1985, c. 114, s. 1; 1987, c. 832, s. 2; 1998-95, s. 22; 2001-424, s. 34.23(c), (d); 2009-451, s. 27A.4(a).)

§ 105-113.81. Exemptions.

(a)   Major Disaster. - Wholesalers and importers of malt beverages and wine are not required to remit excise taxes on malt beverages or wine rendered unsalable by a major disaster. To qualify for this exemption, the wholesaler or importer shall prove to the satisfaction of the Secretary that a major disaster occurred. A major disaster is the destruction, spoilage, or rendering unsalable of 50 or more cases, or the equivalent, of malt beverages or 25 or more cases, or the equivalent, of wine.

(b)   Sales to Oceangoing Vessels. - Wholesalers and importers of malt beverages and wine are not required to remit excise taxes on malt beverages and wine sold and delivered for use on oceangoing vessels. An oceangoing vessel is a ship that plies the high seas in interstate or foreign commerce, in the transport of freight or passengers, or both, for hire exclusively. To qualify for this exemption the beverages shall be delivered to an officer or agent of the vessel for use on that vessel. Sales made to officers, agents, crewmen, or passengers for their personal use are not exempt.

(c)   Sales to Armed Forces of the United States. - Wholesalers and importers of malt beverages and wine are not required to remit excise taxes on malt beverages and wine sold to the Armed Forces of the United States. The Secretary may require malt beverages and wine sold to the Armed Forces of the United States to be marked "For Military Use Only" to facilitate identification of those beverages.

(d)   Out-of-State Sales. - Wholesalers and importers of malt beverages and wine are not required to remit excise taxes on malt beverages and wine shipped out of this State for resale outside the State.

(e)   Tasting. - Resident breweries and wineries are not required to remit excise taxes on malt beverages and wine given free of charge to customers, visitors, and employees on the manufacturer's licensed premises for consumption on those premises. (1963, c. 992, s. 1; 1967, c. 759, s. 24; 1971, c. 872, s. 2; 1975, c. 586, s. 3; 1985, c. 114, s. 1; 2011-183, s. 71.)

§ 105-113.81A: Repealed by Session Laws 2009-451, s. 14.19(f), effective July 1, 2009.

§ 105-113.82. Distribution of part of beer and wine taxes.

(a)   Amount. - The Secretary must distribute annually a percentage of the net amount of excise taxes collected on the sale of malt beverages and wine during the preceding 12-month period ending March 31 to the counties or cities in which the retail sale of these beverages is authorized in the entire county or city. The percentages to be distributed are as follows:

(1)   Of the tax on malt beverages levied under G.S. 105-113.80(a), twenty and forty-seven hundredths percent (20.47%).

(2)   Of the tax on unfortified wine levied under G.S. 105-113.80(b), forty-nine and forty-four hundredths percent (49.44%).

(3)   Of the tax on fortified wine levied under G.S. 105-113.80(b), eighteen percent (18%).

(a1)   Method. - If malt beverages, unfortified wine, or fortified wine may be licensed to be sold at retail in both a county and a city located in the county, both the county and city receive a portion of the amount distributed, that portion to be determined on the basis of population. If one of these beverages may be licensed to be sold at retail in a city located in a county in which the sale of the beverage is otherwise prohibited, only the city receives a portion of the amount distributed, that portion to be determined on the basis of population. The amounts distributable under subsection (a) of this section must be computed separately.

(b)   Repealed by Session Laws 2000, c. 173, s. 3, effective August 2, 2000.

(c)   Exception. - Notwithstanding subsections (a) and (a1) of this section, in a county in which ABC stores have been established by petition, the revenue shall be distributed as though the entire county had approved the retail sale of a beverage whose retail sale is authorized in part of the county.

(d)   Time. - The revenue shall be distributed to cities and counties within 60 days after March 31 of each year. The General Assembly finds that the revenue distributed under this section is local revenue, not a State expenditure, for the purpose of Section 5(3) of Article III of the North Carolina Constitution. Therefore, the Governor may not reduce or withhold the distribution.

(e)   Population Estimates. - To determine the population of a city or county for purposes of the distribution required by this section, the Secretary shall use the most recent annual estimate of population certified by the State Budget Officer.

(f)   City Defined. - As used in this section, the term "city" means a city as defined in G.S. 153A-1(1) or an urban service district defined by the governing body of a consolidated city-county.

(g)   Use of Funds. - Funds distributed to a county or city under this section may be used for any public purpose.

(h)   Disqualification. - No municipality may receive any funds under this section if it was incorporated with an effective date of on or after January 1, 2000, and is disqualified from receiving funds under G.S. 136-41.2. No municipality may receive any funds under this section, incorporated with an effective date on or after January 1, 2000, unless a majority of the mileage of its streets is open to the public. The previous sentence becomes effective with respect to distribution of funds on or after July 1, 1999. (1985, c. 114, s. 1; 1987, c. 836, s. 2; 1989 (Reg. Sess., 1990), c. 813, s. 5; 1991, c. 689, s. 28(b); 1993, c. 321, s. 26(g); c. 485, s. 2; 1995, c. 17, s. 1; 1996, 2nd Ex. Sess., c. 18, s. 25.2(a); 1997-261, s. 109; 1999-458, s. 10; 2000-173, s. 3; 2002-120, s. 1; 2004-203, s. 5(d); 2005-435, s. 34(a); 2006-162, s. 1; 2007-527, s. 4; 2009-451, s. 27A.4(b); 2011-330, s. 7.)

Part 5. Administration.

§ 105-113.83. Payment of excise taxes.

(a)   Liquor. - The excise tax on liquor levied under G.S. 105-113.80(c) is payable monthly by the local ABC board to the Secretary. The tax shall be paid on or before the 15th day of the month following the month in which the tax was collected.

(b)   Beer and Wine. - The excise taxes on malt beverages and wine levied under G.S. 105-113.80(a) and (b), respectively, are payable to the Secretary by the resident wholesaler or importer who first handles the beverages in this State. The excise taxes levied under G.S. 105-113.80(b) on wine shipped directly to consumers in this State pursuant to G.S. 18B-1001.1 must be paid by the wine shipper permittee. The taxes on malt beverages and wine are payable only once on the same beverages. The tax is due on or before the 15th day of the month following the month in which the beverage is first sold or otherwise disposed of in this State by the wholesaler, importer, or wine shipper permittee. When excise taxes are paid on wine or malt beverages, the wholesaler, importer, or wine shipper permittee must submit to the Secretary verified reports on forms provided by the Secretary detailing sales records for the month for which the taxes are paid. The report must indicate the amount of excise tax due, contain the information required by the Secretary, and indicate separately any transactions to which the excise tax does not apply.

(c)   Railroad Sales. - Each person operating a railroad train in this State on which alcoholic beverages are sold must submit monthly reports of the amount of alcoholic beverages sold in this State and must remit the applicable excise tax due on the sale of these beverages when the report is submitted. The report is due on or before the 15th day of the month following the month in which the beverages are sold. The report must be made on a form prescribed by the Secretary. (1985, c. 114, s. 1; 1998-95, s. 23; 2003-402, s. 10; 2004-170, s. 7; 2005-435, s. 26.)

§ 105-113.84. Report of resident brewery, resident winery, nonresident vendor, or wine shipper permittee.

A resident brewery, resident winery, nonresident vendor, and wine shipper permittee must file a monthly report with the Secretary. The report must list the amount of beverages delivered to North Carolina wholesalers, importers, and purchasers under G.S. 18B-1001.1 during the month. The report is due by the 15th day of the month following the month covered by the report. The report must be filed on a form approved by the Secretary and must contain the information required by the Secretary. (1985, c. 114, s. 1; 1998-95, s. 24; 2000-173, s. 4; 2003-402, s. 11.)

§ 105-113.85. Discount.

Each wholesaler or importer who files a timely return and sends a timely payment may deduct from the amount payable a discount of two percent (2%). This discount covers losses due to spoilage and breakage, expenses incurred in

223

preparing the records and reports required by this Article, and the expense of furnishing a bond. (1985, c. 114, s. 1; 2000-173, s. 5; 2001-414, s. 5; 2003-284, s. 45A.2(a); 2004-84, s. 2(d).)

§ 105-113.86. Bonds.

(a)   Wholesalers and Importers. - A wholesaler or importer shall furnish a bond in an amount of not less than five thousand dollars ($5,000) nor more than fifty thousand dollars ($50,000). The bond shall be conditioned on compliance with this Article, shall be payable to the State, shall be in a form acceptable to the Secretary, and shall be secured by a corporate surety or by a pledge of obligations of the federal government, the State, or a political subdivision of the State. The Secretary shall proportion the bond amount to the anticipated tax liability of the wholesaler or importer. The Secretary shall periodically review the sufficiency of bonds furnished by wholesalers and importers, and shall increase the amount of a bond required of a wholesaler or importer when the amount of the bond furnished no longer covers the wholesaler's or importer's anticipated tax liability.

(b)   Nonresident Vendors. - The Secretary may require the holder of a nonresident vendor ABC permit to furnish a bond in an amount not to exceed two thousand dollars ($2,000). The bond shall be conditioned on compliance with this Article, shall be payable to the State, shall be in a form acceptable to the Secretary, and shall be secured by a corporate surety or by a pledge of obligations of the federal government, the State, or a political subdivision of the State. (1985, c. 114, s. 1; 1987, c. 18; 1998-95, s. 25.)

§ 105-113.87. Refund for excise tax paid on sacramental wine.

(a)   Refund Allowed. - A person who purchases wine for the purpose stated in G.S. 18B-103(8) may obtain a refund from the Secretary for the amount of the excise tax levied under this Article. The Secretary shall make refunds annually.

(b)   Application. - An applicant for a refund authorized by this section shall file a written request with the Secretary for the refund due for the prior calendar year on or before April 15. The Secretary may by rule prescribe what information and records shall be supplied by the applicant to qualify for the refund. No refund may be made if the application is filed more than three years after the date it is due.

(c)   Repealed by Session Laws 1998-212, s. 29A.14(e). (1985, c. 114, s. 1; 1998-212, s. 29A.14(e).)

§ 105-113.88. Record-keeping requirements.

A person who is required to file a report or return under this Article must keep a record of all documents used to determine information the person provides in a report or return. The records must be kept for three years from the due date of the report or return to which the records apply. (1939, c. 158, s. 520; 1945, c. 903, s. 1; 1971, c. 872, s. 2; 1973, c. 476, s. 193; 1981, c. 747, s. 28; 1985, c. 114, s. 1; 2000-173, s. 6.)

§ 105-113.89. Other applicable administrative provisions.

The administrative provisions of Article 9 of this Chapter apply to this Article. (1985, c. 114, s. 1; 1998-95, s. 26.)

§§ 105-113.90 through 105-113.91: Repealed by Session Laws 1985, c. 114, s. 1.

§ 105-113.92: Repealed by Session Laws 1981, c. 747, s. 25.

§ 105-113.93: Repealed by Session Laws 1985, c. 114, s. 1.

§ 105-113.94: Repealed by Session Laws 1975, c. 53, s. 3.

§§ 105-113.95 through 105-113.104: Repealed by Session Laws 1985, c. 114, s. 1.

Article 2D.

Unauthorized Substances Taxes.

§ 105-113.105. Purpose.

The purpose of this Article is to levy an excise tax to generate revenue for State and local law enforcement agencies and for the General Fund. Nothing in this Article may in any manner provide immunity from criminal prosecution for a person who possesses an illegal substance. (1989, c. 772, s. 1; 1995, c. 340, s. 1; 1997-292, s. 1; 1998-98, s. 59.)

§ 105-113.106. Definitions.

The following definitions apply in this Article:

(1)   Controlled Substance. - Defined in G.S. 90-87.

(2)   Repealed by Session Laws 1995, c. 340, s. 1.

(3)   Dealer. - Any of the following:

a.   A person who actually or constructively possesses more than 42.5 grams of marijuana, seven or more grams of any other controlled substance that is sold by weight, or 10 or more dosage units of any other controlled substance that is not sold by weight.

b.   A person who in violation of Chapter 18B of the General Statutes possesses illicit spirituous liquor for sale.

c.   A person who in violation of Chapter 18B of the General Statutes possesses mash.

d.   A person who in violation of Chapter 18B of the General Statutes possesses an illicit mixed beverage for sale.

(4)   Repealed by Session Laws 1995, c. 340, s. 1.

(4a)   Illicit mixed beverage. - A mixed beverage, as defined in G.S. 18B-101, composed in whole or in part from spirituous liquor on which the charge imposed by G.S. 18B-804(b)(8) has not been paid, but not including a premixed cocktail served from a closed package containing only one serving.

(4b)   Illicit spirituous liquor. - Spirituous liquor, as defined in G.S. 105-113.68, not authorized by the North Carolina Alcoholic Beverage Control Commission.

Some examples of illicit spirituous liquor are the products known as "bootleg liquor", "moonshine", "non-tax-paid liquor", and "white liquor".

(4c)   Local law enforcement agency. - A municipal police department, a county police department, or a sheriff's office.

(4d)   Low-street-value drug. - Any of the following controlled substances:

a.   An anabolic steroid as defined in G.S. 90-91(k).

b.   A depressant described in G.S. 90-89(4), 90-90(4), 90-91(b), or 90-92(a).

c.   A hallucinogenic substance described in G.S. 90-89(3) or G.S. 90-90(5).

d.   A stimulant described in G.S. 90-89(5), 90-90(3), 90-91(j), 90-92(a)(3), or 90-93(a)(3).

e.   A controlled substance described in G.S. 90-91(c), (d), or (e), 90-92(a)(3), or (a)(5), or 90-93(a)1.

(5)   Repealed by Session Laws 1995, c. 340, s. 1.

(6)   Marijuana. - All parts of the plant of the genus Cannabis, whether growing or not; the seeds of this plant; the resin extracted from any part of this plant; and every compound, salt, derivative, mixture, or preparation of this plant, its seeds, or its resin.

(6a)   Mash. - The fermentable starchy mixture from which spirituous liquor can be distilled.

(7)   Person. - Defined in G.S. 105-228.90.

(8)   Secretary. - Defined in G.S. 105-228.90.

(8a)   State law enforcement agency. - Any State agency, force, department, or unit responsible for enforcing criminal laws.

(9)   Unauthorized substance. - A controlled substance, an illicit mixed beverage, illicit spirituous liquor, or mash. (1989, c. 772, s. 1; 1993, c. 354, s. 10; 1995, c. 340, s. 1; 1997-292, s. 1; 1999-337, s. 19; 2000-119, ss. 3, 4.)

§ 105-113.107. Excise tax on unauthorized substances.

(a)   Controlled Substances. - An excise tax is levied on controlled substances possessed, either actually or constructively, by dealers at the following rates:

(1)   At the rate of forty cents (40¢) for each gram, or fraction thereof, of harvested marijuana stems and stalks that have been separated from and are not mixed with any other parts of the marijuana plant.

(1a)   At the rate of three dollars and fifty cents ($3.50) for each gram, or fraction thereof, of marijuana, other than separated stems and stalks taxed under subdivision (1) of this [sub]section, or synthetic cannabinoids.

(1b)   At the rate of fifty dollars ($50.00) for each gram, or fraction thereof, of cocaine.

(2)   At the rate of two hundred dollars ($200.00) for each gram, or fraction thereof, of any other controlled substance that is sold by weight.

(2a)   At the rate of fifty dollars ($50.00) for each 10 dosage units, or fraction thereof, of any low-street-value drug that is not sold by weight.

(3)   At the rate of two hundred dollars ($200.00) for each 10 dosage units, or fraction thereof, of any other controlled substance that is not sold by weight.

(a1)   Weight. - A quantity of marijuana or other controlled substance is measured by the weight of the substance whether pure or impure or dilute, or by dosage units when the substance is not sold by weight, in the dealer's possession. A quantity of a controlled substance is dilute if it consists of a detectable quantity of pure controlled substance and any excipients or fillers.

(b)   Illicit Spirituous Liquor. - An excise tax is levied on illicit spirituous liquor possessed by a dealer at the following rates:

(1)   At the rate of thirty-one dollars and seventy cents ($31.70) for each gallon, or fraction thereof, of illicit spirituous liquor sold by the drink.

(2)   At the rate of twelve dollars and eighty cents ($12.80) for each gallon, or fraction thereof, of illicit spirituous liquor not sold by the drink.

(c)   Mash. - An excise tax is levied on mash possessed by a dealer at the rate of one dollar and twenty-eight cents ($1.28) for each gallon or fraction thereof.

(d)   Illicit Mixed Beverages. - A tax is levied on illicit mixed beverages sold by a dealer at the rate of twenty dollars ($20.00) on each four liters and a proportional sum on lesser quantities. (1989, c. 772, s. 1; 1995, c. 340, s. 1; 1997-292, s. 1; 1998-218, s. 1; 2012-79, s. 2.2(a).)

§ 105-113.107A. Exemptions.

(a)   Authorized Possession. - The tax levied in this Article does not apply to a substance in the possession of a dealer who is authorized by law to possess the substance. This exemption applies only during the time the dealer's possession of the substance is authorized by law.

(b)   Certain Marijuana Parts. - The tax levied in this Article does not apply to the following marijuana:

(1)   Harvested mature marijuana stalks when separated from and not mixed with any other parts of the marijuana plant.

(2)   Fiber or any other product of marijuana stalks described in subdivision (1) of this subsection, except resin extracted from the stalks.

(3)   Marijuana seeds that have been sterilized and are incapable of germination.

(4)   Roots of the marijuana plant. (1995, c. 340, s. 1; 1997-292, s. 1.)

§ 105-113.108. Reports; revenue stamps.

(a)   Revenue Stamps. - The Secretary shall issue stamps to affix to unauthorized substances to indicate payment of the tax required by this Article. Dealers shall report the taxes payable under this Article at the time and on the return prescribed by the Secretary. Notwithstanding any other provision of law, dealers are not required to give their name, address, social security number, or

229

other identifying information on the return, and the return is not required to be verified by oath or affirmation. Upon payment of the tax, the Secretary shall issue stamps in an amount equal to the amount of the tax paid. Taxes may be paid and stamps may be issued either by mail or in person.

(b)   Reports. - Every local law enforcement agency and every State law enforcement agency must report to the Department within 48 hours after seizing an unauthorized substance, or making an arrest of an individual in possession of an unauthorized substance, listed in this subsection upon which a stamp has not been affixed. The report must be in the form prescribed by the Secretary and it must include the time and place of the arrest or seizure, the amount, location, and kind of substance, the identification of an individual in possession of the substance and that individual's social security number, and any other information prescribed by the Secretary. The report must be made when the arrest or seizure involves any of the following unauthorized substances upon which a stamp has not been affixed as required by this Article:

(1)   More than 42.5 grams of marijuana.

(2)   Seven or more grams of any other controlled substance that is sold by weight.

(3)   Ten or more dosage units of any other controlled substance that is not sold by weight.

(4)   Any illicit mixed beverage.

(5)   Any illicit spirituous liquor.

(6)   Mash. (1989, c. 772, s. 1; 1995, c. 340, s. 1; 1997-292, s. 1; 2000-119, s. 5; 2004-170, s. 8.)

§ 105-113.109. When tax payable.

The tax imposed by this Article is payable by any dealer who actually or constructively possesses an unauthorized substance in this State upon which the tax has not been paid, as evidenced by a stamp. The tax is payable within 48 hours after the dealer acquires actual or constructive possession of a non-tax-paid unauthorized substance, exclusive of Saturdays, Sundays, and legal holidays of this State, in which case the tax is payable on the next working day. Upon payment of the tax, the dealer shall permanently affix the appropriate stamps to the unauthorized substance. Once the tax due on an unauthorized substance has been paid, no additional tax is due under this Article even though the unauthorized substance may be handled by other dealers. (1989, c. 772, s. 1; 1995, c. 340, s. 1; 1997-292, s. 1.)

§ 105-113.110: Repealed by Session Laws 1995, c. 340, s. 1.

§ 105-113.110A. Administration.

Article 9 of this Chapter applies to this Article. (1989 (Reg. Sess., 1990), c. 814, s. 7; 1995, c. 340, s. 1; 1997, c. 292, s. 1; 1998-218, s. 2.)

§ 105-113.111. Assessments.

Notwithstanding any other provision of law, an assessment against a dealer who possesses an unauthorized substance to which a stamp has not been affixed as required by this Article shall be made as provided in this section. The Secretary shall assess a tax, applicable penalties, and interest based on personal knowledge or information available to the Secretary. The Secretary shall notify the dealer in writing of the amount of the tax, penalty, and interest due, and demand its immediate payment. The notice and demand shall be either mailed to the dealer at the dealer's last known address or served on the dealer in person. If the dealer does not pay the tax, penalty, and interest immediately upon receipt of the notice and demand, the Secretary shall collect the tax, penalty, and interest pursuant to the jeopardy collection procedures in G.S. 105-241.23 or the general collection procedures in G.S. 105-242, including causing execution to be issued immediately against the personal property of the dealer, unless the dealer files with the Secretary a bond in the amount of the asserted liability for the tax, penalty, and interest. The Secretary shall use all means available to collect the tax, penalty, and interest from any property in which the dealer has a legal, equitable, or beneficial interest. The dealer may seek review of the assessment as provided in Article 9 of this Chapter. (1989, c. 772, s. 1;

1989 (Reg. Sess., 1990), c. 1039, s. 2; 1991 (Reg. Sess., 1992), c. 900, s. 20(d); 1995, c. 340, s. 1; 1997-292, s. 1; 2007-491, s. 8.)

§ 105-113.112. Confidentiality of information.

(a)   Information obtained by the Department in the course of administering the tax imposed by this Article, including information on whether the Department has issued a revenue stamp to a person, is confidential tax information and is subject to the provisions of G.S. 105-259.

(b)   Information obtained by the Department from the taxpayer in the course of administering the tax imposed by this Article, including information on whether the Department has issued a revenue stamp to a person, may not be used as evidence, as defined in G.S. 15A-971, by a prosecutor in a criminal prosecution of the taxpayer for an offense related to the manufacturing, possession, transportation, distribution, or sale of the unauthorized substance. Under this prohibition, no officer, employee, or agent of the Department may testify about this information in a criminal prosecution of the taxpayer for an offense related to the manufacturing, possession, transportation, distribution, or sale of the unauthorized substance. This subsection implements the protections against double jeopardy and self-incrimination set out in Amendment V of the United States Constitution and the restrictions in it apply regardless of whether information may be disclosed under G.S. 105-259. An officer, employee, or agent of the Department who provides evidence or testifies in violation of this subdivision is guilty of a Class 1 misdemeanor. (1989, c. 772, s. 1; 1993, c. 539, s. 702; 1994, Ex. Sess., c. 24, s. 14(c); 1997, c. 292, s. 1; 2005-435, s. 27; 2008-134, s. 68(a); 2013-414, s. 21.)

§ 105-113.113. Use of tax proceeds.

(a)   Special Account. - The Unauthorized Substances Tax Account is established as a special nonreverting account. The Secretary shall credit the proceeds of the tax levied by this Article to the Account.

(b)   Distribution. - The Secretary shall distribute unencumbered tax proceeds in the Unauthorized Substances Tax Account on a quarterly or more frequent basis. Tax proceeds in the Account are unencumbered when they are collectible under G.S. 105-241.22. The Secretary shall distribute seventy-five percent (75%) of the unencumbered tax proceeds in the Account that were collected by assessment to the State or local law enforcement agency that conducted the investigation of a dealer that led to the assessment. If more than one State or local law enforcement agency conducted the investigation, the Secretary shall determine the equitable share for each agency based on the contribution each agency made to the investigation. The Secretary shall credit the remaining unencumbered tax proceeds in the Account to the General Fund.

(c)   Refunds. - The refund of a tax that has already been distributed shall be drawn initially from the Unauthorized Substances Tax Account. The amount of refunded taxes that were distributed to a law enforcement agency under this section and any interest shall be subtracted from succeeding distributions from the Account to that law enforcement agency. The amount of refunded taxes that were credited to the General Fund under this section and any interest shall be subtracted from succeeding credits to the General Fund from the Account. (1991 (Reg. Sess., 1992), c. 900, s. 20(c); 1995, c. 340, s. 1; 1997-292, s. 1; 2007-491, s. 9.)

Article 3.

Franchise Tax.

§ 105-114. Nature of taxes; definitions.

(a)   Nature of Taxes. - The taxes levied in this Article upon persons and partnerships are for the privilege of engaging in business or doing the act named.

(a1)   Scope. - The taxes levied in this Article upon corporations are privilege or excise taxes levied upon:

(1)   Corporations organized under the laws of this State for the existence of the corporate rights and privileges granted by their charters, and the enjoyment, under the protection of the laws of this State, of the powers, rights, privileges and immunities derived from the State by the form of such existence; and

(2)   Corporations not organized under the laws of this State for doing business in this State and for the benefit and protection which these corporations receive from the government and laws of this State in doing business in this State.

(a2)   Condition for Doing Business. - If the corporation is organized under the laws of this State, the payment of the taxes levied by this Article is a condition precedent to the right to continue in the corporate form of organization. If the corporation is not organized under the laws of this State, payment of these taxes is a condition precedent to the right to continue to engage in doing business in this State.

(a3)   Tax Year. - The taxes levied in this Article are for the fiscal year of the State in which the taxes become due, except that the taxes levied in G.S. 105-122 are for the income year of the corporation in which the taxes become due.

(a4)   No Double Taxation. - G.S. 105-122 does not apply to holding companies taxed under G.S. 105-120.2. G.S. 105-122 applies to a corporation taxed under another section of this Article only to the extent the taxes levied on the corporation in G.S. 105-122 exceed the taxes levied in other sections of this Article on the corporation or on a limited liability company whose assets must be included in the corporation's tax base under G.S. 105-114.1.

(b)   Definitions. - The following definitions apply in this Article:

(1)   City. - Defined in G.S. 105-228.90.

(1a)   Code. - Defined in G.S. 105-228.90.

(2)   Corporation. - A domestic corporation, a foreign corporation, an electric membership corporation organized under Chapter 117 of the General Statutes or doing business in this State, or an association that is organized for pecuniary gain, has capital stock represented by shares, whether with or without par value, and has privileges not possessed by individuals or partnerships. The term includes a mutual or capital stock savings and loan association or building and loan association chartered under the laws of any state or of the United States. The term includes a limited liability company that elects to be taxed as a corporation under the Code, but does not otherwise include a limited liability company.

(3)   Doing business. - Each and every act, power, or privilege exercised or enjoyed in this State, as an incident to, or by virtue of the powers and privileges granted by the laws of this State.

(4)   Income year. - Defined in G.S. 105-130.2(4b).

(c)   Recodified as G.S. 105-114.1 by Session Laws 2002-126, s. 30G.2.(b), effective January 1, 2003. (1939, c. 158, s. 201; 1943, c. 400, s. 3; 1945, c. 708, s. 3; 1965, c. 287, s. 16; 1967, c. 286; 1969, c. 541, s. 6; 1973, c. 1287, s. 3; 1983, c. 713, s. 66; 1985, c. 656, s. 7; 1985 (Reg. Sess., 1986), c. 853, s. 1; 1987, c. 778, s. 1; 1987 (Reg. Sess., 1988), c. 1015, s. 2; 1989, c. 36, s. 2; 1989 (Reg. Sess., 1990), c. 981, s. 2; 1991, c. 30, s. 2; c. 689, s. 250; 1991 (Reg. Sess., 1992), c. 922, s. 3; 1993, c. 12, s. 4; c. 354, s. 11; c. 485, s. 5; 1997-118, s. 4; 1998-98, ss. 60, 76; 1999-337, s. 20; 2000-173, s. 8; 2001-327, s. 2(b); 2002-126, s. 30G.2(b); 2005-435, s. 59.2(a); 2006-66, s. 24A.2(a); 2006-162, ss. 3(b), 22; 2008-107, s. 28.7(a).)

§ 105-114.1. Limited liability companies.

(a)   Definitions. - The following definitions apply in this section:

(1)   Affiliated group. - Defined in section 1504 of the Code.

(2)   Capital interest. - The right under a limited liability company's governing law to receive a percentage of the company's assets upon dissolution after payments to creditors.

(3)   Entity. - A person that is not a human being.

(4)   Governing law. - The law under which a limited liability company is organized.

(5)   Noncorporate limited liability company. - A limited liability company that does not elect to be taxed as a corporation under the Code.

(b)   Controlled Companies. - If a corporation or an affiliated group of corporations owns more than fifty percent (50%) of the capital interests in a noncorporate limited liability company, the corporation or group of corporations must include in its three tax bases pursuant to G.S. 105-122 the same

235

percentage of (i) the noncorporate limited liability company's capital stock, surplus, and undivided profits; (ii) fifty-five percent (55%) of the noncorporate limited liability company's appraised ad valorem tax value of property; and (iii) the noncorporate limited liability company's actual investment in tangible property in this State, as appropriate.

(c)   Constructive Ownership. - Ownership of the capital interests in a noncorporate limited liability company is determined by reference to the constructive ownership rules for partnerships, estates, and trusts in section 318(a)(2)(A) and (B) of the Code with the following modifications:

(1)   The term "capital interest" is substituted for "stock" each place it appears.

(2)   A noncorporate limited liability company and any noncorporate entity other than a partnership, estate, or trust is treated as a partnership.

(3)   The operating rule of section 318(a)(5) of the Code applies without regard to section 318(a)(5)(C).

(d)   No Double Inclusion. - If a corporation is required to include a percentage of a noncorporate limited liability company's assets in its tax bases under this Article pursuant to subsection (b) of this section, its investment in the noncorporate limited liability company is not included in its computation of capital stock base under G.S. 105-122(b).

(e)   Affiliated Group. - If the owner of the capital interests in a noncorporate limited liability company is an affiliated group of corporations, the percentage to be included pursuant to subsection (b) of this section by each group member that is doing business in this State is determined by multiplying the capital interests in the noncorporate limited liability company owned by the affiliated group by a fraction. The numerator of the fraction is the capital interests in the noncorporate limited liability company owned by the group member, and the denominator of the fraction is the capital interests in the noncorporate limited liability company owned by all group members that are doing business in this State.

(f)   Exemption. - This section does not apply to assets owned by a noncorporate limited liability company if the total book value of the noncorporate limited liability company's assets never exceeded one hundred fifty thousand dollars ($150,000) during its taxable year.

(g)   Timing. - Ownership of the capital interests in a noncorporate limited liability company is determined as of the last day of its taxable year. The adjustments pursuant to subsections (b) and (d) of this section must be made to the owner's next following return filed under this Article. If a noncorporate limited liability company and a corporation or an affiliated group of corporations have engaged in a pattern of transferring assets between them with the result that each did not own the capital interests on the last day of its taxable year, the ownership of the capital interests in the noncorporate limited liability company must be determined as of the last day of the corporation or group of corporations' taxable year.

(h)   Penalty. - A taxpayer who, because of fraud with intent to evade tax, underpays the tax under this Article on assets attributable to it under this section is guilty of a Class H felony in accordance with G.S. 105-236(7). (2002-126, s. 30G.2(b); 2004-74, ss. 1, 2; 2004-170, s. 8.1; 2006-66, s. 24A.2(b); 2008-107, s. 28.7(b); 2013-157, s. 25.)

§ 105-115. Repealed by Session Laws 1989 (Reg. Sess., 1990), c. 1002, s. 1.

§ 105-116. (Repealed effective July 1, 2014) Franchise or privilege tax on electric power, water, and sewerage companies.

(a)   Tax. - An annual franchise or privilege tax is imposed on the following:

(1)   An electric power company engaged in the business of furnishing electricity, electric lights, current, or power.

(2),   (2a) Repealed by Session Laws 1998-22, s. 2, effective July 1, 1999.

(3)   A water company engaged in owning or operating a water system subject to regulation by the North Carolina Utilities Commission.

(4)   A public sewerage company engaged in owning or operating a public sewerage system.

The tax on an electric power company is three and twenty-two hundredths percent (3.22%) of the company's taxable gross receipts from the business of

237

furnishing electricity, electric lights, current, or power. The tax on a water company is four percent (4%) of the company's taxable gross receipts from owning or operating a water system subject to regulation by the North Carolina Utilities Commission. The tax on a public sewerage company is six percent (6%) of the company's taxable gross receipts from owning or operating a public sewerage company. A company's taxable gross receipts are its gross receipts from business inside the State less the amount of gross receipts from sales reported under subdivision (b)(2). A company that engages in more than one business taxed under this section shall pay tax on each business.

(b)   Return and Payment. - The tax imposed by this section is payable quarterly or monthly as specified in this subsection. A return is due quarterly.

A water company or public sewerage company must pay tax quarterly when filing a return. An electric power company must pay tax in accordance with the schedule and requirements that apply to payments of sales and use tax under G.S. 105-164.16 and must file a return quarterly.

A quarterly return covers a calendar quarter and is due by the last day of the month that follows the quarter covered by the return. A taxpayer must submit a return on a form provided by the Secretary. The return must include the taxpayer's gross receipts from all property it owned or operated during the reporting period in connection with its business taxed under this section. A taxpayer must report its gross receipts on an accrual basis. A return must contain the following information:

(1)   The taxpayer's gross receipts for the reporting period from business inside and outside this State, stated separately.

(2)   The taxpayer's gross receipts from commodities or services described in subsection (a) that are sold to a vendee subject to the tax levied by this section or to a joint agency established under Chapter 159B of the General Statutes or a city having an ownership share in a project established under that Chapter.

(3)   The amount of and price paid by the taxpayer for commodities or services described in subsection (a) that are purchased from others engaged in business in this State and the name of each vendor.

(4)   For an electric power company the entity's gross receipts from the sale within each city of the commodities and services described in subsection (a).

(c)   Repealed by Session Laws 1998-22, s. 2, effective July 1, 1999.

(d)   Distribution. - Part of the taxes imposed by this section on electric power companies is distributed to cities under G.S. 105-116.1. If a taxpayer's return does not state the taxpayer's taxable gross receipts derived within a city, the Secretary must determine a practical method of allocating part of the taxpayer's taxable gross receipts to the city.

(e)   Local Tax. - So long as there is a distribution to cities from the tax imposed by this section, no city shall impose or collect any greater franchise, privilege or license taxes, in the aggregate, on the businesses taxed under this section, than was imposed and collected on or before January 1, 1947.

(e1)   An electric power company engaged in the business of furnishing electricity, electric lights, current, or power that collects the annual franchise or privilege tax pursuant to subsection (a) of this section and remits the tax collected to the Secretary shall not be subject to any additional franchise or privilege tax imposed upon it by any city or county.

(f)   Repealed by Session Laws 1998-22, s. 2, effective July 1, 1999. (1939, c. 158, s. 203; 1949, c. 392, s. 2; 1951, c. 643, s. 3; 1955, c. 1313, s. 2; 1957, c. 1340, s. 3; 1959, c. 1259, s. 3; 1963, c. 1169, s. 1; 1965, c. 517; 1967, c. 519, ss. 1, 3; c. 1272, ss. 1, 3; 1971, c. 298, s. 1; c. 833, s. 1; 1973, c. 476, s. 193; c. 537, s. 3; c. 1287, s. 3; c. 1349; 1975, c. 812; 1983 (Reg. Sess., 1984), c. 1097, ss. 2, 16; 1987 (Reg. Sess., 1988), c. 882, s. 4.4; 1989 (Reg. Sess., 1990), c. 813, s. 3; c. 814, s. 10; c. 945, ss. 3, 17; 1991, c. 598, s. 4; c. 689, s. 28(c); 1991 (Reg. Sess., 1992), c. 1007, s. 2; 1993, c. 321, s. 26(h); 1997-118, s. 2; 1997-426, s. 3; 1998-22, s. 2; 1998-98, s. 72; 1998-217, s. 32(a); 2000-140, s. 62; 2001-427, s. 6(c), (d); 2002-72, s. 10; 2002-120, s. 8; 2006-33, s. 10; 2006-162, s. 31; 2013-316, s. 4.1(a); 2013-414, s. 1(a).)

§ 105-116.1. (Repealed effective July 1, 2014) Distribution of gross receipts taxes to cities.

(a)   Definitions. - The following definitions apply in this section:

(1)   Freeze deduction. - The amount by which the percentage distribution amount of a city was required to be reduced in fiscal year 1995-96 in determining the amount to distribute to the city.

(2)   Percentage distribution amount. - Three and nine hundredths percent (3.09%) of the gross receipts derived by an electric power company from sales within a city that are taxable under G.S. 105-116.

(b)   Distribution. - The Secretary must distribute to the cities part of the taxes collected under this Article on electric power companies. Each city's share for a calendar quarter is the percentage distribution amount for that city for that quarter minus one-fourth of the city's hold-back amount and one-fourth of the city's proportionate share of the annual cost to the Department of administering the distribution. The Secretary must make the distribution within 75 days after the end of each calendar quarter. The General Assembly finds that the revenue distributed under this section is local revenue, not a State expenditure, for the purpose of Section 5(3) of Article III of the North Carolina Constitution. Therefore, the Governor may not reduce or withhold the distribution.

(c)   Limited Hold-Harmless Adjustment. - The hold-back amount for a city that, in the 1995-96 fiscal year, received from gross receipts taxes on electric power companies and natural gas companies less than ninety-five percent (95%) of the amount it received in the 1990-91 fiscal year but at least sixty percent (60%) of the amount it received in the 1990-91 fiscal year is the amount determined by the following calculation:

(1)   Adjust the city's 1995-96 distribution by adding the city's freeze deduction attributable to receipts from electric power companies and natural gas companies to the amount distributed to the city for that year.

(2)   Compare the adjusted 1995-96 amount with the city's 1990-91 distribution.

(3)   If the adjusted 1995-96 amount is less than or equal to the city's 1990-91 distribution, the hold-back amount for the city is zero.

(4)   If the adjusted 1995-96 amount is more than the city's 1990-91 distribution, the hold-back amount for the city is the city's freeze deduction attributable to receipts from electric power companies and natural gas companies minus the difference between the city's 1990-91 distribution and the city's 1995-96 distribution.

(c1)   Additional Limited Hold-Harmless Adjustment. - The hold-back amount for a city that, in the 1995-96 fiscal year, received from gross receipts taxes on electric power companies and natural gas companies less than sixty percent

(60%) of the amount it received in the 1990-91 fiscal year is the amount determined by the following calculation:

(1)   Adjust the city's 1999-2000 distribution by adding the city's freeze deduction attributable to receipts from electric power companies and natural gas companies to the amount distributed to the city for that year.

(2)   Compare the adjusted 1999-2000 amount with the city's 1990-91 distribution.

(3)   If the adjusted 1999-2000 amount is less than or equal to the city's 1990-91 distribution, the hold-back amount for the city is zero.

(4)   If the adjusted 1999-2000 amount is more than the city's 1990-91 distribution, the hold-back amount for the city is the city's freeze deduction attributable to receipts from electric power companies and natural gas companies minus the difference between the city's 1990-91 distribution and the city's 1999-2000 distribution.

(d)   Allocation of Hold-Harmless Adjustment. - The hold-back amount for a city that, in the 1995-96 fiscal year, received from gross receipts taxes on electric power companies and natural gas companies at least ninety-five percent (95%) of the amount it received in the 1990-91 fiscal year is the amount determined by the following calculation:

(1)   Determine the amount by which the freeze deduction attributable to receipts from electric power companies and natural gas companies is reduced for all cities whose hold-back amount is determined under subsections (c) and (c1) of this section. This amount is the total hold-harmless adjustment.

(2)   Determine the amount of gross receipts taxes that would be distributed for the quarter to cities whose hold-back amount is determined under this subsection if these cities received their percentage distribution amount minus one-fourth of their freeze deduction attributable to receipts from electric power companies and natural gas companies.

(3)   For each city included in the calculation in subdivision (2) of this subsection, determine that city's percentage share of the amount determined under that subdivision.

241

(4)   Add to the city's freeze deduction attributable to receipts from electric power companies and natural gas companies an amount equal to the city's percentage share under subdivision (3) of this subsection multiplied by the total hold-harmless adjustment.

(e)   Disqualification. - No municipality may receive any funds under this section if it was incorporated with an effective date of on or after January 1, 2000, and is disqualified from receiving funds under G.S. 136-41.2. No municipality may receive any funds under this section, incorporated with an effective date on or after January 1, 2000, unless a majority of the mileage of its streets is open to the public. The previous sentence becomes effective with respect to distribution of funds on or after July 1, 1999. (1997-118, s. 1; 1997-426, s. 3.1; 1997-439, s. 3; 1997-456, s. 55.5; 1998-22, s. 3; 1999-458, s. 11; 2000-128, s. 2; 2001-430, s. 11; 2002-120, s. 2; 2005-435, s. 34(b); 2013-316, s. 4.1(a).)

§§ 105-117 through 115-118: Repealed by Session Laws 1995 (Regular Session, 1996), c. 646, s. 3.

§ 105-119: Repealed by Session Laws 2000-173, s. 7.

§ 105-120: Repealed by Session Laws 2001-430, s. 12, effective January 1, 2002, and applies to taxable services reflected on bills dated on or after January 1, 2002.

§ 105-120.1: Repealed by Session Laws 2000-173, s. 7.

§ 105-120.2. Franchise or privilege tax on holding companies.

(a)   Every corporation, domestic and foreign, incorporated or, by an act, domesticated under the laws of this State or doing business in this State that, at the close of its taxable year, is a holding company as defined in subsection (c) of this section, shall, pursuant to the provisions of G.S. 105-122, do all of the following:

(1)   File a return.

(2)   Determine the total amount of its issued and outstanding capital stock, surplus and undivided profits.

242

(3)   Apportion such outstanding capital stock, surplus and undivided profits to this State.

(b)   (1)   Every corporation taxed under this section shall annually pay to the Secretary of Revenue, at the time the return is due, a franchise or privilege tax at the rate of one dollar and fifty cents ($1.50) per one thousand dollars ($1,000) of the amount determined under subsection (a) of this section, but in no case shall the tax be more than seventy-five thousand dollars ($75,000) nor less than thirty-five dollars ($35.00).

(2)   Notwithstanding the provisions of subdivision (1) of this subsection, if the tax produced pursuant to application of this paragraph (2) exceeds the tax produced pursuant to application of subdivision (1), then the tax is levied at the rate of one dollar and fifty cents ($1.50) per one thousand dollars ($1,000) on the greater of the following:

a.   Fifty-five percent (55%) of the appraised value as determined for ad valorem taxation of all the real and tangible personal property in this State of each such corporation plus the total appraised value of intangible property returned for taxation of intangible personal property as computed under G.S. 105-122(d).

b.   The total actual investment in tangible property in this State of such corporation as computed under G.S. 105-122(d).

(c)   For purposes of this section, a "holding company" is a corporation that satisfies at least one of the following conditions:

(1)   It has no assets other than ownership interests in corporations in which it owns, directly or indirectly, more than fifty percent (50%) of the outstanding voting stock or voting capital interests.

(2)   It receives during its taxable year more than eighty percent (80%) of its gross income from corporations in which it owns directly or indirectly more than fifty percent (50%) of the outstanding voting stock or voting capital interests.

(d)   Repealed by Session Laws 1985, c. 656, s. 39.

(e)   Counties, cities and towns shall not levy a franchise tax on corporations taxed under this section. The tax imposed under the provisions of G.S. 105-122 shall not apply to businesses taxed under the provisions of this section.

(f)   Repealed by Session Laws 2011-330, s. 3, effective June 27, 2011. (1975, c. 130, s. 1; 1985, c. 656, s. 39; 1985 (Reg. Sess., 1986), c. 854, s. 1; 1987 (Reg. Sess., 1988), c. 882, s. 4.2; 1991, c. 30, s. 4; 1998-98, s. 72; 2006-196, s. 9; 2011-330, s. 3; 2012-79, s. 2.3; 2013-414, s. 1(b).)

§ 105-121: Repealed by Session Laws 1945, c. 752, s. 1.

§ 105-121.1. Mutual burial associations.

An annual franchise or privilege tax on all domestic mutual burial associations shall be due and payable to the Secretary of Revenue on or before the first day of April of each year. The amount of this franchise or privilege tax shall be based on the membership of such associations according to the following schedule:

Membership less than 3,000 .... $15.00

Membership of 3,000 to 5,000 .... 20.00

Membership of 5,000 to 10,000 .... 25.00

Membership of 10,000 to 15,000 .... 30.00

Membership of 15,000 to 20,000 .... 35.00

Membership of 20,000 to 25,000 .... 40.00

Membership of 25,000 to 30,000 .... 45.00

Membership of 30,000 or more
.... 50.00

(1943, c. 60, s. 2; 1973, c. 476, s. 193.)

§ 105-122. Franchise or privilege tax on domestic and foreign corporations.

(a)   An annual franchise or privilege tax is imposed on a corporation doing business in this State. The tax is determined on the basis of the books and records of the corporation as of the close of its income year. A corporation subject to the tax must file a return under affirmation with the Secretary at the place and in the manner prescribed by the Secretary. The return must be signed by the president, vice-president, treasurer, or chief financial officer of the corporation. The return is due on or before the fifteenth day of the fourth month following the end of the corporation's income year.

(b)   Determination of Capital Base. - A corporation taxed under this section shall determine the total amount of its issued and outstanding capital stock, surplus, and undivided profits. No reservation or allocation from surplus or undivided profits is allowed except as provided below:

(1)   Definite and accrued legal liabilities.

(1a)   Billings in excess of costs that are considered a deferred liability under the percentage of completion method of revenue recognition.

(2)   Taxes accrued, dividends declared, and reserves for depreciation of tangible assets and for amortization of intangible assets as permitted for income tax purposes.

(3)   When including deferred tax liabilities, a corporation may reduce the amount included in its base by netting against that amount deferred tax assets. The reduction may not decrease deferred tax liabilities below zero (0).

(4)   Reserves for the cost of any air-cleaning device or sewage or waste treatment plant, including waste lagoons, and pollution abatement equipment purchased or constructed and installed which reduces the amount of air or water pollution resulting from the emission of air contaminants or the discharge of sewage and industrial wastes or other polluting materials or substances into the

245

outdoor atmosphere or streams, lakes, or rivers, upon condition that the corporation claiming such deductible liability shall furnish to the Secretary a certificate from the Department of Environment and Natural Resources or from a local air pollution control program for air-cleaning devices located in an area where the Environmental Management Commission has certified a local air pollution control program pursuant to G.S. 143-215.112 certifying that the Environmental Management Commission or local air pollution control program has found as a fact that the air-cleaning device, waste treatment plant or pollution abatement equipment purchased or constructed and installed as above described has actually been constructed and installed and that such plant or equipment complies with the requirements of the Environmental Management Commission or local air pollution control program with respect to such devices, plants or equipment, that such device, plant or equipment is being effectively operated in accordance with the terms and conditions set forth in the permit, certificate of approval, or other document of approval issued by the Environmental Management Commission or local air pollution control program and that the primary purpose thereof is to reduce air or water pollution resulting from the emission of air contaminants or the discharge of sewage and waste and not merely incidental to other purposes and functions.

(5)   Reserves for the cost of purchasing and installing equipment or constructing facilities for the purpose of recycling or resource recovering of or from solid waste or for the purpose of reducing the volume of hazardous waste generated shall be treated as deductible for the purposes of this section upon condition that the corporation claiming such deductible liability shall furnish to the Secretary a certificate from the Department of Environment and Natural Resources certifying that the Department of Environment and Natural Resources has found as a fact that the equipment or facility has actually been purchased, installed or constructed, that it is in conformance with all rules and regulations of the Department of Environment and Natural Resources, and the recycling or resource recovering is the primary purpose of the facility or equipment.

(6)   Reserves for the cost of constructing facilities of any private or public utility built for the purpose of providing sewer service to residential and outlying areas shall be treated as deductible for the purposes of this section; the deductible liability allowed by this section shall apply only with respect to such pollution abatement plants or equipment constructed or installed on or after January 1, 1955.

(7)   The cost of treasury stock.

(8)   In the case of an international banking facility, the capital base shall be reduced by the excess of the amount as of the end of the taxable year of all assets of an international banking facility which are employed outside the United States over liabilities of the international banking facility owed to foreign persons. For purposes of such reduction, foreign persons shall have the same meaning as defined in G.S. 105-130.5(b)(13)d.

Every corporation doing business in this State which is a parent, subsidiary, or affiliate of another corporation shall add to its capital stock, surplus, and undivided profits all indebtedness owed to a parent, subsidiary, or affiliated corporation as a part of its capital used in its business and as a part of the base for franchise tax under this section. If any part of the capital of the creditor corporation is capital borrowed from a source other than a parent, subsidiary, or affiliate, the debtor corporation, which is required under this subsection to include in its tax base the amount of debt by reason of being a parent, subsidiary, or affiliate of the creditor corporation, may deduct from the debt included a proportionate part determined on the basis of the ratio of the borrowed capital of the creditor corporation to the total assets of the creditor corporation. If the creditor corporation is also taxable under the provisions of this section, the creditor corporation is allowed to deduct from the total of its capital, surplus, and undivided profits the amount of any debt owed to it by a parent, subsidiary or affiliated corporation to the extent that the debt has been included in the tax base of the parent, subsidiary, or affiliated debtor corporation reporting for taxation under the provisions of this section.

(b1)   Definitions. - The following definitions apply in subsection (b) of this section:

(1)   Affiliate. - The same meaning as specified in G.S. 105-130.2.

(2)   Indebtedness. - All loans, credits, goods, supplies, or other capital of whatsoever nature furnished by a parent, subsidiary, or affiliated corporation, other than indebtedness endorsed, guaranteed, or otherwise supported by one of these corporations.

(3)   Parent. - The same meaning as specified in G.S. 105-130.2.

(4)   Subsidiary. - The same meaning as specified in G.S. 105-130.2.

(c)   Repealed by Session Laws 2007-491, s. 2, effective January 1, 2008.

(c1)   Apportionment. - A corporation that is doing business in this State and in one or more other states must apportion its capital stock, surplus, and undivided profits to this State. A corporation must use the apportionment method set out in subdivision (1) of this subsection unless the Department has authorized it to use a different method under subdivision (2) of this subsection. The portion of a corporation's capital stock, surplus, and undivided profits determined by applying the appropriate apportionment method is considered the amount of capital stock, surplus, and undivided profits the corporation uses in its business in this State.

(1)   Statutory. - A corporation that is subject to income tax under Article 4 of this Chapter must apportion its capital stock, surplus, and undivided profits by using the fraction it applies in apportioning its income under that Article. A corporation that is not subject to income tax under Article 4 of this Chapter must apportion its capital stock, surplus, and undivided profits by using the fraction it would be required to apply in apportioning its income if it were subject to that Article. The apportionment method set out in this subdivision is considered the statutory method of apportionment and is presumed to be the best method of determining the amount of a corporation's capital stock, surplus, and undivided profits attributable to the corporation's business in this State.

(2)   Alternative. - A corporation that believes the statutory apportionment method set out in subdivision (1) of this subsection subjects a greater portion of its capital stock, surplus, and undivided profits to tax under this section than is attributable to its business in this State may make a written request to the Secretary for permission to use an alternative method. The request must set out the reasons for the corporation's belief and propose an alternative method. The corporation has the burden of establishing by clear, cogent, and convincing proof that the statutory apportionment method subjects a greater portion of the corporation's capital stock, surplus, and undivided profits to tax under this section than is attributable to its business in this State and that the proposed alternative method is a better method of determining the amount of the corporation's capital stock, surplus, and undivided profits attributable to the corporation's business in this State.

The Secretary must issue a written decision on a corporation's request for an alternative apportionment method. If the decision grants the request, it must describe the alternative method the corporation is authorized to use and state the tax years to which the alternative method applies. A decision may apply to no more than three tax years. A corporation may renew a request to use an alternative apportionment method by following the procedure in this subdivision.

A decision of the Secretary on a request for an alternative apportionment method is final and is not subject to administrative or judicial review. A corporation authorized to use an alternative method may apportion its capital stock, surplus, and undivided profits in accordance with the alternative method or the statutory method.

(3)   Repealed by Session Laws 2011-330, s. 5, effective June 27, 2011.

(d)   After determining the proportion of its total capital stock, surplus and undivided profits as set out in subsection (c1) of this section, which amount shall not be less than fifty-five percent (55%) of the appraised value as determined for ad valorem taxation of all the real and tangible personal property in this State of each corporation nor less than its total actual investment in tangible property in this State, every corporation taxed under this section shall annually pay to the Secretary of Revenue, at the time the return is due, a franchise or privilege tax at the rate of one dollar and fifty cents ($1.50) per one thousand dollars ($1,000) of the total amount of capital stock, surplus and undivided profits as provided in this section. The tax imposed in this section shall not be less than thirty-five dollars ($35.00) and is for the privilege of carrying on, doing business, and/or the continuance of articles of incorporation or domestication of each corporation in this State. Appraised value of tangible property including real estate is the ad valorem valuation for the calendar year next preceding the due date of the franchise tax return. The term "total actual investment in tangible property" as used in this section means the total original purchase price or consideration to the reporting taxpayer of its tangible properties, including real estate, in this State plus additions and improvements thereto less reserve for depreciation as permitted for income tax purposes, and also less any indebtedness incurred and existing by virtue of the purchase of any real estate and any permanent improvements made thereon. In computing "total actual investment in tangible personal property" a corporation may deduct reserves for the entire cost of any air-cleaning device or sewage or waste treatment plant, including waste lagoons, and pollution abatement equipment purchased or constructed and installed which reduces the amount of air or water pollution resulting from the emission of air contaminants or the discharge of sewage and industrial wastes or other polluting materials or substances into the outdoor atmosphere or into streams, lakes, or rivers, upon condition that the corporation claiming this deduction shall furnish to the Secretary a certificate from the Department of Environment and Natural Resources or from a local air pollution control program for air-cleaning devices located in an area where the Environmental Management Commission has certified a local air pollution control program pursuant to G.S. 143-215.112 certifying that said Department or local air

249

pollution control program has found as a fact that the air-cleaning device, waste treatment plant or pollution abatement equipment purchased or constructed and installed as above described has actually been constructed and installed and that the device, plant or equipment complies with the requirements of the Environmental Management Commission or local air pollution control program with respect to the devices, plants or equipment, that the device, plant or equipment is being effectively operated in accordance with the terms and conditions set forth in the permit, certificate of approval, or other document of approval issued by the Environmental Management Commission or local air pollution control program and that the primary purpose is to reduce air or water pollution resulting from the emission of air contaminants or the discharge of sewage and waste and not merely incidental to other purposes and functions. The cost of constructing facilities of any private or public utility built for the purpose of providing sewer service to residential and outlying areas is treated as deductible for the purposes of this section; the deductible liability allowed by this section applies only with respect to pollution abatement plants or equipment constructed or installed on or after January 1, 1955.

(d1)   Credits. - A corporation is allowed a credit against the tax imposed by this section for a taxable year equal to one-half of the amount of tax payable during the taxable year under Article 5E of this Chapter. The credit allowed by this subsection may not exceed the amount of tax imposed by this section for the taxable year, reduced by the sum of all other credits allowed against that tax, except tax payments made by or on behalf of the taxpayer.

(e)   Any corporation which changes its income year, and files a "short period" income tax return pursuant to G.S. 105-130.15 shall file a franchise tax return in accordance with the provisions of this section in the manner and as of the date specified in subsection (a) of this section. Such corporation shall be entitled to deduct from the total franchise tax computed (on an annual basis) on such return the amount of franchise tax previously paid which is applicable to the period subsequent to the beginning of the new income year.

(f)   The return and tax required by this section are in addition to all other reports required or taxes levied and assessed in this State.

(g)   Counties, cities and towns shall not levy a franchise tax on corporations taxed under this section.

(h)   Repealed by Session Laws 1981 (Regular Session, 1982), c. 1211, s. 5. (1939, c. 158, s. 210; 1941, c. 50, s. 4; 1943, c. 400, s. 3; 1945, c. 708, s. 3;

1947, c. 501, s. 3; 1951, c. 643, s. 3; 1953, c. 1302, s. 3; 1955, c. 1100, s. 2½; c. 1350, s. 17; 1957, c. 1340, s. 3; 1959, c. 1259, s. 3; 1963, c. 1169, s. 1; 1967, c. 286; c. 892, ss. 10, 11; c. 1110, s. 2; 1973, c. 476, s. 193; c. 695, s. 17; c. 1262, s. 23; c. 1287, s. 3; 1975, c. 764, s. 2; 1977, c. 771, s. 4; 1981, c. 704, s. 18; c. 855, s. 3; 1981 (Reg. Sess., 1982), c. 1211, s. 5; 1985, c. 656, s. 40; 1985 (Reg. Sess., 1986), c. 826, s. 6; c. 854, s. 1; 1987 (Reg. Sess., 1988), c. 882, s. 4.3; 1989, c. 148, s. 1; c. 727, ss. 218(39), 219(27); 1991, c. 30, s. 5; 1993, c. 532, s. 11; 1995 (Reg. Sess., 1996), c. 560, s. 1; 1997-443, s. 11A.119(a); 1998-22, ss. 8, 9; 1998-98, ss. 72, 77; 1998-217, s. 43; 1999-337, s. 21; 2001-427, s. 12(a); 2003-416, s. 5(j); 2006-95, s. 1.1; 2006-162, s. 2; 2007-491, ss. 2, 10, 11; 2008-134, ss. 3(a), (b); 2009-422, s. 1; 2009-445, s. 2; 2010-31, s. 31.9(a); 2010-89, s. 2(c); 2011-145, s. 31A.2(a); 2011-330, s. 5; 2012-79, s. 1.14(a); 2013-414, ss. 1(c), 2(a).)

§ 105-122.1. Credit for additional annual report fees paid by limited liability companies subject to franchise tax.

A limited liability company subject to tax under this Article is allowed a credit against the tax imposed by this Article equal to the difference between the annual report fee for corporations under G.S. 55-1-22(a)(23) and the annual report fee for limited liability companies under G.S. 57D-1-22. The credit allowed by this section may not exceed the amount of tax imposed by this Article for the taxable year reduced by the sum of all credits allowed, except payments of tax made by or on behalf of the taxpayer. (2006-66, s. 24A.2(c); 2007-323, s. 30.6(b); 2013-157, s. 26.)

§ 105-123: Repealed by Session Laws 1991, c. 30, s. 1.

§ 105-124. Repealed by Session Laws 1959, c. 1259, s. 9.

§ 105-125. Exempt corporations.

(a)   Exemptions. - The following corporations are exempt from the taxes levied by this Article. Upon request of the Secretary, an exempt corporation must establish its claim for exemption in writing:

(1)   A charitable, religious, fraternal, benevolent, scientific, or educational corporation not operated for profit.

(2)　　An insurance company subject to tax under Article 8B of this Chapter.

(3)　　A mutual ditch or irrigation association, a mutual or cooperative telephone association or company, a mutual canning association, a cooperative breeding association, or a similar corporation of a purely local character deriving receipts solely from assessments, dues, or fees collected from members for the sole purpose of meeting expenses.

(4)　　A cooperative marketing association that operates solely for the purpose of marketing the products of members or other farmers and returns to the members and farmers the proceeds of sales, less the association's necessary operating expenses, including interest and dividends on capital stock, on the basis of the quantity of product furnished by them. The association's operations may include activities directly related to these marketing activities.

(5)　　A production credit association organized under the federal Farm Credit Act of 1933.

(6)　　A club organized and operated exclusively for pleasure, recreation, or other nonprofit purposes, a civic league operated exclusively for the promotion of social welfare, a business league, or a board of trade.

(7)　　A chamber of commerce or merchants' association not organized for profit, no part of the net earnings of which inures to the benefit of a private stockholder, an individual, or another corporation.

(8)　　An organization, such as a condominium association, a homeowners' association, or a cooperative housing corporation not organized for profit, the membership of which is limited to the owners or occupants of residential units in the condominium, housing development, or cooperative housing corporation. To qualify for the exemption, the organization must be operated exclusively for the management, operation, preservation, maintenance, or landscaping of the residential units owned by the organization or its members or of the common areas and facilities that are contiguous to the residential units and owned by the organization or by its members. To qualify for the exemption, no part of the net earnings of the organization may inure, other than through the performance of related services for the members of the organization, to the benefit of any person.

(9)   Except as otherwise provided by law, an organization exempt from federal income tax under the Code.

Provided, that an entity that qualifies as a real estate mortgage investment conduit, as defined in section 860D of the Code, is exempt from all of the taxes levied in this Article. Upon request by the Secretary of Revenue, a real estate mortgage investment conduit must establish in writing its qualification for this exemption.

(b)   Certain Investment Companies. - A corporation doing business in North Carolina that meets one or more of the following conditions may, in determining its capital stock, surplus, and undivided profits base for franchise tax, deduct the aggregate market value of its investments in the stocks, bonds, debentures, or other securities or evidences of debt of other corporations, partnerships, individuals, municipalities, governmental agencies, or governments:

(1)   A regulated investment company. - A regulated investment company is an entity that qualifies as a regulated investment company under section 851 of the Code.

(2)   A REIT, unless the REIT is a captive REIT. - The terms "REIT" and "captive REIT" have the same meanings as defined in G.S. 105-130.12. (1939, c. 158, s. 213; 1951, c. 937, s. 3; 1955, c. 1313, s. 1; 1957, c. 1340, s. 3; 1963, c. 601, s. 3; c. 1169, s. 1; 1967, c. 1110, s. 2; 1971, c. 820, s. 3; c. 833, s. 1; 1973, c. 476, s. 193; c. 1053, s. 2; c. 1287, s. 3; 1975, c. 591, s. 1; 1983, c. 28, s. 2; c. 713, s. 67; 1985 (Reg. Sess., 1986), c. 826, s. 4; 1991, c. 30, s. 6; 1993, c. 485, s. 4; c. 494, s. 1; 2008-107, s. 28.7(c); 2011-330, s. 8.)

§ 105-126. Repealed by Session Laws 1959, c. 1259, s. 9.

§ 105-127. When franchise or privilege taxes payable.

(a)   Every corporation, domestic or foreign, that is required to file a return with the Secretary shall, unless otherwise provided, pay annually the franchise tax as required by G.S. 105-122.

(b)   Repealed by Session Laws 1998-98, s. 78, effective August 14, 1998.

(c)   It shall be the duty of the treasurer or other officer having charge of any such corporation, domestic or foreign, upon which a tax is herein imposed, to transmit the amount of the tax due to the Secretary of Revenue within the time provided by law for payment of same.

(d),   (e) Repealed by Session Laws 2002-72, s. 11, effective August 12, 2002.

(f)   After the end of the income year in which a domestic corporation is dissolved pursuant to Part 1 of Article 14 of Chapter 55 of the General Statutes, the corporation is no longer subject to the tax levied in this Article unless the Secretary of Revenue finds that the corporation has engaged in business activities in this State not appropriate to winding up and liquidating its business and affairs. (1939, c. 158, s. 215; 1973, c. 476, s. 193; 1991, c. 30, s. 7; 1993, c. 485, s. 6; 1998-98, s. 78; 2002-72, s. 11; 2011-330, s. 9; 2013-414, s. 1(d).)

§ 105-128. Power of attorney.

The Secretary of Revenue shall have the authority to require a proper power of attorney of each and every agent for any taxpayer under this Article. (1939, c. 158, s. 217; 1973, c. 476, s. 193.)

§ 105-129. Extension of time for filing returns.

A return required by this Article is due on or before the date set in this Article. A taxpayer may ask the Secretary for an extension of time to file a return under G.S. 105-263. (1939, c. 158, s. 216; 1955, c. 1350, s. 17; 1959, c. 1259, s. 9; 1973, c. 476, s. 193; 1977, c. 1114, s. 6; 1989 (Reg. Sess., 1990), c. 984, s. 7; 1997-300, s. 2.)

§ 105-129.1: Repealed by Session Laws 1989, c. 582, s. 1.

Article 3A.

Tax Incentives For New And Expanding Businesses.

§§ 105-129.2 through 105-129.13: Repealed effective for business activities occurring on or after January 1, 2007.

§ 105-129.14: Reserved for future codification purposes.

Article 3B.

Business And Energy Tax Credits.

§ 105-129.15. Definitions.

The following definitions apply in this Article:

(1)   Business property. - Tangible personal property that is used by the taxpayer in connection with a business or for the production of income and is capitalized by the taxpayer for tax purposes under the Code. The term does not include, however, a luxury passenger automobile taxable under section 4001 of the Code or a watercraft used principally for entertainment and pleasure outings for which no admission is charged.

(2)   Cost. - In the case of property owned by the taxpayer, cost is determined pursuant to regulations adopted under section 1012 of the Code, subject to the limitation on cost provided in section 179 of the Code. In the case of property the taxpayer leases from another, cost is value as determined pursuant to G.S. 105-130.4(j)(2), unless the property is renewable energy property for which the taxpayer claims either a federal energy credit under section 48 of the Code or a federal grant in lieu of that credit and makes a lease pass-through election under the Code. In this circumstance, the cost of the leased renewable energy property is the cost determined under the Code.

(3)   Recodified as § 105-129.15(5).

255

(4)   Hydroelectric generator. - A machine that produces electricity by water power or by the friction of water or steam.

(4a)   Repealed by Session Laws 2002-87, s. 3, effective August 22, 2002.

(4b)   Installation of renewable energy property. - Renewable energy property that, standing alone or in combination with other machinery, equipment, or real property, is able to produce usable energy on its own.

(5)   Purchase. - Defined in section 179 of the Code.

(6)   Renewable biomass resources. - Organic matter produced by terrestrial and aquatic plants and animals, such as standing vegetation, aquatic crops, forestry and agricultural residues, spent pulping liquor, landfill wastes, and animal wastes.

(7)   Renewable energy property. - Any of the following machinery and equipment or real property:

a.   Biomass equipment that uses renewable biomass resources for biofuel production of ethanol, methanol, and biodiesel; anaerobic biogas production of methane utilizing agricultural and animal waste or garbage; or commercial thermal or electrical generation. The term also includes related devices for converting, conditioning, and storing the liquid fuels, gas, and electricity produced with biomass equipment.

b.   Combined heat and power system property. - Defined in section 48 of the Code.

c.   Geothermal equipment that meets either of the following descriptions:

1.   It is a heat pump that uses the ground or groundwater as a thermal energy source to heat a structure or as a thermal energy sink to cool a structure.

2.   It uses the internal heat of the earth as a substitute for traditional energy for water heating or active space heating or cooling.

d.   Hydroelectric generators located at existing dams or in free-flowing waterways, and related devices for water supply and control, and converting, conditioning, and storing the electricity generated.

e.   Solar energy equipment that uses solar radiation as a substitute for traditional energy for water heating, active space heating and cooling, passive heating, daylighting, generating electricity, distillation, desalination, detoxification, or the production of industrial or commercial process heat. The term also includes related devices necessary for collecting, storing, exchanging, conditioning, or converting solar energy to other useful forms of energy.

f.   Wind equipment required to capture and convert wind energy into electricity or mechanical power, and related devices for converting, conditioning, and storing the electricity produced or relaying the electricity by cable from the turbine motor to the power grid.

(8)   Renewable fuel. - Either of the following:

a.   Biodiesel, as defined in G.S. 105-449.60.

b.   Ethanol either unmixed or in mixtures with gasoline that are seventy percent (70%) or more ethanol by volume. (1996, 2nd Ex. Sess., c. 13, s. 3.12; 1997-277, s. 3; 1998-55, s. 2; 1999-342, s. 2; 1999-360, s. 1; 2000-173, s. 1(a); 2001-431, s. 1; 2002-87, s. 3; 2004-153, s. 1; 2005-413, s. 4; 2006-162, s. 23; 2009-548, s. 1; 2010-167, s. 2(a).)

§§ 105-129.15A, 105-129.16: Repealed by Session Laws 2005-413, ss. 6 and 7, effective September 20, 2005.

§ 105-129.16A. (Repealed effective for renewable energy property placed into service on or after January 1, 2016) Credit for investing in renewable energy property.

(a)   Credit. - If a taxpayer that has constructed, purchased, or leased renewable energy property places it in service in this State during the taxable year, the taxpayer is allowed a credit equal to thirty-five percent (35%) of the cost of the property. In the case of renewable energy property that serves a nonbusiness purpose, the credit must be taken for the taxable year in which the property is placed in service. For all other renewable energy property, the entire credit may not be taken for the taxable year in which the property is placed in service but must be taken in five equal installments beginning with the taxable

257

year in which the property is placed in service. Upon request of a taxpayer that leases renewable energy property, the lessor of the property must give the taxpayer a statement that describes the renewable energy property and states the cost of the property. No credit is allowed under this section to the extent the cost of the renewable energy property was provided by public funds. For the purposes of this section, "public funds" does not include grants made under section 1603 of the American Recovery and Reinvestment Tax Act of 2009.

(b)   Expiration. - If, in one of the years in which the installment of a credit accrues, the renewable energy property with respect to which the credit was claimed is disposed of, taken out of service, or moved out of State, the credit expires and the taxpayer may not take any remaining installment of the credit. The taxpayer may, however, take the portion of an installment that accrued in a previous year and was carried forward to the extent permitted under G.S. 105-129.17.

(c)   Ceilings. - The credit allowed by this section may not exceed the applicable ceilings provided in this subsection.

(1)   Business. - A ceiling of two million five hundred thousand dollars ($2,500,000) applies to each installation of renewable energy property placed in service for a business purpose. Renewable energy property is placed in service for a business purpose if the useful energy generated by the property is offered for sale or is used on-site for a purpose other than providing energy to a residence.

(2)   Nonbusiness. - The following ceilings apply to renewable energy property placed in service for a nonbusiness purpose:

a.   One thousand four hundred dollars ($1,400) per dwelling unit for solar energy equipment for domestic water heating, including pool heating.

b.   Three thousand five hundred dollars ($3,500) per dwelling unit for solar energy equipment for active space heating, combined active space and domestic hot water systems, and passive space heating.

c.   Eight thousand four hundred dollars ($8,400) for each installation of geothermal equipment.

d.   Ten thousand five hundred dollars ($10,500) for each installation of any other renewable energy property.

(3)   (Effective for taxable years beginning on or after January 1, 2011) Eco-Industrial Park. - A ceiling of five million dollars ($5,000,000) applies to each installation of renewable energy property placed in service at an Eco-Industrial Park certified under G.S. 143B-437.08 for a business purpose described in subdivision (1) of this subsection.

(d)   No Double Credit. - A taxpayer that claims any other credit allowed under this Chapter with respect to renewable energy property may not take the credit allowed in this section with respect to the same property. A taxpayer may not take the credit allowed in this section for renewable energy property the taxpayer leases from another unless the taxpayer obtains the lessor's written certification that the lessor will not claim a credit under this Chapter with respect to the property.

(e)   Sunset. - This section is repealed effective for renewable energy property placed into service on or after January 1, 2016. (1999-342, s. 2; 2005-413, s. 5; 2009-548, s. 2; 2010-4, s. 1; 2010-147, s. 5.4; 2010-167, s. 2(b).)

§ 105-129.16B: Recodified as G.S. 105-129.41 by Session Laws 2002-87, s. 2, as amended by Session Laws 2003-416, s. 1, effective August 22, 2002, and applicable to credits for buildings for which a federal tax credit is first claimed for a taxable year beginning on or after January 1, 2002.

§ 105-129.16C: Repealed effective for taxable years beginning on or after January 1, 2006.

§ 105-129.16D. (Repealed effective for facilities placed in service on or after January 1, 2014) Credit for constructing renewable fuel facilities.

(a)   Dispensing Credit. - A taxpayer that constructs and installs and places in service in this State a qualified commercial facility for dispensing renewable fuel is allowed a credit equal to fifteen percent (15%) of the cost to the taxpayer of constructing and installing the part of the dispensing facility, including pumps, storage tanks, and related equipment, that is directly and exclusively used for dispensing or storing renewable fuel. A facility is qualified if the equipment used to store or dispense renewable fuel is labeled for this purpose and clearly identified as associated with renewable fuel.

The entire credit may not be taken for the taxable year in which the facility is placed in service but must be taken in three equal annual installments beginning with the taxable year in which the facility is placed in service. If, in one of the years in which the installment of a credit accrues, the portion of the facility directly and exclusively used for dispensing or storing renewable fuel is disposed of or taken out of service, the credit expires and the taxpayer may not take any remaining installment of the credit. The taxpayer may, however, take the portion of an installment that accrued in a previous year and was carried forward to the extent permitted under G.S. 105-129.17.

(b)   Production Credit. - A taxpayer that constructs and places in service in this State a commercial facility for processing renewable fuel is allowed a credit equal to twenty-five percent (25%) of the cost to the taxpayer of constructing and equipping the facility. The entire credit may not be taken for the taxable year in which the facility is placed in service but must be taken in seven equal annual installments beginning with the taxable year in which the facility is placed in service. If, in one of the years in which the installment of a credit accrues, the facility with respect to which the credit was claimed is disposed of or taken out of service, the credit expires and the taxpayer may not take any remaining installment of the credit. The taxpayer may, however, take the portion of an installment that accrued in a previous year and was carried forward to the extent permitted under G.S. 105-129.17.

Notwithstanding subsection (d) of this section, this section is repealed effective for facilities placed in service on or after January 1, 2017, in the case of a taxpayer that meets both of the following conditions:

(1)   Signs a letter of commitment with the Department of Commerce on or before September 1, 2013, stating the taxpayer's intent to construct and place into service in this State a commercial facility for processing renewable fuel.

(2)   Begins construction of the facility on or before December 31, 2013.

(b1)   Alternative Production Credit. - In lieu of the credit allowed under subsection (b) of this section, a taxpayer that constructs and places in service in this State three or more commercial facilities for processing renewable fuel and that invests a total amount of at least four hundred million dollars ($400,000,000) in the facilities is allowed a credit equal to thirty-five percent

(35%) of the cost to the taxpayer of constructing and equipping the facilities. In order to claim the credit, the taxpayer must obtain a written determination from the Secretary of Commerce that the taxpayer is expected to invest within a five-year period a total amount of at least four hundred million dollars ($400,000,000) in three or more facilities. The credit must be taken in seven equal annual installments beginning with the taxable year in which the first facility is placed in service. If, in one of the years in which the installment of credit accrues, a facility with respect to which the credit was claimed is disposed of or taken out of service and the investment requirements of this subsection are no longer satisfied, the credit expires and the taxpayer may take any remaining installment of the credit only to the extent allowed under subsection (b) of this section. The taxpayer may, however, take the portion of an installment under this subsection that accrued in a previous year and was carried forward to the extent permitted under G.S. 105-129.17. Notwithstanding the provisions of G.S. 105-129.17, a taxpayer may carry forward unused portions of the credit allowed under this subsection for the succeeding 10 years.

If a taxpayer that claimed a credit under this subsection fails to meet the requirements of this subsection but meets the requirements of subsection (b) of this section, the taxpayer forfeits the difference between the alternative credit claimed under this subsection and the credit allowed under subsection (b) of this section. A taxpayer that forfeits part of the alternative credit under this subsection is liable for the additional taxes avoided plus interest at the rate established under G.S. 105-241.21, computed from the date the additional taxes would have been due if the credit had not been allowed. The additional taxes and interest are due 30 days after the date the credit is forfeited. A taxpayer that fails to pay the additional taxes and interest by the due date is subject to penalties provided in G.S. 105-236.

(c)   No Double Credit. - A taxpayer may not claim the credits allowed under subsections (b) and (b1) of this section with respect to the same facility. A taxpayer that claims any other credit allowed under this Chapter with respect to the costs of constructing and installing a facility may not take the credit allowed in this section with respect to the same costs.

(d)   Sunset. - This section is repealed effective for facilities placed in service on or after January 1, 2014. (2004-153, s. 2; 2006-66, s. 24.7(a); 2006-259, s. 19.5(a); 2007-323, s. 31.9(a); 2010-95, s. 2; 2010-167, s. 1(a); 2012-36, s. 2; 2013-363, s. 11.3(a).)

§ 105-129.16E. Expired effective January 1, 2010, pursuant to the terms of former subsection (d) of this section.

§ 105-129.16F. (Repealed for taxable years beginning on or after January 1, 2014) Credit for biodiesel producers.

(a)   Credit. - A biodiesel provider that produces at least 100,000 gallons of biodiesel during the taxable year is allowed a credit equal to the per gallon excise tax the producer paid under Article 36C of this Chapter on the biodiesel. For the purposes of this section, "biodiesel" is liquid fuel derived in whole from agricultural products, animal fats, or wastes from agricultural products or animal fats. The credit does not apply to tax paid on diesel fuel included in a biodiesel blend. The credit may not exceed five hundred thousand dollars ($500,000) and is subject to the limitations of G.S. 105-129.17.

(b)   Sunset. - This section is repealed for taxable years beginning on or after January 1, 2014. (2006-66, s. 24.8(a); 2010-167, s. 1(b); 2012-36, s. 3.)

§ 105-129.16G. (Expiring for taxable years beginning on or after January 1, 2014) Work Opportunity Tax Credit.

(a)   Credit. - A taxpayer who is allowed a federal tax credit under Part IV, Subpart F of the Code for the taxable year is allowed a credit against the tax imposed by this Part. The credit is equal to a percentage of the amount of credit allowed under the Code for wages paid during the taxable year for positions located in this State. A position is located in this State if more than fifty percent (50%) of the employee's duties are performed in the State. The percentage is as follows:

(1)   For taxable year 2013, three percent (3%).

(2)   For all other taxable years, six percent (6%).

(b)   Sunset. - This section expires for taxable years beginning on or after January 1, 2014. (2007-323, s. 31.21(a); 2008-134, s. 2(a); 2012-36, s. 4; 2013-10, s. 4.)

§ 105-129.16H. (For contingent repeal, see subsection (d)) Credit for donating funds to a nonprofit organization or unit of State or local government to enable the nonprofit or government unit to acquire renewable energy property.

(a)   Credit. - A taxpayer who donates money to a tax-exempt nonprofit organization or a unit of State or local government for the purpose of providing funds for the organization or government unit to construct, purchase, or lease renewable energy property is allowed a credit under this section if the donation is used for its intended purpose. A tax-exempt nonprofit organization is an organization that is exempt from tax under section 501(c)(3) of the Code.

The amount of the credit allowed in this section is the taxpayer's share of the credit the nonprofit organization or the unit of State or local government could claim under G.S. 105-129.16A if the nonprofit organization or government unit were subject to tax. The taxpayer's share of the credit is calculated by dividing the taxpayer's donation by the cost of the renewable energy property constructed, purchased, or leased by the nonprofit organization or government unit and placed in service during the taxable year and then multiplying this percentage by the amount of the credit the nonprofit organization or government unit could claim if it were subject to tax. A taxpayer must take the credit allowed by this section for the taxable year in which the property is placed in service. The installment requirements in G.S. 105-129.16A for nonresidential property do not apply to the credit allowed in this section.

(b)   Records. - A nonprofit organization or a unit of State or local government must keep a record of all donations it receives for the purpose of providing funds for the organization to construct, purchase, or lease renewable energy property and of the amount of the donations used for this purpose. If a nonprofit organization or government unit places renewable energy property in service that is purchased in whole or in part from donations made for this purpose, the nonprofit organization or government unit must give each taxpayer who made a donation a statement setting out the amount of the credit for which the taxpayer qualifies under this section. The statement must describe the renewable energy property placed in service and state the cost of the property, the amount of the credit the nonprofit organization or government unit could claim under G.S. 105-129.16A if it were subject to tax, and the taxpayer's share of the credit allowed in this section. If the donations made for the renewable energy property exceed the cost of the property, the nonprofit organization or government unit must prorate each taxpayer's share of the credit. The sum of the credits allowed under this section to taxpayers who make donations to a nonprofit organization or a government unit may not exceed the amount of the

263

credit the nonprofit organization or government unit could claim under G.S. 105-129.16A if it were subject to tax.

(c)   No Double Benefit. - A taxpayer who claims a credit under this section based on a donation to a nonprofit organization or a unit of State or local government is not allowed to deduct this donation as a charitable contribution.

(d)   Sunset. - This section is repealed as of the date that G.S. 105-129.16A is repealed. The repeal applies to donations made for renewable energy property placed in service on or after the date the section is repealed. (2007-397, s. 13(a); 2008-107, s. 28.25(a); 2008-134, s. 70; 2013-414, s. 32.)

§ 105-129.16I. (Repealed effective for a renewable energy property facility placed in service on or after January 1, 2014) Credit for a renewable energy property facility.

(a)   Credit. - A taxpayer that places in service in this State a commercial facility for the manufacture of renewable energy property or a major component subassembly for a solar array or a wind turbine is allowed a credit. A taxpayer places a facility in service if it constructs the facility or converts its existing manufacturing facility to change the product it manufactures. For a taxpayer that constructs a facility, the credit is twenty-five percent (25%) of the taxpayer's cost to construct and equip the facility. For a taxpayer that converts a facility, the credit is twenty-five percent (25%) of the taxpayer's cost to convert and equip the existing facility. A taxpayer that claims any other credit allowed under this Chapter with respect to the facility may not take the credit allowed in this section with respect to that facility.

(b)   Installments. - The entire credit may not be taken for the taxable year in which the facility is placed in service but must be taken in five equal annual installments beginning with the taxable year in which the facility is placed in service. If, in one of the years in which the installment of a credit accrues, the facility with respect to which the credit was claimed is disposed of or taken out of service, the credit expires and the taxpayer may not take any remaining installment of the credit. The taxpayer may, however, take the portion of an installment that accrued in a previous year and was carried forward to the extent permitted under G.S. 105-129.17.

(c)   Sunset. - This section is repealed effective for a renewable energy property facility placed in service on or after January 1, 2014. (2010-167, s. 3(a).)

§ 105-129.16J. Temporary unemployment insurance refundable tax credit.

(a)   Credit. - A small business that makes contributions during the taxable year to the State Unemployment Insurance Fund with respect to wages paid for employment in this State is allowed a credit equal to twenty-five percent (25%) of the contributions. A small business is a business whose cumulative gross receipts from business activity for the taxable year do not exceed one million dollars ($1,000,000).

(b)   Refundable. - Notwithstanding G.S. 105-129.17, the credit allowed by this section is subject to the following:

(1)   The credit may only be claimed against the income taxes imposed by Article 4 of this Chapter.

(2)   If the credit exceeds the amount of tax imposed by Article 4 of this Chapter for the taxable year reduced by the sum of all credits allowable, the excess is refundable. The refundable excess is governed by the provisions governing a refund of an overpayment by the taxpayer of the tax imposed in that Article. In computing the amount of tax against which multiple credits are allowed, nonrefundable credits are subtracted before refundable credits.

(c)   Applicability. - This section applies only to taxable years 2010 and 2011. (2010-31, s. 31.1A(a).)

§ 105-129.17. Tax election; cap.

(a)   Tax Election. - The credit allowed in G.S. 105-129.16A is allowed against the franchise tax levied in Article 3 of this Chapter, the income taxes levied in Article 4 of this Chapter, or the gross premiums tax levied in Article 8B of this Chapter. All other credits allowed in this Article are allowed against the franchise tax levied in Article 3 of this Chapter or the income taxes levied in Article 4 of this Chapter. The taxpayer must elect the tax against which a credit will be claimed when filing the return on which the first installment of the credit is claimed. This election is binding. Any carryforwards of a credit must be claimed against the same tax.

(b)   Cap. - The credits allowed in this Article may not exceed fifty percent (50%) of the tax against which they are claimed for the taxable year, reduced by the sum of all other credits allowed against that tax, except tax payments made by or on behalf of the taxpayer. This limitation applies to the cumulative amount of credit, including carryforwards, claimed by the taxpayer under this Article against each tax for the taxable year. Any unused portion of the credits may be carried forward for the succeeding five years. (1996, 2nd Ex. Sess., c. 13, s. 3.12; 1997-277, s. 3; 1999-342, s. 2; 1999-360, ss. 1, 13; 2000-140, ss. 63(a), 88; 2001-431, s. 3; 2002-87, s. 5; 2009-548, s. 3.)

§ 105-129.18. (See Editor's note for repeal) Substantiation.

To claim a credit allowed by this Article, the taxpayer must provide any information required by the Secretary of Revenue. Every taxpayer claiming a credit under this Article must maintain and make available for inspection by the Secretary of Revenue any records the Secretary considers necessary to determine and verify the amount of the credit to which the taxpayer is entitled. The burden of proving eligibility for a credit and the amount of the credit rests upon the taxpayer, and no credit may be allowed to a taxpayer that fails to maintain adequate records or to make them available for inspection. (1996, 2nd Ex. Sess., c. 13, s. 3.12; 1997-277, s. 3; 1999-342, s. 2; 1999-360, ss. 1, 14; 2000-140, ss. 63(b), 88.)

§ 105-129.19. Report.

The Department must include in the economic incentives report required by G.S. 105-256 the following information itemized by credit and by taxpayer:

(1)   The number of taxpayers that took the credits allowed in this Article.

(2)   The cost of renewable energy property with respect to which credits were taken.

(2a)   Repealed by Session Laws 2002-87, s. 6, effective August 22, 2002.

(3)   The total cost to the General Fund of the credits taken. (1996, 2nd Ex. Sess., c. 13, s. 3.12; 1997-277, s. 3; 1999-342, s. 2; 1999-360, ss. 1, 15; 2000-140, ss. 63(c), 88; 2001-414, s. 10; 2002-87, s. 6; 2005-429, s. 2.3; 2010-166, s. 1.2.)

§§ 105-129.20 through 105-129.24. Reserved for future codification purposes.

Article 3C.

Tax Incentives For Recycling Facilities.

§ 105-129.25. Definitions.

The following definitions apply in this Article:

(1)   Reserved.

(2)   Reserved.

(3)   Repealed by Session Laws 2010-166, s. 2.1, effective July 1, 2010.

(4)   Machinery and equipment. - Engines, machinery, tools, and implements used or designed to be used in the business for which the credit is claimed. The term does not include real property as defined in G.S. 105-273 or rolling stock as defined in G.S. 105-333.

(5)   Major recycling facility. - A recycling facility that qualifies under G.S. 105-129.26(a).

(6)   Owner. - A person who owns or leases a recycling facility.

(7)   Post-consumer waste material. - Any product that was generated by a business or consumer, has served its intended end use, and has been

267

separated from the solid waste stream for the purpose of recycling. The term includes material acquired by a recycling facility either directly or indirectly, such as through a broker or an agent.

(8)   Purchase. - Defined in section 179 of the Code.

(9)   Recycling facility. - A manufacturing plant at least three-fourths of whose products are made of at least fifty percent (50%) post-consumer waste material measured by weight or volume. The term includes real and personal property located at or on land in the same county and reasonably near the plant site and used to perform business functions related to the plant or to transport materials and products to or from the plant. The term also includes utility infrastructure and transportation infrastructure to and from the plant. (1998-55, s. 12; 2010-166, s. 2.1.)

§ 105-129.26. Qualification; forfeiture.

(a)   Major Recycling Facility. - A recycling facility qualifies for the tax benefits provided in this Article and in Article 5 of this Chapter for major recycling facilities if it meets all of the following conditions:

(1)   The facility is located in an area that, at the time the owner began construction of the facility, was an enterprise tier one area pursuant to G.S. 105-129.3.

(2)   The Secretary of Commerce has certified that the owner will, by the end of the fourth year after the year the owner begins construction of the recycling facility, invest at least three hundred million dollars ($300,000,000) in the facility and create at least 250 new, full-time jobs at the facility.

(3)   The jobs at the recycling facility meet the wage standard in effect pursuant to G.S. 105-129.4(b) as of the date the owner begins construction of the facility.

(b)   Repealed by Session Laws 2010-166, s. 2.1, effective July 1, 2010.

(c)   Forfeiture. - If the owner of a major recycling facility fails to make the required minimum investment or create the required number of new jobs within the period certified by the Secretary of Commerce under this section, the

268

recycling facility no longer qualifies for the applicable recycling facility tax benefits provided in this Article and in Article 5 of this Chapter and forfeits all tax benefits previously received under those Articles. Forfeiture does not occur, however, if the failure was due to events beyond the owner's control. Upon forfeiture of tax benefits previously received, the owner is liable under Part 1 of Article 4 of this Chapter for a tax equal to the amount of all past taxes under Articles 3, 4, and 5 previously avoided as a result of the tax benefits received plus interest at the rate established in G.S. 105-241.21, computed from the date the taxes would have been due if the tax benefits had not been received. The tax and interest are due 30 days after the date of the forfeiture. An owner that fails to pay the tax and interest is subject to the penalties provided in G.S. 105-236.

(d)   Substantiation. - To claim a credit allowed by this Article, the owner must provide any information required by the Secretary of Revenue. Every owner claiming a credit under this Article shall maintain and make available for inspection by the Secretary of Revenue any records the Secretary considers necessary to determine and verify the amount of the credit to which the owner is entitled. The burden of proving eligibility for the credit and the amount of the credit shall rest upon the owner, and no credit shall be allowed to an owner that fails to maintain adequate records or to make them available for inspection.

(e)   Report. - The Department must include in the economic incentives report required by G.S. 105-256 the following information itemized by taxpayer:

(1)   The number and location of major recycling facilities qualified under this Article.

(2)   The number of new jobs created by each recycling facility.

(3)   The amount of investment in each recycling facility.

(4)   The amount of credits taken under this Article. (1998-55, s. 12; 2005-429, s. 2.4; 2007-491, s. 44(1)a; 2010-166, ss. 1.3, 2.1; 2013-414, s. 33.)

§ 105-129.27. Credit for investing in major recycling facility.

(a)   Credit. - An owner that purchases or leases machinery and equipment for a major recycling facility in this State during the taxable year is allowed a

269

credit equal to fifty percent (50%) of the amount payable by the owner during the taxable year to purchase or lease the machinery and equipment.

(b)   Taxes Credited. - The credit provided in this section is allowed against the franchise tax levied in Article 3 of this Chapter and the income tax levied in Part 1 of Article 4 of this Chapter. Any other nonrefundable credits allowed the owner are subtracted before the credit allowed by this section.

(c)   Carryforwards. - The credit provided in this section may not exceed the amount of tax against which it is claimed for the taxable year, reduced by the sum of all other credits allowed against that tax, except tax payments made by or on behalf of the owner. Any unused portion of the credit may be carried forward for the succeeding 25 years.

(d)   Change in Ownership of Facility. - The sale, merger, consolidation, conversion, acquisition, or bankruptcy of a recycling facility, or any transaction by which the facility is reformulated as another business, does not create new eligibility in a succeeding owner with respect to a credit for which the predecessor was not eligible under this section. A successor business may, however, take any carried-over portion of a credit that its predecessor could have taken if it had a tax liability.

(e)   Forfeiture. - If any machinery or equipment for which a credit was allowed under this section is not placed in service within 30 months after the credit was allowed, the credit is forfeited. A taxpayer that forfeits a credit under this section is liable for all past taxes avoided as a result of the credit plus interest at the rate established under G.S. 105-241.21, computed from the date the taxes would have been due if the credit had not been allowed. The past taxes and interest are due 30 days after the date the credit is forfeited; a taxpayer that fails to pay the past taxes and interest by the due date is subject to the penalties provided in G.S. 105-236.

(f)   No Double Credit. - A recycling facility that is eligible for the credit allowed in this section is not allowed the credit for investing in machinery and equipment provided in G.S. 105-129.9 or G.S. 105-129.88. (1998-55, s. 12; 1999-369, s. 5.3; 2007-491, s. 44(1)a; 2009-445, s. 3(a); 2010-166, s. 2.1.)

§ 105-129.28: Repealed by Session Laws 1998-55, s, 19, effective for taxable years beginning on or after January 1, 2008.

§§ 105-129.29 through 105-129.34. Reserved for future codification purposes.

Article 3D.

Historic Rehabilitation Tax Credits.

§ 105-129.35. Credit for rehabilitating income-producing historic structure.

(a)   Credit. - A taxpayer who is allowed a federal income tax credit under section 47 of the Code for making qualified rehabilitation expenditures for a certified historic structure located in this State is allowed a credit equal to twenty percent (20%) of the expenditures that qualify for the federal credit. If the certified historic structure is a facility that at one time served as a State training school for juvenile offenders, the amount of the credit is equal to forty percent (40%) of the expenditures that qualify for the federal credit. To claim the credit allowed by this subsection, the taxpayer must provide a copy of the certification obtained from the State Historic Preservation Officer verifying that the historic structure has been rehabilitated in accordance with this subsection.

(b)   Notwithstanding the provisions of G.S. 105-131.8 and G.S. 105-269.15, a pass-through entity that qualifies for the credit provided in this section may allocate the credit among any of its owners in its discretion as long as an owner's adjusted basis in the pass-through entity, as determined under the Code, at the end of the taxable year in which the certified historic structure is placed in service, is at least forty percent (40%) of the amount of credit allocated to that owner. Owners to whom a credit is allocated are allowed the credit as if they had qualified for the credit directly. A pass-through entity and its owners must include with their tax returns for every taxable year in which an allocated credit is claimed a statement of the allocation made by the pass-through entity and the allocation that would have been required under G.S. 105-131.8 or G.S. 105-269.15.

(c)   Definitions. - The following definitions apply in this section:

(1)   Certified historic structure. - Defined in section 47 of the Code.

(2)   Pass-through entity. - Defined in G.S. 105-228.90.

(3)   Qualified rehabilitation expenditures. - Defined in section 47 of the Code.

271

(4)   State Historic Preservation Officer. - Defined in G.S. 105-129.36. (1993, c. 527, ss. 1, 2; 1997-139, ss. 1, 2; 1998-98, ss. 36, 69; 1999-389, ss. 2, 5, 6; 2001-476, s. 19(a); 2003-284, s. 35A.1; 2003-415, ss. 1, 2; 2003-416, s. 4(c); 2004-170, s. 14; 2006-40, s. 2; 2007-461, s. 1.)

§ 105-129.36. Credit for rehabilitating nonincome-producing historic structure.

(a)   Credit. - A taxpayer who is not allowed a federal income tax credit under section 47 of the Code and who makes rehabilitation expenses for a State-certified historic structure located in this State is allowed a credit equal to thirty percent (30%) of the rehabilitation expenses. If the certified historic structure is a facility that at one time served as a State training school for juvenile offenders, the amount of the credit is equal to forty percent (40%) of the expenditures that qualify for the federal credit. To qualify for the credit, the taxpayer's rehabilitation expenses must exceed twenty-five thousand dollars ($25,000) within a 24-month period. To claim the credit allowed by this subsection, the taxpayer must provide a copy of the certification obtained from the State Historic Preservation Officer verifying that the historic structure has been rehabilitated in accordance with this subsection.

(b)   Definitions. - The following definitions apply in this section:

(1)   Certified rehabilitation. - Repairs or alterations consistent with the Secretary of the Interior's Standards for Rehabilitation and certified as such by the State Historic Preservation Officer.

(2)   Rehabilitation expenses. - Expenses incurred in the certified rehabilitation of a certified historic structure and added to the property's basis. The term does not include the cost of acquiring the property, the cost attributable to the enlargement of an existing building, the cost of sitework expenditures, or the cost of personal property.

(3)   State-certified historic structure. - A structure that is individually listed in the National Register of Historic Places or is certified by the State Historic Preservation Officer as contributing to the historic significance of a National Register Historic District or a locally designated historic district certified by the United States Department of the Interior.

272

(4)   State Historic Preservation Officer. - The Deputy Secretary of Archives and History or the Deputy Secretary's designee who acts to administer the historic preservation programs within the State.

(c)   Recodified as G.S. 105-129.36A by Session Laws 2003-284, s. 35A.2, effective July 15, 2003. (1993, c. 527, ss. 1, 2; 1997-139, ss. 1, 2; 1998-98, ss. 36, 69; 1999-389, ss. 3, 5, 6; 2002-159, s. 35(e); 2003-284, ss. 35A.2, 35A.3; 2006-40, ss. 3, 4.)

§ 105-129.36A. Rules; fees.

(a)   Rules. - The North Carolina Historical Commission, in consultation with the State Historic Preservation Officer, may adopt rules needed to administer the certification process required by this section.

(b)   Fees. - The North Carolina Historical Commission, in consultation with the State Historic Preservation Officer, may adopt a schedule of fees for providing certifications required by this Article. In establishing the fee schedule, the Commission shall consider the administrative and personnel costs incurred by the Department of Cultural Resources. An application fee may not exceed one percent (1%) of the completed qualifying rehabilitation expenditures. The proceeds of the fees are receipts of the Department of Cultural Resources and must be used for performing its duties under this Article. (1993, c. 527, ss. 1, 2; 1997-139, ss. 1, 2; 1998-98, ss. 36, 69; 1999-389, ss. 3, 5, 6; 2002-159, s. 35(e); 2003-284, s. 35A.2.)

§ 105-129.37. Tax credited; credit limitations.

(a)   Tax Credited. - The credits provided in this Article are allowed against the income taxes levied in Article 4 of this Chapter.

(b)   Credit Limitations. - The entire credit may not be taken for the taxable year in which the property is placed in service but must be taken in five equal installments beginning with the taxable year in which the property is placed in service. Any unused portion of the credit may be carried forward for the succeeding five years. A credit allowed under this Article may not exceed the amount of the tax against which it is claimed for the taxable year reduced by the

273

sum of all credits allowed, except payments of tax made by or on behalf of the taxpayer.

(c)   Forfeiture for Disposition. - A taxpayer who is required under section 50 of the Code to recapture all or part of the federal credit for rehabilitating an income-producing historic structure located in this State forfeits the corresponding part of the State credit allowed under G.S. 105-129.35 with respect to that historic structure. If the credit was allocated among the owners of a pass-through entity, the forfeiture applies to the owners in the same proportion that the credit was allocated.

(d)   Forfeiture for Change in Ownership. - If an owner of a pass-through entity that has qualified for the credit allowed under G.S. 105-129.35 disposes of all or a portion of the owner's interest in the pass-through entity within five years from the date the rehabilitated historic structure is placed in service and the owner's interest in the pass-through entity is reduced to less than two-thirds of the owner's interest in the pass-through entity at the time the historic structure was placed in service, the owner forfeits a portion of the credit. The amount forfeited is determined by multiplying the amount of credit by the percentage reduction in ownership and then multiplying that product by the forfeiture percentage. The forfeiture percentage equals the recapture percentage found in the table in section 50(a)(1)(B) of the Code. The remaining allowable credit is allocated equally among the five years in which the credit is claimed.

(e)   Exceptions to Forfeiture. - Forfeiture as provided in subsection (d) of this section is not required if the change in ownership is the result of any of the following:

(1)   The death of the owner.

(2)   A merger, consolidation, or similar transaction requiring approval by the shareholders, partners, or members of the taxpayer under applicable State law, to the extent the taxpayer does not receive cash or tangible property in the merger, consolidation, or other similar transaction.

(f)   Liability From Forfeiture. - A taxpayer or an owner of a pass-through entity that forfeits a credit under this section is liable for all past taxes avoided as a result of the credit plus interest at the rate established under G.S. 105-241.21, computed from the date the taxes would have been due if the credit had not been allowed. The past taxes and interest are due 30 days after the date the credit is forfeited. A taxpayer or owner of a pass-through entity that fails to pay

274

the taxes and interest by the due date is subject to the penalties provided in G.S. 105-236. (1993, c. 527, ss. 1, 2; 1997-139, ss. 1, 2; 1998-98, ss. 36, 69; 1999-389, ss. 4, 5, 6; 2007-491, s. 44(1)a.)

§ 105-129.38. (See note for repeal) Report.

The Department must include in the economic incentives report required by G.S. 105-256 the following information itemized by taxpayer:

(1)   The number of taxpayers that took the credits allowed in this Article.

(2)   The amount of rehabilitation expenses and qualified rehabilitation expenditures with respect to which credits were taken.

(3)   The total cost to the General Fund of the credits taken. (2005-429, s. 2.5; 2010-166, s. 1.4.)

§ 105-129.39. Sunset.

This Article expires for qualified rehabilitation expenditures and rehabilitation expenses incurred on or after January 1, 2015. (2010-166, s. 1.5; 2012-36, s. 12(a).)

Article 3E.

Low-Income Housing Tax Credits.

(See Editor's note for repeal of this Article.)

§ 105-129.40. (See Editor's note for repeal) Scope and definitions.

(a)   Scope. - G.S. 105-129.41 applies to buildings that are awarded a federal credit allocation before January 1, 2003. G.S. 105-129.42 applies to buildings that are awarded a federal credit allocation on or after January 1, 2003.

275

(b)   Definitions. - The definitions in section 42 of the Code and the following definitions apply in this Article:

(1)   Housing Finance Agency. - The North Carolina Housing Finance Agency established in G.S. 122A-4.

(2)   Pass-through entity. - Defined in G.S. 105-228.90. (2002-87, s. 1; 2003-416, s. 3.)

§ 105-129.41. (See note for repeal) Credit for low-income housing awarded a federal credit allocation before January 1, 2003.

(a)   Credit. - A taxpayer that is allowed for the taxable year a federal income tax credit for low-income housing under section 42 of the Code with respect to a qualified North Carolina low-income building, is allowed a credit under this Article equal to a percentage of the total federal credit allowed with respect to that building. For the purposes of this section, the total federal credit allowed is the total allowed during the 10-year federal credit period plus the disallowed first-year credit allowed in the 11th year. For the purposes of this section, the total federal credit is calculated based on qualified basis as of the end of the first year of the credit period and is not recalculated to reflect subsequent increases in qualified basis. For buildings that meet condition (c)(1) or (c)(1a) of this section, the credit percentage is seventy-five percent (75%). For other buildings, the credit percentage is twenty-five percent (25%).

(a1)   Tax Election. - The credit allowed in this section is allowed against the franchise tax levied in Article 3 of this Chapter, the income taxes levied in Article 4 of this Chapter, or the gross premiums tax levied in Article 8B of this Chapter. The taxpayer must elect the tax against which the credit will be claimed when filing the return on which the first installment of the credit is claimed. This election is binding. Any carryforwards of the credit must be claimed against the same tax.

(a2)   Cap. - The credit allowed in this section may not exceed fifty percent (50%) of the tax against which it is claimed for the taxable year, reduced by the sum of all other credits made by or on behalf of the taxpayer. This limitation applies to the cumulative amount of credit, including carryforwards, claimed by the taxpayer under this section against each tax for the taxable year. Any unused portion of the credit may be carried forward for the succeeding five years.

(b)   Timing. - The credit must be taken in equal installments over the five years beginning in the first taxable year in which the federal credit is claimed for that building. During the first taxable year in which the credit allowed under this section may be taken with respect to a building, the amount of the installment must be multiplied by the applicable fraction under section 42(f)(2)(A) of the Code. Any reduction in the amount of the first installment as a result of this multiplication is carried forward and may be taken in the first taxable year after the fifth installment is allowed under this section.

(b1)   Allocation. - Notwithstanding the provisions of G.S. 105-131.8 and G.S. 105-269.15, a pass-through entity that qualifies for the credit provided in this section may allocate the credit among any of its owners in its discretion as long as an owner's adjusted basis in the pass-through entity, as determined under the Code at the end of the taxable year in which the federal credit is first claimed, is at least forty percent (40%) of the amount of credit allocated to that owner. Owners to whom a credit is allocated are allowed the credit as if they had qualified for the credit directly. A pass-through entity and its owners must include with their tax returns for every taxable year in which an allocated credit is claimed a statement of the allocation made by the pass-through entity and the allocation that would have been required under G.S. 105-131.8 or G.S. 105-269.15.

(c)   Qualifying Buildings. - As used in this section the term "qualified North Carolina low-income building" means a qualified low-income building that was allocated a federal credit under section 42(h)(1) of the Code, was not allowed a federal credit under section 42(h)(4) of the Code, and meets any of the following conditions:

(1)   It is located in an area that, at the time the federal credit is allocated to the building, is a tier one or two enterprise area, as defined in G.S. 105-129.3.

(1a)   Expired pursuant to Session Laws 2000-56, s. 10(f), effective January 1, 2005.

(2)   It is located in an area that, at the time the federal credit is allocated to the building, is a tier three or four enterprise area, and forty percent (40%) of its residential units are both rent-restricted and occupied by individuals whose

277

income is fifty percent (50%) or less of area median gross income as defined in the Code.

(3)   It is located in an area that, at the time the federal credit is allocated to the building, is a tier five enterprise area, and forty percent (40%) of its residential units are both rent-restricted and occupied by individuals whose income is thirty-five percent (35%) or less of area median gross income as defined in the Code.

(d)   Expiration. - If, in one of the five years in which an installment of the credit under this section accrues, the taxpayer is no longer eligible for the corresponding federal credit with respect to the same qualified North Carolina low-income building, then the credit under this section expires and the taxpayer may not take any remaining installment of the credit. If, in one of the five years in which an installment of the credit under this section accrues, the building no longer qualifies as a low-income building under subdivision (2) or (3) of subsection (c) of this section because less than forty percent (40%) of its residential units are both rent-restricted and occupied by individuals who meet the income requirements, then the credit under this section expires and the taxpayer may not take any remaining installments of the credit. The taxpayer may, however, take the portion of an installment that accrued in a previous year and was carried forward to the extent permitted under G.S. 105-129.17.

(e)   Forfeiture for Disposition. - If the taxpayer is required under section 42(j) of the Code to recapture all or part of a federal credit under that section with respect to a qualified North Carolina low-income building, the taxpayer must report the recapture event to the Secretary and to the Housing Finance Agency. The taxpayer forfeits the corresponding part of the credit allowed under this section with respect to that qualified North Carolina low-income building. If the credit was allocated among the owners of a pass-through entity, the forfeiture applies to the owners in the same proportion that the credit was allocated. This subsection does not apply when the recapture of part or all of the federal credit is the result of an event that occurs after the credit period described in subsection (b) of this section.

(f)   Forfeiture for Change in Ownership. - If an owner of a pass-through entity that has qualified for the credit allowed under this section disposes of all or a portion of the owner's interest in the pass-through entity within five years from the date the federal credit is first claimed and the owner's interest in the pass-through entity is reduced to less than two-thirds of the owner's interest in the pass-through entity at the time the federal credit is first claimed, the owner

278

must report the change to the Secretary and to the Housing Finance Agency. The owner forfeits a portion of the credit. The amount forfeited is determined by multiplying the amount of credit by the percentage reduction in ownership and then multiplying that product by the forfeiture percentage. The forfeiture percentage equals the recapture percentage found in the table in section 50(a)(1)(B) of the Code. The remaining allowable credit is allocated equally among the five years in which the credit is claimed. Forfeiture as provided in this subsection is not required if the change in ownership is the result of any of the following:

(1)   The death of the owner.

(2)   A merger, consolidation, or similar transaction requiring approval by the shareholders, partners, or members of the taxpayer under applicable State law, to the extent the taxpayer does not receive cash or tangible property in the merger, consolidation, or other similar transaction.

(g)   Liability From Forfeiture. - A taxpayer or an owner of a pass-through entity that forfeits a credit under this section is liable for all past taxes avoided as a result of the credit plus interest at the rate established under G.S. 105-241.21, computed from the date the taxes would have been due if the credit had not been allowed. The past taxes and interest are due 30 days after the date the credit is forfeited. A taxpayer or owner of a pass-through entity that fails to pay the taxes and interest by the due date is subject to the penalties provided in G.S. 105-236. (1999-360, s. 11; 2000-56, s. 7; 2000-140, s. 88; 2001-431, s. 2; 2002-87, s. 2; 2003-416, s. 1; 2007-491, s. 44(1)a.)

§ 105-129.42. (See note for repeal) Credit for low-income housing awarded a federal credit allocation on or after January 1, 2003.

(a)   Definitions. - The following definitions apply in this section:

(1)   Qualified Allocation Plan. - The plan governing the allocation of federal low-income housing tax credits for a particular year, as approved by the Governor after a public hearing and publication in the North Carolina Register.

(2)   Qualified North Carolina low-income housing development. - A qualified low-income project or building that is allocated a federal tax credit under section 42(h)(1) of the Code and is described in subsection (c) of this section.

279

(3)   Qualified residential unit. - A housing unit that meets the requirements of section 42 of the Code.

(b)   Credit. - A taxpayer who is allocated a federal low-income housing tax credit under section 42 of the Code to construct or substantially rehabilitate a qualified North Carolina low-income housing development is allowed a credit equal to a percentage of the development's qualified basis, as determined pursuant to section 42 of the Code. For the purpose of this section, qualified basis is calculated based on the information contained in the carryover allocation and is not recalculated to reflect subsequent increases or decreases. No credit is allowed for a development that uses tax-exempt bond financing.

(c)   Developments and Amounts. - The following table sets out the housing developments that are qualified North Carolina low-income housing developments and are allowed a credit under this section. The table also sets out the percentage of the development's qualified basis for which a credit is allowed. The designation of a county or city as Low Income, Moderate Income, or High Income and determinations of affordability are made by the Housing Finance Agency in accordance with the Qualified Allocation Plan in effect as of the time the federal credit is allocated. A change in the income designation of a county or city after a federal credit is allocated does not affect the percentage of the developer's qualified basis for which a credit is allowed. The affordability requirements set out in the chart apply for the duration of the federal tax credit compliance period. If in any year a taxpayer fails to meet these affordability requirements, the credit is forfeited under subsection (h) of this section.

Percentage of

Basis for

                Type of Development
Which Credit

                                                                        is

Allowed

Forty percent (40%) of the qualified residential units

are affordable to households whose income is fifty
Thirty percent

percent (50%) or less of area median income and the
(30%)

units are in a Low-Income county or city.

Fifty percent (50%) of the qualified residential units

are affordable to households whose income is fifty
Twenty percent

percent (50%) or less of the area median income and
(20%)

the units are in a Moderate-Income county or city.

Fifty percent (50%) of the qualified residential units

are affordable to households whose income is forty
Ten percent

percent (40%) or less of the area median income and
(10%)

the units are in a High-Income county or city.

Twenty-five percent (25%) of the qualified residential

units are affordable to households whose income is
Ten percent

thirty percent (30%) or less of the area median income
(10%)

281

and the units are in a High-Income county or city.

(d)   Election. - When a taxpayer to whom a federal low-income housing credit is allocated submits to the Housing Finance Agency a request to receive a carryover allocation for that credit, the taxpayer must elect a method for receiving the tax credit allowed by this section. A taxpayer may elect to receive the credit in the form of either a direct tax refund or a loan generated by transferring the credit to the Housing Finance Agency. Neither a direct tax refund nor a loan received as the result of the transfer of the credit is considered taxable income under this Chapter.

Under the direct tax refund method, a taxpayer elects to apply the credit allowed by this section to the taxpayer's liability under Article 4 of this Chapter. If the credit allowed by this section exceeds the amount of tax imposed by Article 4 for the taxable year, reduced by the sum of all other credits allowable, the Secretary must refund the excess. In computing the amount of tax against which multiple credits are allowed, nonrefundable credits are subtracted before this credit. The provisions that apply to an overpayment of tax apply to the refundable excess of a credit allowed under this section.

Under the loan method, a taxpayer elects to transfer the credit allowed by this section to the Housing Finance Agency and receive a loan from that Agency for the amount of the credit. The terms of the loan are specified by the Housing Finance Agency in accordance with the Qualified Allocation Plan.

(e)   Exception When No Carryover. - If a taxpayer does not submit to the Housing Finance Agency a request to receive a carryover allocation, the taxpayer must elect the method for receiving the credit allowed by this section when the taxpayer submits to the Agency federal Form 8609. A taxpayer to whom this subsection applies claims the credit for the taxable year in which the taxpayer submits federal Form 8609.

(f)   Pass-Through Entity. - Notwithstanding the provisions of G.S. 105-131.8 and G.S. 105-269.15, a pass-through entity that qualifies for the credit provided in this Article does not distribute the credit among any of its owners. The pass-through entity is considered the taxpayer for purposes of claiming the credit allowed by this Article. If a return filed by a pass-through entity indicates that the entity is paying tax on behalf of the owners of the entity, the credit allowed under this Article does not affect the entity's payment of tax on behalf of its owners.

(g)   Return and Payment. - A taxpayer may claim the credit allowed by this section on a return filed for the taxable year in which the taxpayer receives a carryover allocation of a federal low-income housing credit. The return must state the name and location of the qualified low-income housing development for which the credit is claimed.

If a taxpayer chooses the loan method for receiving the credit allowed under this section, the Secretary must transfer to the Housing Finance Agency the amount of credit allowed the taxpayer. The Agency must loan the taxpayer the amount of the credit on terms consistent with the Qualified Allocation Plan. The Housing Finance Agency is not required to make a loan to a qualified North Carolina low-income housing development until the Secretary transfers the credit amount to the Agency.

If the taxpayer chooses the direct tax refund method for receiving the credit allowed under this section, the Secretary must transfer to the Housing Finance Agency the refundable excess of the credit allowed the taxpayer. The Agency holds the refund due the taxpayer in escrow, with no interest accruing to the taxpayer during the escrow period. The Agency must release the refund to the taxpayer upon the occurrence of the earlier of the following:

(1)   The Agency determines that the taxpayer has complied with the Qualified Allocation Plan and has completed at least fifty percent (50%) of the activities included in the development's qualified basis.

(2)   Within 30 days after the date the development is placed in service.

(h)   Forfeiture. - A taxpayer that receives a credit under this section must immediately report any recapture event under section 42 of the Code to the Housing Finance Agency. If the taxpayer or any of its owners are required under section 42(j) of the Code to recapture all or part of a federal credit with respect to a qualified North Carolina low-income development, the taxpayer forfeits the corresponding part of the credit allowed under this section. This requirement does not apply in the following circumstances:

(1)   When the recapture of part or all of the federal credit is the result of an event that occurs in the sixth or a subsequent calendar year after the calendar year in which the development was awarded a federal credit allocation.

(2)   The taxpayer elected to transfer the credit allowed by this section to the Housing Finance Agency.

(i)   Liability From Forfeiture. - A taxpayer that forfeits all or part of the credit allowed under this section is liable for all past taxes avoided and any refund claimed as a result of the credit plus interest at the rate established under G.S. 105-241.21. The interest is computed from the date the Secretary transferred the credit amount to the Housing Finance Agency. The past taxes, refund, and interest are due 30 days after the date the credit is forfeited. A taxpayer that fails to pay the taxes, refund, and interest by the due date is subject to the penalties provided in G.S. 105-236. (2002-87, s. 1; 2003-416, ss. 6-8; 2004-110, s. 4.2; 2007-491, s. 44(1)a.)

§ 105-129.43. (See Editor's note for repeal) Substantiation.

A taxpayer allowed a credit under this Article must maintain and make available for inspection any information or records required by the Secretary of Revenue or the Housing Finance Agency. The burden of proving eligibility for a credit and the amount of the credit rests upon the taxpayer. (2002-87, s. 1.)

§ 105-129.44. (See note for repeal) Report.

The Department must include in the economic incentives report required by G.S. 105-256 the following information itemized by taxpayer:

(1)   The number of taxpayers that took the credit allowed in this Article.

(2)   The location of each qualified North Carolina low-income building or housing development for which a credit was taken.

(3)   The total cost to the General Fund of the credits taken. (2002-87, s. 1; 2005-429, s. 2.6; 2010-166, s. 1.6.)

§ 105-129.45. Sunset.

This Article is repealed effective January 1, 2015. The repeal applies to developments to which federal credits are allocated on or after January 1, 2015. (2002-87, s. 1; 2004-110, s. 4.1; 2008-107, s. 28.3(a).)

§ 105-129.46: Reserved for future codification purposes.

§ 105-129.47: Reserved for future codification purposes.

§ 105-129.48: Reserved for future codification purposes.

§ 105-129.49: Reserved for future codification purposes.

Article 3F.

Research and Development.

§ 105-129.50. (See note for repeal) Definitions.

The definitions in section 41 of the Code apply in this Article. In addition, the following definitions apply in this Article:

(1)   Development tier one area. - Defined in G.S. 143B-437.08.

(2)   Full-time job. - Defined in G.S. 105-129.81.

(3)   Reserved.

(4)   North Carolina university research expenses. - Any amount the taxpayer paid or incurred to a research university for qualified research performed in this State or basic research performed in this State.

(4a)   (Repealed effective for taxable years beginning on or after January 1, 2014) Participating community college. - A community college, as defined in G.S. 115D-2, that offers an associate in applied science degree in simulation and game development.

(5)   Period of measurement. - Defined in the Small Business Size Regulations of the federal Small Business Administration.

285

(6)   Qualified North Carolina research expenses. - Qualified research expenses, other than North Carolina university research expenses, for research performed in this State.

(7)   Receipts. - Defined in the Small Business Size Regulations of the federal Small Business Administration.

(8)   Related person. - Defined in G.S. 105-163.010.

(9)   Research university. - An institution of higher education that meets one or both of the following conditions:

a.   It is classified as one of the following in the most recent edition of "A Classification of Institutions of Higher Education", the official report of The Carnegie Foundation for the Advancement of Teaching:

1.   Doctoral/Research Universities, Extensive or Intensive.

2.   Masters Colleges and Universities, I or II.

3.   Baccalaureate Colleges, Liberal Arts or General.

b.   It is a constituent institution of The University of North Carolina.

(10)   Small business. - A business whose annual receipts, combined with the annual receipts of all related persons, for the applicable period of measurement did not exceed one million dollars ($1,000,000). (2004-124, s. 32D.2; 2010-147, s. 3.2; 2011-330, s. 4; 2013-316, s. 2.3(b).)

§ 105-129.51. (See note for repeal) Taxpayer standards and sunset.

(a)   A taxpayer is eligible for a credit allowed in this Article if it satisfies the requirements of G.S. 105-129.83(c), (d), (e), (f), and (g) relating to wage standard, health insurance, environmental impact, safety and health programs, and overdue tax debts, respectively.

(b)   This Article is repealed for taxable years beginning on or after January 1, 2016.

286

(c)   Repealed by Session Laws 2004-124, s. 32D.4, effective for taxable years beginning on or after January 1, 2006. (2004-124, ss. 32D.2, s. 32D.4; 2006-252, s. 2.20; 2008-107, s. 28.2(a); 2010-147, s. 3.3; 2013-316, s. 2.3(c).)

§ 105-129.52. (Effective for taxable years beginning before January 1, 2011 - see note) Tax election; cap.

(a)   Tax Election. - The credit allowed in this Article is allowed against the franchise tax levied in Article 3 of this Chapter or the income taxes levied in Article 4 of this Chapter. The taxpayer must elect the tax against which a credit will be claimed when filing the return on which the credit is first claimed. This election is binding. Any carryforwards of a credit must be claimed against the same tax.

(b)   Cap. - A credit allowed in this Article may not exceed fifty percent (50%) of the amount of tax against which it is claimed for the taxable year, reduced by the sum of all other credits allowed against that tax, except tax payments made by or on behalf of the taxpayer. This limitation applies to the cumulative amount of credit, including carryforwards, claimed by the taxpayer under this Article against each tax for the taxable year. Any unused portion of a credit allowed in this Article may be carried forward for the succeeding 15 years. (2004-124, s. 32D.2.)

§ 105-129.52. (Effective for taxable years beginning on or after January 1, 2011 - see note for repeal) Tax election; cap.

(a)   Tax Election. - A credit allowed in this Article is allowed against the franchise tax levied in Article 3 of this Chapter or the income taxes levied in Article 4 of this Chapter. The taxpayer must elect the tax against which a credit will be claimed when filing the return on which the credit is first claimed. This election is binding. Any carryforwards of a credit must be claimed against the same tax.

(b)   Cap. - A credit allowed in this Article may not exceed fifty percent (50%) of the amount of tax against which it is claimed for the taxable year, reduced by the sum of all other credits allowed against that tax, except tax payments made by or on behalf of the taxpayer. This limitation applies to the cumulative amount of credit, including carryforwards, claimed by the taxpayer under this Article against each tax for the taxable year. Any unused portion of a credit allowed in this Article may be carried forward for the succeeding 15 years. (2004-124, s. 32D.2; 2010-96, s. 40.3; 2010-147, s. 3.4.)

§ 105-129.53. (See notes) Substantiation.

To claim a credit allowed by this Article, the taxpayer must provide any information required by the Secretary. Every taxpayer claiming a credit under this Article must maintain and make available for inspection by the Secretary any records the Secretary considers necessary to determine and verify the amount of the credit to which the taxpayer is entitled. The burden of proving eligibility for a credit and the amount of the credit rests upon the taxpayer, and no credit may be allowed to a taxpayer that fails to maintain adequate records or to make them available for inspection. (2004-124, s. 32D.2.)

§ 105-129.54. Report.

The Department must include in the economic incentives report required by G.S. 105-256 the following information itemized by credit and by taxpayer:

(1)   (Effective for taxable years beginning before January 1, 2014) The number of taxpayers that took a credit allowed in this Article. The credit allowed under G.S. 105-129.55 must be itemized by the categories of small business, low-tier, university research, Eco-Industrial Park, and other. The credit allowed under G.S. 105-129.56 must be itemized by the categories of higher education collaboration and other.

(1)   (Effective for taxable years beginning on or after January 1, 2014) The number of taxpayers that took a credit allowed in this Article, itemized by the categories of small business, low-tier, university research, Eco-Industrial Park, and other.

(2)   The amount of each credit taken in each category.

(3)   The total cost to the General Fund of the credits taken. (2004-124, s. 32D.2; 2005-429, s. 2.7; 2010-147, s. 3.5; 2010-166, s. 1.7; 2013-316, s. 2.3(d).)

§ 105-129.55. (Effective for taxable years beginning before January 1, 2011 - see note) Credit for North Carolina research and development.

(a)   Qualified North Carolina Research Expenses. - A taxpayer that has qualified North Carolina research expenses for the taxable year is allowed a credit equal to a percentage of the expenses, determined as provided in this subsection. Only one credit is allowed under this subsection with respect to the same expenses. If more than one subdivision of this subsection applies to the same expenses, then the credit is equal to the higher percentage, not both percentages combined. If part of the taxpayer's qualified North Carolina research expenses qualifies under subdivision (2) of this subsection and the remainder qualifies under subdivision (3) of this subsection, the applicable percentages apply separately to each part of the expenses.

(1)   Small business. - If the taxpayer was a small business as of the last day of the taxable year, the applicable percentage is three and one-quarter percent (3.25%).

(2)   Low-tier research. - For expenses with respect to research performed in a development tier one area, the applicable percentage is three and one-quarter percent (3.25%).

(3)   Other research. - For expenses not covered under subdivision (1) or (2) of this subsection, the percentages provided in the table below apply to the taxpayer's qualified North Carolina research expenses during the taxable year at the following levels:

Expenses Over	Up To	Rate
-0-	$50 million	1.25%
$50 million	$200 million	2.25%
$200 million	-	3.25%

(b) North Carolina University Research Expenses. - A taxpayer that has North Carolina university research expenses for the taxable year is allowed a credit equal to twenty percent (20%) of the expenses. (2004-124, s. 32D.2; 2006-252, s. 2.1; 2007-323, s. 31.8(a).)

§ 105-129.55. (Effective for taxable years beginning on or after January 1, 2011 - see note for repeal) Credit for North Carolina research and development.

(a) Qualified North Carolina Research Expenses. - A taxpayer that has qualified North Carolina research expenses for the taxable year is allowed a credit equal to a percentage of the expenses, determined as provided in this section. Only one credit is allowed under this section with respect to the same expenses. If more than one subdivision of this section applies to the same expenses, then the credit is equal to the higher percentage, not both percentages combined. If part of the taxpayer's qualified North Carolina research expenses qualifies under more than one subdivision of this section, the applicable percentages apply separately to each part of the expenses.

(1) Small business. - If the taxpayer was a small business as of the last day of the taxable year, the applicable percentage is three and one-quarter percent (3.25%).

(2) Low-tier research. - For expenses with respect to research performed in a development tier one area, the applicable percentage is three and one-quarter percent (3.25%).

(2a) University research. - For North Carolina university research expenses, the applicable percentage is twenty percent (20%).

(2b) Eco-Industrial Park. - For expenses with respect to research performed in an Eco-Industrial Park certified under G.S. 143B-437.08, the applicable percentage is thirty-five percent (35%).

(3) Other research. - For expenses not covered under another subdivision of this section, the percentages provided in the table below apply to the taxpayer's qualified North Carolina research expenses during the taxable year at the following levels:

Expenses Over   Up To   Rate

-0-	$50 million	1.25%
$50 million	$200 million	2.25%
$200 million	-	3.25%

(b)   Repealed by Session Laws 2010-147, s. 5.5, effective January 1, 2011. (2004-124, s. 32D.2; 2006-252, s. 2.1; 2007-323, s. 31.8(a); 2010-147, s. 5.5.)

§ 105-129.56. (Repealed effective for taxable years beginning on or after January 1, 2014) Interactive digital media.

(a)   IDM Defined. - Interactive digital media is a product that meets all of the following requirements:

(1)   It is produced for distribution on electronic media, including distribution by file download over the Internet.

(2)   It contains a computer-controlled virtual universe with which an individual who uses the program may interact in order to achieve a goal.

(3)   It contains a significant amount of at least three of the following five types of data: animated images, fixed images, sound, text, and 3D geometry.

(b)   Credit. - A taxpayer that develops in this State interactive digital media or a digital platform or engine for use in interactive digital media is allowed a credit equal to a percentage of the taxpayer's expenses that exceed fifty thousand dollars ($50,000) and that are paid during the taxable year in developing the media, platform, or engine. The percentage that applies to the expenses is determined under subsection (c) of this section. The expenses to which the credit applies are as follows:

(1)   Compensation and wages for a full-time job on which withholding payments are remitted to the Department under Article 4A of this Chapter.

(2)   Employee fringe contributions on compensation and wages included under subdivision (1) of this subsection, including health, pension, and welfare contributions.

291

(3)   Amounts paid to a participating community college or a research university for services performed in this State.

(c)   Percentage. - The percentage of the credit allowed under this section is as follows:

(1)   Higher education collaboration. - Twenty percent (20%) for allowable expenses paid to a participating community college or a research university.

(2)   Other. - Fifteen percent (15%) for allowable expenses not covered in subdivision (1) of this subsection.

(d)   Limitations. - The amount of credit allowed a taxpayer under this section may not exceed seven million five hundred thousand dollars ($7,500,000). The credit allowed by this section does not apply to interactive digital media that meets any of the following descriptions:

(1)   It is developed by the taxpayer for internal use.

(2)   It is an interpersonal communications service, such as videoconferencing, wireless telecommunications, a text-based channel, or a chat room.

(3)   It is an Internet site that is primarily static and primarily designed to provide information about one or more persons, businesses, companies, or firms.

(4)   It is a gambling or casino game.

(5)   It is political advertising.

(6)   It contains material that is obscene, as defined in G.S. 14-190.1, or that is harmful to minors, as defined in G.S. 14-190.13.

(e)   No Double Benefit. - A taxpayer that claims a credit under this section may not claim any of the following with respect to the expenses used to determine the credit under this section:

(1)   A credit allowed under any other section of this Chapter.

(2)   A grant from the Job Development Investment Grant Program, set out in Part 2G of Article 10 of Chapter 143B of the General Statutes.

(3)   A grant from the One North Carolina Fund, set out in Part 2H of Article 10 of Chapter 143B of the General Statutes. (2010-147, s. 3.6; 2013-316, s. 2.3(b).)

§ 105-129.57: Reserved for future codification purposes.

§ 105-129.58: Reserved for future codification purposes.

§ 105-129.59: Reserved for future codification purposes.

Article 3G.

Tax Incentives for Major Computer Manufacturing Facilities.

§ 105-129.60: Repealed by Session Laws 2010-166, s. 2.2, effective July 1, 2010.

§ 105-129.61: Repealed by Session Laws 2010-166, s. 2.2, effective July 1, 2010.

§ 105-129.62: Repealed by Session Laws 2010-166, s. 2.2, effective July 1, 2010.

§ 105-129.63: Repealed by Session Laws 2010-166, s. 2.2, effective July 1, 2010.

§ 105-129.64: Repealed by Session Laws 2010-166, s. 2.2, effective July 1, 2010.

§ 105-129.65: Repealed by Session Laws 2010-166, s. 2.2, effective July 1, 2010.

§ 105-129.65A: Repealed by Session Laws 2010-166, s. 2.2, effective July 1, 2010.

§ 105-129.66: Repealed by Session Laws 2010-166, s. 2.2, effective July 1, 2010.

§ 105-129.67: Reserved for future codification purposes.

§ 105-129.68: Reserved for future codification purposes.

§ 105-129.69: Reserved for future codification purposes.

Article 3H.

Mill Rehabilitation Tax Credit.

(See G.S. 105-129.75 for repeal of this Article.)

§ 105-129.70. (See note for repeal) Definitions.

The following definitions apply in this Article:

(1)   Certified historic structure. - Defined in section 47 of the Code.

(2)   Certified rehabilitation. - Defined in G.S. 105-129.36.

(3)   Cost certification. - The certification obtained by the State Historic Preservation Officer from the taxpayer of the amount of the qualified rehabilitation expenditures or the rehabilitation expenses incurred with respect to a certified rehabilitation of an eligible site.

(3a)   Development tier area. - Defined in G.S. 143B-437.08.

(4)   Eligibility certification. - The certification obtained from the State Historic Preservation Officer that the applicable facility comprises an eligible site.

(5)   Eligible site. - A site located in this State that satisfies all of the following conditions:

a.   It was used as a manufacturing facility or for purposes ancillary to manufacturing, as a warehouse for selling agricultural products, or as a public or private utility.

b.   It is a certified historic structure or a State-certified historic structure.

c.   It has been at least eighty percent (80%) vacant for a period of at least two years immediately preceding the date the eligibility certification is made.

d.   Repealed by Session Laws 2008-107, s. 28.4(a), effective for taxable years beginning on or after January 1, 2008.

(6)   Repealed by Session Laws 2006-252, s. 2.22, effective January 1, 2007.

(7)   Pass-through entity. - Defined in G.S. 105-228.90.

(8)   Qualified rehabilitation expenditures. - Defined in section 47 of the Code.

(9)   Rehabilitation expenses. - Defined in G.S. 105-129.36.

(10)   State-certified historic structure. - Defined in G.S. 105-129.36.

(11)   State Historic Preservation Officer. - Defined in G.S. 105-129.36. (2006-40, s. 1; 2006-252, s. 2.22; 2008-107, s. 28.4(a).)

Vision Books Order Form

Fax Orders:	1-980-299-5965
Phone Orders:	1-704-898-0770
E-mail Orders:	www.visionbooks.org
Mail Orders:	Vision Books, LLC P.O. Box 42406 Charlotte, NC 28215

Shipp To:
Name_____
Address_____
City_____State_____Zip_____
Phone_____Fax_____
Email_____@_____

Bill To: We can bill a third party on your behalf.
Name_____
Address_____
City_____State_____Zip_____
Phone____(_____)_____Fax_____
Email_____@_____

Pamphlet Number ($15.00 Each)	Qty	Total Cost
_____	_____	_____
_____	_____	_____
_____	_____	_____
_____	_____	_____
_____	_____	_____
_____	_____	_____
_____	_____	_____
_____	_____	_____
Full Volume Set 1-92	92 Pamphlets	1,380.00

Free Shipping Shipping & Handling on Full Volume Orders
Add $1.00 Shipping & Handling per pamphlet $_____

Total Cost $_____

Thank you for your support. Management!

DID YOU ENJOY THIS BOOK?

Vision Books, LLC would like to hear from you! If you or someone you know has been fasely imprisoned, we would like to hear your story. If the 'North Carolina Criminal Law and Procedure' has had an effect in your life or if you have suggestions, we would like to hear from you. Send your letters to:

Vision Books, LLC
Attn: Staff Writers
P.O. Box 42406
Charlotte, NC 28215
Email: staff@visionbooks.org

Order Additional Copies:

Fax Orders: 1-980-299-5965

Phone Orders: 1-704-898-0770

E-mail Orders: www.visionbooks.org

Mail Orders: Vision Books, LLC
P.O. Box 42406
Charlotte, NC 28215

www.ingramcontent.com/pod-product-compliance
Lightning Source LLC
Chambersburg PA
CBHW051630170526
45167CB00001B/134